THE HARD ROAD TO REFORM

The Politics of Zimbabwe's Global Political Agreement

THE HARD ROAD TO REFORM

The Politics of Zimbabwe's Global Political Agreement

edited by

BRIAN RAFTOPOULOS

Published by
Weaver Press, Box A1922, Avondale, Harare. 2013
<www.weaverpresszimbabwe.com>
in association with the Solidarity Peace Trust,
Port Shepstone. 2013
<www.solidaritypeacetrust.org>

© Each individual chapter the author. This collection,
Brian Raftopoulos, 2013

© Tsvangirayi Mukwazhi for photographs on pp. 43, 46, 82, 85, 127
© Shari Eppel for photographs on pp.236, 237

Typeset by Weaver Press
Cover Design: Danes Design, Harare
Printed by: Sable Press, Harare

The authors, editor and publishers would like to express their gratitude to OSISA for their support in the development of this text.
<www.osisa.org>

All rights reserved. No part of the publication may be reproduced, stored in a retrieval system or transmitted in any form by any means – electronic, mechanical, photocopying, recording, or otherwise – without the express written permission
of the publisher.

ISBN: 978-1-77922-216-0

Contents

Introduction: Brian Raftopoulos xi

Chapter 1: Brian Raftopoulos – *An Overview of the GPA: National Conflict, Regional Agony and International Dilemma.* 1

Chapter 2: James Muzondidya – *The Opposition Dilemma in Zimbabwe: A Critical Review of the Politics of the Movement for Democratic Change (MDC) Parties under the GPA Transitional Framework 2009-2012.* 39

Chapter 3: Gerald Mazarire – *ZANU-PF and the Government of National Unity* 71

Chapter 4: Bertha Chiroro – *Responses of Civil Society to the Inclusive Government: The Challenges of turning Confrontation into Engagement.* 117

Chapter 5: Sabelo J. Ndlovu-Gatsheni – *Politics Behind Politics: African Union, SADC and the GPA in Zimbabwe.* 142

Chapter 6: Munyaradzi Nyakudya – *Sanctioning the Government of National Unity: A Review of Zimbabwe's Relations with the West in the Framework of the GPA.* 171

Chapter 7: Shari Eppel – *Repairing a Fractured Nation: Challenges and Opportunities in Post-GPA Zimbabwe.* 211

Select Bibliography 251

Contributors

Bertha Chiroro is a research specialist at the Africa Institute of South Africa, in Pretoria. She has an M.Phil. in Political Science from the University of Durham, UK. She has done research and published on a range of issues on democracy and governance, gender and elections. Her research interests range from Civil Society mobilisation for Sustainable Development to Elections and Political Processes in Africa.

Shari Eppel is a Zimbabwean, and director of Solidarity Peace Trust. She has worked with victims of torture for nearly twenty years, and is now studying for an MA in Forensic Anthropology. Once qualified, she intends to resume the work done by Amani Trust in the 1990s in Matabeleland involving 'healing the dead', a process whereby human remains are exhumed and returned to families for decent and customary reburials. Eppel has worked in the field of transitional justice for more than a decade and was the primary author of the CCJP/LRF history: *Breaking the Silence, Building True Peace: A Report on the Disturbances in Matabeleland and the Midlands 1980-1987*, which remains the definitive history of the Gukurahundi period in Zimbabwe.

Gerald Chikozho Mazarire is the former head of the History Department of the University of Zimbabwe where he served for ten years before moving to the Midlands State University as a Senior Lecturer in History. He is currently a Post-Doctoral Fellow at the University of Stellenbosch in South Africa.

James Muzondidya is a Research Manager at the Zimbabwe Institute – a political think tank based in Harare. He conducts research on politics and history, citizenship and identity.

Sabelo J. Ndlovu-Gatsheni is a professor in the Department of Development Studies at the University of South Africa and Head of the Archie Mafeje Research Institute based at the same university. He previously taught History and

Development Studies at Midlands State University (2000-2004); International Studies at Monash University (2005-2007); African Studies at the Ferguson Centre for African and Asian Studies at the Open University (2008-2009) and held the position of Senior Researcher at the South Africa Institute of International Affairs in 2010. He has published widely on Zimbabwean, South African and African history and politics. His recent major publications include *The Ndebele Nation: Reflections on Hegemony, Memory and Historiography*; *Do 'Zimbabweans' Exist? Trajectories of Nationalism, National Identity Formation and Crisis in a Postcolonial State*; *Grotesque or Redemptive Nationalism? Rethinking Contemporary Politics in Zimbabwe*; *Coloniality of Power in Postcolonial Africa: Myths of Decolonization*; and *Empire, Global Coloniality and African Subjectivity*.

Munyaradzi Nyakudya is a lecturer in History at the University of Zimbabwe, with a special interest in African colonial and post-colonial history. His most recent studies have focused on governance issues, the education sector and peace and security studies. He is the founding chairman of the Zimbabwe Peace and Security Education and Training (ZIPSET) Network.

Brian Raftopoulos is a leading Zimbabwean scholar and activist. Formally a Professor of Development Studies at the University of Zimbabwe, he moved to Cape Town at the end of March 2006 and is currently the Director of Research and Advocacy in the Solidarity Peace Trust, an NGO dealing with human rights issues in Zimbabwe. He has published widely on Zimbabwean history, historiography, and politics and is a regular contributor to public debates in Zimbabwe. At present, Professor Raftopoulos is also Mellon Senior Research Mentor at the Centre for Humanities Research at the University of the Western Cape. He is on the Advisory Editorial Board of the *Journal of Southern African Studies* and an Editor of *Kronos* a journal of Southern African histories, based at the University of the Western Cape. As an activist he was a founder member of the National Constitutional Assembly in 1998, the first Chair of the Crisis in Zimbabwe Coalition in 2001, and continues to work closely with the labour movement in Zimbabwe as a board member of the Labour and Development Institute of Zimbabwe.

Acknowledgements

I would like to thank the organisations and individuals who made this publication possible. Firstly, thanks must go to OSISA for funding the project and to Solidarity Peace Trust for organising and providing the administrative support for the book. Secondly, thanks to the authors for their continued commitment to advancing the cause of scholarship in Zimbabwe; many of them participated in the *'Becoming Zimbabwe'* project in 2009, and it has been a great pleasure to work with this group of scholars once again. In addition, would like to thank the Centre for Humanities Research, University of the Western Cape for its continued hospitality and support. Thirdly, thanks are due to Sana Raftopoulos for her original ideas in developing the book cover; her work has been well incorporated into the final product. Fourthly, I am grateful to David Moore for our ongoing discussions on the GPA and to Tyrone Savage for his editorial comments on one of the chapters at a very difficult stage. Last but by no means least the authors would like to thank Irene Staunton and Murray McCartney from Weaver Press for their excellent editorial work and continued efforts in keeping the publishing industry alive in Zimbabwe.

Brian Raftopoulos
January, 2013

Introduction
BRIAN RAFTOPOULOS

Since the signing of the Global Political Agreement (GPA) in September 2008 the outcome of the process has been fiercely contested, and by the end of 2012 remained in the balance. The Agreement, which set out to prepare the political process for a generally acceptable election after the debacle of 2008, has been marked by severe ebbs and flows. This is all too characteristic of the battle for the state that has constituted the politics of the GPA. At almost every stage of the mediation from 2007 and the implementation of the GPA from February 2009, intense conflicts over the interpretation of the accord have left their debris on the political terrain. At the heart of this contestation has been the struggle over the meaning of 'sovereignty'.

Around its conceptions of sovereignty ZANU-PF has woven dense layers of political discourse combined with its continued monopolisation of state violence and coercion. As many observers[1] have noted, the naming of 'enemies' and 'outsiders' by the Mugabe state in the context of a selective script around liberation and national community has been a key dimension of the 'state's performance of its "stateness".[2] This politics of sovereignty, heightened in Zimbabwe since the late 1990s, was perceptively and starkly described by Eric Worby a decade ago. He noted that it was less about who is included under the rubric of citizenship, than about who decides who is included, and who decides who lives and who dies.[3]

Moreover, in the framework of a highly contested political framework like the GPA, the deployment of security, and intimidation and punishment, have remained key resources in ZANU-PF's battle to retain state power. Within the politics of the Inclusive Government the major aim of this strategy has been to manipulate and stall the reform provisions of the GPA. This has been done with the intention of regrouping and consolidating after plunging to the nadir of its legitimacy in the 2008 electoral defeat. ZANU-PF has not only relied on violence and coercion to claw back political space within this period. A combination of the uneven effects of the changes on the land over the last decade, the abuse of income from the Marange diamond mines to extend its patronage,[4] the resonance of the indigenisation message in the context of shrunken opportunities for economic advancement, and reiteration of the liberation, anti-imperialist discourse in the face of the continued debate over Western 'sanctions,' have posed difficult challenges for the opposing players in the GPA.

Confronted with this formidable array of state resources and obstructive interventions the MDC formations and their allies in the civic movement have had to adapt to find ways to push their agendas. Challenges have ranged from the problems of learning the art of statecraft, to the leadership and organisational shortcomings within both MDC formations, and the difficulty of developing a language that could not be easily assimilated into the securitized, regime change discourse of post 9/11 global politics. All these issues continue to pose real challenges.

The central objective of this book is to carry out a political assessment of the GPA within the parameters of these broad challenges. It seeks to understand the conditions which gave rise to the GPA, the factors influencing the mediation and the politics that has unfolded under the agreement. The book also examines the contestations at national level within the broader dynamics of regional and international interventions, and to locate this confluence of forces within the longer term dynamics of post-1980 Zimbabwe.

Locating the Global Political Agreement

The GPA was not the first Inclusive Government or Government of National Unity in Zimbabwe. In 1980, the new independent government, dominated by ZANU-PF, began its life as a unity government composed of the other liberation movement, PF ZAPU, and representatives of the former settler government. This arrangement was driven by the balance of political and economic power which expressed the continuing economic influence of the white alliance, regional political pressure, the influence of the Western powers on the early transition, and the emerging aspirations of the ruling African elite.[5] This attempt at an early unity project was carried out within the context of a nationalist history whose claims of unity were always carried out on highly contested terrain characterised by a series of fractures resulting from the colonial situation.⁶ The complexity of this historical moment was compounded by the particularity of Zimbabwe as neither an early nor a late decoloniser, but one that stood, in Ndlovu's words, 'uneasily astride the fading socialist world and the emerging neoliberal world.'⁷ Thus the discourse of ZANU-PF's state building project in the 1980s was an uneasy ideological mixture, combining radical socialist rhetoric with the soothing messaging of reconciliation, and the deadly force of ethnic suppression during the period of Gukurahundi in Matabeleland and the Midlands.⁸

By the late 1980s the second attempt at a Unity Government was carried out at the end of the turmoil and terror of the Gukurahundi violence that effectively neutralised Joshua Nkomo's PF ZAPU, and consolidated the state-party project of Mugabe's party. As Eppel writes, the resulting 1987 Unity Accord 'had as its explicit and sole objective the complete annihilation of ZAPU as a separate entity'.⁹ Eppel's analysis shows that the violence and the unity pact in this early period took place in a context markedly different from the post 2000 context. The key features characterising the background to the Unity Accord were: the narrow regional base of ZAPU support; the intensity and extent of repression against ZAPU in a short period of time (1983-85); the limited information available on the extent of the atrocities; the absence of a broader empathy for the victims of the repression; the lack of concern and response by Western countries; and the power and cohesion of ZANU-PF during this first decade of independence. The result was less about power sharing and more about the 'absorption of one party into another'.

Thus by the end of the first decade of independence ZANU-PF had established its dominance over the state and any other party with ambitions for state power, even as the economic strength of the white community remained clearly evident. With ZAPU largely silenced, the politics of 'accommodation' could not conceal the domination of ZANU-PF, and the simmering tensions in the political landscape. While the formal political ambitions of ZAPU were tied to the trajectory of its dominant partner in the Accord, the resentment and potential for mobilisaton for a future opposition in Matabeleland could not be so easily assimilated and contained under the strictures of the unity agreement.

The growth of opposition forces from the era of neoliberal economic policy in the 1990s to the widespread crisis of nationalist legitimacy and state authority in the 2000s, led to a series of election challenges from the opposition. The parliamentary defeat of ZANU-PF in March 2008 and of Mugabe in the first round of the presidential election resulted in a third attempt at an inclusive government with the signing of the GPA between ZANU-PF and the two MDC formations in September 2008. Unlike in 1987, ZANU-PF was now faced with a strong national opposition at a time when its weakened existence depended largely on the use of coercion. In the face of regional and international opposition to the growing violence of the Mugabe regime, and the hostility of key Western countries to the fast track programme, – epitomised by the sanctions put in place by the US and EU in the 2000s – ZANU-PF's isolation became a factor in ways that it had not been during the Gukurahundi period.

Under the GPA ZANU-PF was for the first time faced with the reality of sharing power, even though much of the 'hard power' of the state remained in its hands. The challenges presented by the GPA led to a new realignment of political and economic forces as the battle for state power intensified. A broad overview of these issues is provided by Raftopoulos in the first chapter, which sets out the national, regional and international dynamics leading to the signing of the GPA. Through an assessment of the factors that gave rise to the SADC mediation and the challenges posed by the contested 2008 election, the chapter reviews the struggles that emerged over the implementation of the GPA; these are also analysed through the regional and international constructions of the country's political challenges. The first chapter thus provides a wide canvas of events over the last four years, followed by more detailed treatment of the issues in those that follow.

A recent volume on Zimbabwe's political regime transition describes it as a protracted struggle for domination between ZANU-PF and the two MDC formations, in which the transition 'looks quite uncertain.'[10] A somewhat Manichean picture is thus presented of this contest:

> Two sets of opposing forces are locked in a bitter and protracted contest for supremacy. These are the old regime forces (which have historically held power) personified by incumbent President Mugabe and his Zimbabwe African Union Patriotic Front (ZANU-PF) party on the one hand, and, on the other hand, the two formations of the Movement for Democratic Change (MDC), which until the Inclusive Government (IG), have historically been out of power. Until 2008, the former had ruled Zimbabwe as a dominant and de facto one-party regime, resisting any changes that threatened its continued prolongation in power and the perquisites that power brings. The two MDC formations have been

fighting for change for over a decade, with Morgan Tsvangirai ... personifying their epic struggle.[11]

In this schema, influenced by the work of O'Donnell and Schmitter[12] and Bratton and Nicholas[13], change is defined by a political transition through elections.

In an important sense the picture presented above captures a key element of the ongoing struggle for democratisation in Zimbabwe, and the GPA represented a frustration of that struggle, even as the various parties found it necessary to enter into it for different reasons. However, the narrow focus of Masunungure and Shumba's analysis of political regime transition through elections misses the broader changes taking place in Zimbabwe's political economy. The idea of transition in this argument assumes a certain normative direction in which change should occur even if the road to that transition is not linear. We argue that transition under the GPA refers to conflicting notions of change, rather than assuming that the change agenda applies only to the MDC formations. Thus the political regime change agenda of the MDCs and the political developments within these formations should be analysed against the changes in the configuration of ZANU-PF's dominant power structures in the context of the general crisis of hegemony that the latter has experienced since the late 1990s, in which new forms of economic accumulation have developed. The politics of ZANU-PF is not only one of destruction and obstruction; it is also constitutive of the new social and economic forces that have emerged in the last 10-15 years. In Gramscian terms, faced with a major organic crisis across the social formation as a whole, ZANU-PF has attempted not only to defend its existing structures, but to 'cure them within certain limits and to overcome them.'[14]

ZANU-PF's attempts, under the GPA, to deal with the challenges created by its own policies have taken different forms. In terms of economic policy, in addition to the new beneficiaries created in the problematic fast track land reform programme,[15] ZANU-PF has since 2009 placed central emphasis on the policy of indigenisation. In a report at its 13th National People's Congress held in December 2012 the party outlined this programme as follows:

Our strategic focus is on facilitating movement on indigenisation per se to focus on full economic empowerment with direct and measurable benefits to the people.

The heightened drive towards sustainable economic empower-

ment for the masses is anchored on a triangular approach focusing on creating and growing opportunities, training and business skills development and the provision of funding for indigenous business ventures particularly start ups and those run by previously disadvantaged individuals with an overarching goal of ensuring their entry and meaningful participation in the mainstream economy.[16]

While this policy has become a central part of ZANU-PF's campaign strategy ahead of the next election, it is also clear that it is part of the ongoing politics of patronage by the Mugabe regime. In recent years there has been increasing concern about the lack of transparency over the revenue from the Marange diamond mines and the ZANU-PF patronage networks that have emerged. In his 2012 Mid Term Fiscal Policy Review, Finance Minister Tendai Biti complained that against anticipated diamond revenues of US$600m only US$46m had been received in the national fiscus.[17] Biti also complained about the 'expenditure overrun' on employment costs attributable to an overall growth in employment levels of 9,820 during the period January to May 2012, with the largest part of this growth represented by the 5,200 recruits to the Zimbabwe National Army.[18] Thus one of the key messages of Biti's review was the problem of ZANU-PF's patronage through a combination of unaccountable diamond revenues and expansion in the security section. Against this trend the Finance Minister called for greater 'austerity' and the 'return to cash budgeting'.[19]

The problem of ZANU-PF's politics of patronage has also been apparent in local government. As McGregor has shown by reviewing violence and threats against local councilors, civil servants and civic bodies, ZANU-PF has relied on 'coercive measures, and irregular enticements to try to maintain the local state as a system of patronage when challenged under the Inclusive Government'. Her analysis points to the ways in which the privatisation and deregulation of local authority controls 'provided opportunities and resources to fuel ZANU-PF accumulation and patronage through party linked business'. Moreover, as the privatisation and deregulation were carried out at the same time that recentralisation policies were underway, 'the combination allowed for a greater inter-penetration of party/state business ... deepening the capacity of the local state to act as a vehicle of accumulation, and for partisan distribution of local state allocated goods'.[20]

The second part of ZANU-PF's strategy under the GPA has been the continued use, or threat, of selective violence and coercion. As Cheeseman has noted, one of the key factors in assessing the interaction between parties in a unity government is the distribution of violence.[21] The chapters by Muzondidya and Mazarire explore the effects of this legacy of violence on the politics of both the MDC formations and ZANU-PF during this period. Mazarire traces the importance of the military in ZANU-PF appointments since at least the late 1970s, as well as the ways in which the grassroots structures of the party have for the most part been 'guided' by the leadership. He notes that since 1977 Mugabe has carried out a restructuring exercise that resulted in a more centralised administration, building a permanent alliance between the President's Office and the departments of defence, security and the commissariat. The effects of this alliance have continued to make themselves felt in ZANU-PF's obstructive politics and the patronage networks that have been extended during the GPA period.

This obstructive politics has also manifested itself in the blockages that Mugabe's party has placed before the implementation of various democratising provisions of the GPA. In the constitutional reform process, under Article VI of the GPA, a draft constitution was produced in July 2012 after three years of delays, obstructions, logistical and financial squabbles and a problematic outreach programme under the Parliamentary Select Committee process, COPAC. While the COPAC draft is clearly a compromise document, it contains some important changes such as controls on executive power, more accountability of the judicial and security services, a more independent national prosecuting authority, devolution, and broader citizenship rights. Importantly, in terms of process, all the parties to the agreement were signatories to the draft, leading to the logical assumption that at all times the principals of the parties and their respective leaderships were fully informed of the discussions of the COPAC team.[22]

In response to this, ZANU-PF initiated a strategy intended to foil the process. In August 2012 Mugabe presented the leaders of the MDC formations with a ZANU-PF redraft of the COPAC document on the grounds that the latter was written without regard to the views gathered during the outreach process. The redraft, described by ZANU-PF as 'non-negotiable', attempted to undermine the GPA and once again force the Zimbabwe citizenry into a new election, either with a ZANU-PF constitutional construction, or without a new constitution. The redraft effectively dismissed the major reforms included in the COPAC draft and proposed a return to the kind of executive powers and party/state rule that ZANU-PF had constructed since 1980.

At the COPAC All Stakeholders Conference held on 22 October 2012, Mugabe made the assertion that given the ongoing disagreement over the draft it was the principals of the three parties who would make the final decision. After initially objecting strongly to Mugabe's move, both MDC formations agreed to a cabinet committee composed of a slightly restructured COPAC management committee to resolve the outstanding issues in the draft. In the interim, at ZANU-PF's National People's Conference held in early December 2012, Mugabe reasserted his position on the constitution:

> *Looking back to April 2009 when the Copac was set up, after a long, inexplicable and wasted 44 months, it is clear that the electoral cowards, and enemies of the values and ideals of our liberation struggle have violated public trust by abusing their participation in the GPA mandated constitution-making process.*
>
> *Their prime motive is to delay the holding of elections in order to extend their ill-gotten stay in that awkward animal called the Inclusive Government whose policy gridlock and non-performance have been a monumental betrayal of our people's legitimate expectations.*[23]

Mugabe further asserted that 'we will go for elections in March with or without a new constitution'.[24]

In addition to the constitutional reform process, ZANU-PF has also hindered the workings of the Zimbabwe Human Rights Commission (ZHRC) and the Joint Monitoring and Implementation Committee (JOMIC), to give just two more examples. On 16 December the Chair of the ZHRC, Prof. Reg Austin, tendered his resignation, noting that the establishment of the Commission has been a 'tale of unreadiness, delay, lack of commitment and serious focus'. Elaborating on his frustration he criticised the legal framework of the ZHRC Act, which he maintained 'effectively grants the executive (the Minister) a wide discretion, today and in the future to silence the Commission' on the grounds that its investigation of a complaint 'may prejudice the defence, external relations, internal security or economic interests of the State'. It was this discretionary power to gag the ZHRC which Austin found 'unacceptable'.[25] With regard to JOMIC, in the face of its growing capacity to broaden its operations and to monitor the implementation of the GPA more effectively, ZANU-PF's JOMIC co-chair, Nicholas Goche, launched an attack on the body in

November 2012. Central to his recriminations was an attempt to deligitimise the secretariat of JOMIC on the grounds that its key members were allies of the MDC formations and were assisting them to extend their organisational presence throughout the country.[26]

The combined effects of these and other obstructive measures were to present the two MDCs with formidable obstacles. As Muzondidya's chapter demonstrates, aside from the major problem of ZANU-PF's unwillingness to loosen its grip on state power, the MDC formations have faced major challenges dealing with administrative and bureaucratic issues within the GPA and in deploying competent people as representatives in government. The intraparty and interparty animosity and conflict of the two formations has also hindered their organisational growth and allowed ZANU-PF, and Mugabe in particular, to play them off against each other, with Mutambara providing the necessary foil. When all these problems are added to the growing trend of corruption, particularly in the MDC-T, it was not surprising that the support base of both formations began to decline. A Freedom House Survey carried out in mid 2012 reported that the MDC-T suffered a fall in support 'from 38% to 20% in the parliamentary vote from 2010 to 2012'. In contrast, ZANU-PF 'experienced a growth in popular support, moving from 17% to 31% in the same period'.[27]

ZANU-PF's history of violence cannot easily be discounted in such surveys, and the memory of such violence continues to be a key factor in Zimbabwean politics. The widespread involvement of people in ZANU-PF's coercion and violence has created a constituency with a stake in such violence. In a recent study of women and political violence in the Midlands, Marongwe has provided a disturbing account of a broader complicity in the then ruling party's violence:

> Many people...participated at...rallies either as cheerleaders, politicians, ordinary women and men, youth militias or also as war veterans. At times these roles were confused and conflated, making the distinction more difficult. Besides these office bearing women in political organisations the majority of ordinary women also helped to foment political violence. These women sang, danced, ululated, wore party regalia and made various performances.[28]

Such a political legacy cannot be discounted in any account of electoral mobilisation. Nevertheless it is also clear, as noted above, that ZANU-PF has not relied solely on violence to maintain its power base. It has also been more effective in the last four years in crafting a 'number of election and party choice platforms around the land, indigenisation, and the effects of foreign interference', as well as its longstanding messaging around the legacy of the liberation struggle.[29] The MDC's message of 'change' and its fight for human rights, while effective in mobilising a largely discontented citizenry for much of the 2000s, has lost some of its force as the MDC formations have become more accountable for policy decisions under the Inclusive Government. The launch of the MDC campaign document, *Jobs, Upliftment, Investment Capital and the Environment* (JUICE), centred around a democratic developmental state 'directing resources towards development-oriented initiatives through enabling legislation, sound policies, budgetary support and strengthening of linkages with the private sector',[30] has yet to make a substantive impact on the policy debates in the country. One major reason for this weakness is ZANU-PF's continued stranglehold over the electronic media; however, it is also clear that the mixed messaging and continued lack of coordination between the two MDC formations and their allies in the civic movement have contributed greatly to its weakened impact.

The civic movement has also dealt with the complex challenges of the GPA in uneven ways. At the heart of the birth of the opposition MDC in the late 1990s, the strength of the civics declined substantially during the economic crisis of the 2000s and the changing mode of MDC politics of this period. The civil society groups were largely marginalised in the SADC facilitation and were also unprepared for the agreement that emerged in 2008. The result of this was an extremely ambivalent approach to the GPA, sometimes resulting in the loss of opportunities to open up more political space during this period. This ambivalence was particularly apparent over the issue of constitutional reform. Unlike the period of the constitutional debate in the late 1990s, when the civic groups under the NCA played a key role in setting the intellectual and political agenda of the discussions, the current period largely witnessed contradictory messaging and weak participation by the these groups. Chiroro's chapter captures these changes, as well as the continuing lack of capacity of the civic movement – apart from its labour component – to deal with economic policy issues. However, she notes that human rights groups have continued to play an indispensable role in monitoring and reporting human rights abuses, and lobbying on these at all levels. The need for a strong civil society remains a central prerequisite for the democratisation of Zimbabwean politics.

Moving to the role of regional and international players in the GPA the chapters by Ndlovu-Gatsheni and Nyakudya track the interventions of SADC, the EU and the US. In many ways Mbeki's determination to ensure that African institutions maintained control of the mediation process on Zimbabwe set the tone for the relations between SADC and the West. Ndlovu-Gatsheni locates Mbeki's approach in his broader Pan Africanist vision, the shared liberation legacy of the regional nationalist movements, and a critical perspective on the persistent imperial ambitions of Western interventions in Africa. The result of this perspective was to contain the influence of the EU and the US on the SADC mediation, which led to the always uneasy attempts by the SA facilitation team to reconcile the need for democratic changes in Zimbabwe with the requirement for political 'stabilisation'.

Nyakudya's chapter follows this with a discussion of the contradictory role of Western diplomacy and the highly problematic influence of the sanctions debate on the SADC facilitation and the implementation of the GPA. An incisive thesis on Zimbabwe's power sharing agreement by Hoekman correctly notes that Western governments were only agreeable to the MDC-T joining the Inclusive Government on condition that ZANU-PF was genuine about power sharing, that there were sufficient guarantees to ensure a transition, and that 'Mugabe's exit was ensured'.[31] The lack of convergence between the West and SADC on these issues led to persistent tensions over the issue of sanctions that for the most part played into the hands of the Mugabe regime. Nyakudya's assessment also discusses the double standards of the West in its sanctions policy. This disparity is particularly apparent in areas of the world where the geopolitical interests of the EU and the US are more pronounced, such as the Middle East. Mbeki picked up on this issue in the aftermath of West's intervention in Libya in 2011, observing that:

> *Unless practically we assume responsibility for the advancement of democracy, the protection of human rights and the realisation of the objective of good governance on our continent, and act to guarantee peace and security, these [Western] powers will intervene in our countries in pursuit of their selfish objectives, legitimising such intervention by presenting themselves as 'friends of Africa', intent to give us the gift of democracy, human rights, peace, good governance and progress, regardless of our wishes.*[32]

Whilst Mbeki was clearly critiquing the problem of Western interventions in Africa, he was also reflecting on the failure of African states, including his own, to protect the democratic and human rights of its citizens.

The final chapter, by Shari Eppel, examines the challenges of the Transitional Justice (TJ) debate as Zimbabwean look to the future. Eppel analyses the weakness of the National Healing structure under the GPA as well as the various civic attempts to address this issue. More specifically, the chapter calls for a broadening of the TJ agenda to include social, economic and cultural/ethnic rights, instead of focusing solely on the documentation of individual violations. The human rights groups in Zimbabwe have built a formidable reputation for documenting violations, and these reports have been essential in lobbying against the abuses of the Mugabe regime. However, the neglect of broader structural violations in the political economy of the country, has led to the marginalisation of these groups from any serious discussions on economic policy alternatives designed to deal with the longstanding violations in this area. This challenge is one that must be addressed by the civic groups.

As this book goes to press in January 2013 the GPA Principals finally reached agreement on the outstanding issues on the draft constitution. Mugabe announced that the parties had 'come to the conclusion of the exercise';[33] with the date of the referendum and new election still to be announced, that will hopefully go some way in resolving the issues that gave rise to the GPA in 2008. Surveying the political trends in the country it appears foolhardy to place so much hope in such an election, given the severe challenges that continue to be faced in implementing the Agreement. This book is an attempt to analyse and assess both the hopes and frustrations of the last four years and to confront the harsh challenges that lie ahead. We hope that we have made a small contribution to an understanding of these challenges.

ENDNOTES

1 T. Ranger, 'Nationalist historiography, patriotic history and the history of the nation: The struggle over the past in Zimbabwe', *Journal of Southern African Studies*, 30(2), 2004, pp. 215-234; B-M. Tendi, *Making History in Mugabe's Zimbabwe: Politics, Intellectuals and the Media*. (Oxford: Peter Lang, 2010); B. Rutherford, 'On the promise and perils of citizenship: heuristic concepts, Zimbabwean example', *Citizenship Studies*, 15(3-4), 2011, pp. 499-512.

2 T.B. Hansen and F. Stepputat, 'Introduction' in T.B. Hansen and F. Stepputat (eds), *Sovereign Bodies. Citizens, Migrants and States in the Postcolonial World* (Princeton: Princeton University Press, 2005), p. 1.

3 E.Worby, 'The End of Modernity in Zimbabwe? Passages from Development to Sovereignty', in A. Hammar, B. Raftopoulos and S. Jensen (eds), *Zimbabwe's Unfinished Business: Rethinking Land, State and Nation in the Context of Crisis* (Harare: Weaver Press, 2003) p. 59.

4 Partnership Africa Canada, *Reap what you Sow: Greed and Corruption in Zimbabwe's Marange Diamond Fields*, Ottawa, Canada, 2012. p. 4. This reports concludes that 'a parallel trade in Marange diamonds continues to thrive, with the full knowledge and complicity of officials in the Ministry of Mines, ZMDC, MMCZ, and military'.

5 I. Mandaza, 'Introduction: The Political Economy of Transition,' in I. Mandaza (ed.), *Zimbabwe, The Political Economy of Transition 1980-1986* (Dakar: CODESRIA, 1986).

6 B. Raftopoulos and A. Mlambo (eds), *Becoming Zimbabwe: A History from the Pre-Colonial Period to 2008* (Harare: Weaver Press; Johannesburg: Jacana Media, 2009.) S. Ndlovu, *Do 'Zimbabweans' Exist? Trajectories of Nationalism, National Identity Formation and Crisis in a Postcolonial State* (Oxford: Peter Lang, 2009). For a similar analysis of the unevenness and contingency of national unity in Zambian history see M. Larmer, *Rethinking African Politics, A History of Opposition in Zambia* (Farnham: Ashgate, 2011).

7 Sabelo Ndlovu, *The Zimbabwe Nation-State Project, A Historical Diagnosis of Identity and Power-Based Conflicts in a Post-Colonial State* (Uppsala: Nordiska Afrikainstitutet, 2011), p. 60.

8 J. Alexander, J. McGregor and T. Ranger, *Violence and Memory, One Hundred Years in the 'Dark Forests' of Matabeleland* (Oxford: James Currey, 2000).

9 S. Eppel, 'An Overview of the circumstances of the Unity Accord of 1987 in comparison to those of the Global Political Agreement of 2008', Political Update, Solidarity Peace Trust, 2009, p. 8.

10 E.V. Masunugure and J.M. Shumba, *Zimbabwe, Mired in Transition* (Harare: Weaver Press, IDAZIM, 2012) pp. xiv-xvi.

11 Ibid, p. xiv.

12 G. O'Donnell and P. Schmitter, *Transitions from Electoral Rule: Tentative Conclusions about Uncertain Democracies* (Baltimore: Johns Hopkins University Press, 1986).

13 M. Bratton and N. van der Walle, *Democratic Experiments in Africa: Regime Transitions in Comparative Perspective* (Cambridge: Cambridge University Press, 1997).

14 A. Gramsci, *Selections from the Prison Notebooks* (London: Lawrence and Wishart, 1982), p. 178. See also S. Hall, *Thatcherism and the Crisis of the Left, The Hard Road to Renewal* (London: Verso, 1990), pp. 104-5.
15 I. Scoones, N. Marongwe, B. Mavedzenge, J. Mahenene, F. Murimbarimba, and C. Sukume, *Zimbabwe's Land Reform: Myths and Realities* (Oxford: James Currey; Harare: Weaver Press; Johannesburg: Jacana Media, 2010).
16 'Indigenisation: The Progress Report', *Sunday Mail*, 9-15 December 2012.
17 Parliament of Zimbabwe, *2012 Mid Term Fiscal Policy Review Statement*, 18 July 2012.
18 Ibid.
19 Ibid.
20 J. McGregor, 'Patronage, "power-sharing" and the politics of urban control in Zimbabwe' (forthcoming, *Journal of Southern African Studies*, 2013.)
21 N. Cheeseman, 'The Internal Dynamics of power-sharing in Africa', *Democratisation*, 18(2), 2011, p. 338.
22 This section draws from B. Raftopoulos, 'Towards another stalemate in Zimbabwe?', Norwegian Peacebuilding Resource Centre, October 2012.
23 'Zanu PF ready for elections', *Sunday Mail*, 9-15 December 2012.
24 Nqabi Matsahzi, 'Robert Mugabe's election rant a pipedream', www.thezimbabwemail.net/zimbabwe Accessed on 05/11/12.
25 Statement from Prof. Reg Austin, Chair of the Zimbabwe Human Rights Commission, 26 December 2012.
26 Statement by ZANU-PF's JOMIC co-chair Nicholas Goche on his party's concerns about the body that monitors compliance with a 2008 power sharing pact between ZANU-PF and the two MDC factions. 14 November 2012.
27 Freedom House, 'Change and "New" Politics in Zimbabwe', Harare, 18 August 2012, p. 5.
28 Ngonidzashe Marongwe, 'Rural women as the invisible victims of militarised political violence: The case of Shurugwe district', Draft PhD thesis, University of the Western Cape, 2012, p. 236.
29 Freedom House, op cit, p. 21.
30 Movement for Democratic Change, 'Jobs, Upliftment, Investment Capital and the Environment (JUICE)', Harare, 2012, p. 15. This document was strongly influenced by the ZCTU's economic policy position. See G. Kanyenze, T. Kondo, P. Chitambara and J. Martens, *Beyond the Enclave: Towards a Pro-Poor and Inclusive Development Strategy for Zimbabwe* (Harare: Weaver Press, 2011).
31 Thys Hoekman, 'The Politics of Negotiation: Opposition and Power-Sharing in Zimbabwe', M.Phil, Oxford University, April 2012, p. 75. This thesis is one of the few discussions of the SADC mediation that looks seriously at the combination of

national, regional and international factors leading to the GPA.
32 Thabo Mbeki, 'Reflections on Peacemaking, State Sovereignty and Democratic Governance in Africa', Dullah Omar Eighth Memorial Lecture, Community Law Centre, University of the Western Cape, 16 February 2012.
33 'Principals resolve COPAC row', *The Herald*, 18 January 2013.

CHAPTER 1

An Overview of the Politics of the Global Political Agreement:
National Conflict, Regional Agony, International Dilemma

BRIAN RAFTOPOULOS

Introduction

On 15 September 2008, ZANU-PF and the two MDC formations signed the SADC-mediated Global Political Agreement (GPA). Its major purpose was to plot a route beyond the contested 2008 presidential elections, and the problem of political legitimacy that this entailed for all the parties and prepare the ground for a more generally acceptable election process. Coming out of the worst ZANU-PF led violence in the country since the state-inflicted Gukurahundi massacres in Matabeleland and the Midlands in the mid 1980s, Zimbabwe emerged from the 2008 elections in a highly polarised state. The economy was in the worst condition of the post-colonial era, with hyperinflation, unemployment, failure of state services, cholera and massive human displacement, serving as the major indicators of this crisis. There were, however, also signs that the land convulsions of the 2000s, though still enormously problematic, had led to some positive growth with new forms of smallholder production and new markets pointing to the potential of a revamped agrarian sector.[1]

Thus the combination of ZANU-PF's redistributive economic interventions, carried out through an authoritarian nationalist politics that brutally repressed the electoral will of the Zimbabwean citizenry, forced SADC to develop a mediation framework that would seek to protect regional sovereignty, respect the legacies of liberation struggles in the region, confront international pressures and provide a framework for democratic transition in the country. Not surprisingly this proved to be a Herculean task, with the SADC mediation encountering numerous obstacles and delays. These have taken the form of obstructive politics from ZANU-PF, the internal political dynamics of the major parties in Zimbabwe, the contradictions of the civic responses, counter-productive positions from the Western countries, and the slowness of SADC in responding to the authoritarian politics of the Mugabe regime. Moreover the position of the SADC facilitators has been questioned, with Presidents Mbeki and Zuma both being accused on different occasions of not acting in 'good faith' by one political party or the other.

In a general sense power-sharing agreements have been subjected to a great deal of criticism. Critics have noted their undermining effects on democratisation and the accountability of politicians, the creation of unsustainable budgets and the establishment of cumbersome institutions that result in policy gridlock.[2] More specifically Zimbabwe's GPA has also been strongly criticised in the academic literature. In their comparative analysis of 'unity government' in Kenya and Zimbabwe, Cheeseman and Tendi conclude that power sharing 'serves to postpone conflict rather than resolve it'. Moreover the authors state that in the Zimbabwean case, 'the combination of institutional and partisan veto players ensured that the power-sharing government was still-born' and that ZANU-PF and military hardliners 'had no intention of respecting the unity deal'.[3]

Other scholars have produced similar criticisms of the GPA. Matyszak's largely legalistic analysis has sought to expose the legal limitations of the agreement with the author noting that 'the bulk of the fifteen-page agreement comprises pious statements devoid of any practical consequence and which are little more than political posturing'.[4] Saunders condemns the GPA as being 'ineffective in meeting its key objectives' and for providing a 'flimsy but sufficient veneer of legitimacy while facilitating ZANU-PF's continued access to strategic levers of power'.⁵ Kriger's position locates the weakness of the GPA in the informal networks and alliances that ZANU-PF has created both inside and outside of state institutions to consolidate the power of the latter. As a result of this process she concludes that this 'parallel government demonstrates the relative powerlessness of the IG [Inclusive Government] and the dominance of ZANU-PF in its competition with the MDC'.⁶

Against such broad dismissals of the GPA process, Muzondidya has provided a more nuanced assessment of the Inclusive Government noting not only the serious shortcomings outlined above, but also stressing the potential of the arrangement given the balance of political forces in the country since 2008.⁷

While this chapter shares many of the criticisms of the GPA offered by these authors, and addresses many of the same questions asked by previous writers, it makes two claims in its contribution. Firstly, it contributes to a more comprehensive understanding of the combination of national, regional and international factors that shaped the decisions around the process and set the limits for the ongoing politics of the 'coalition government'.⁸ Much of the existing analysis of the GPA has not sufficiently addressed the complex interaction between these processes, and has often concentrated on one or other level of this process. Secondly, it aims to produce a more nuanced picture of the GPA, examining the various dynamics involved in its construction and providing a better understanding of the political options available to the different players at a particular conjuncture in Zimbabwe's history.

Quiet Diplomacy and the Zimbabwe Crisis

As the situation in Zimbabwe began to unravel from the 1990s in a complex articulation of long-term questions of democratisation and structural economic inequalities, the politics of the crisis posed serious dilemmas not only for Zimbabweans themselves, but for the southern African region and South Africa in particular.⁹ From the late 1990s, the Mugabe regime spent a great deal of ideological energy on articulating the Zimbabwean crisis as primarily an issue of colonial redress centred on the land question, as well as being part of a broader anti-imperialist and Pan-Africanist struggle on the African continent and in the developing world.¹⁰ On his ascendancy to the South African Presidency in 1999, Thabo Mbeki, confronted with the politics of solidarity and sovereignty in SADC and the AU, was determined to avoid the criticisms of unilateralism that the South African state faced in its positions on Nigeria, Lesotho and the

Democratic Republic of Congo (DRC) in the 1990s. The post 9/11 world and regime change strategy that became central to US foreign policy under George Bush also heightened the sensitivities of African states to opposition movements on the continent perceived as the agents of such a strategy.

The Mbeki government was clear that South Africa should not be viewed as the regional strongman, pushing its own agenda in conflict situations, and hence continuing the ambitions of the apartheid state. Thus, on the Zimbabwe question, South Africa's broader ambition of leading the continent and becoming a global player meant that it had to balance its continental ambitions with maintaining Western support, and link its Pan-Africanist ambitions to its struggle to reform the global order.[11] More specifically Mbeki's position on Zimbabwe was based on a number of assumptions, including: the lack of capacity on the part of the Movement for Democratic Change (MDC) to carry out a transition process on its own; a strong perception within sections of the ANC that the MDC was too close to the West; that the West should not intervene in the Zimbabwe crisis until requested to do so by the region since the language of regime change was deeply damaging to the dialogue in Zimbabwe; the need to reassure Mugabe about his future; and the need to keep the military on side. Mbeki also understood that the problem of succession in ZANU-PF needed to be confronted.[12]

In a paper written in the early 2000s Mbeki set out his assessment of the Zimbabwe problem and his analysis of the 'party of revolution', ZANU-PF:

> *Of critical importance ... is the obvious necessity to ensure that Zimbabwe does not end up in a situation of isolation, confronted by an array of international forces it cannot defeat, condemned to sink into an ever-deepening social and economic crisis that would result in the reversal of so many of the gains of the national democratic revolution. It is also important that the party of revolution should consider its internationalist responsibilities to the rest of the continent and especially to southern Africa, given the reality that events in any one of our countries has an impact on other countries in our region.*[13]

In his analysis Mbeki sought to open a discussion with ZANU-PF that set out the problems of the party, the reasons for the emergence of the opposition, the broader regional and international conditions in which this had taken place, and provided suggestions for a reform process within ZANU-PF. Mbeki's hope was that a reformed ZANU-PF would still be able to recover its support and, if necessary, lead a government of national unity in normalising its relations with the West.

In addition to the above discussion on the rationale for SA's foreign policy, other suggestions have been made to explain Mbeki's 'quiet diplomacy' on Zimbabwe. Tendi argues that Mbeki's position was largely determined by the agreement that Mugabe reached with Commonwealth Secretary-General in the early 1990s not to proceed with radical land reform because this would derail the democratic transition in South Africa. The result was that the ANC felt that they were in debt to Mugabe.[14] Moore offers a more critical evaluation in his analysis of Mbeki's discourse around the National Democratic Revolution (NDR), the first stage of which required the removal of white minority rule, while the second sought to end poverty, underdevelopment and bridge the gulf between blacks and whites. He argues that the latter conceptualisation places Mbeki and Mugabe in close ideological proximity because it allows for the 'elision between "race" and "nation", and then opens the space for "self-determination" along racial lines'. Moore further argues that in spite of keeping white capital on board, Mbeki slips into the same 'kith and kin' argument as Mugabe, thus justifying Mugabe's reduction of all opposition to a British conspiracy, and not paying any significant attention to the massive human rights abuses of the ZANU-PF government.[15] These positions all contribute to a more multi-faceted explanation of Mbeki's policy on Zimbabwe and they should be considered together rather than as singular explanations.[16]

What is clear, however, is that Mbeki and SADC took the issue of 'regime change' and its implications for the region very seriously. In his recent book on the removal of Thabo Mbeki, Frank Chikane, former Director General for the SA Presidency, writes:

The SADC perspective on Zimbabwe was a classic case. SADC was totally opposed to the policy of undemocratic 'regime change' advocated by some of the major Western powers. Notwithstanding the view that Zimbabwe may have made mistakes or have approached certain matters in a way that exposed it to attack, an undemocratic regime change would not be allowed in the region, especially when it was driven by Western powers.

SADC determined that if this was allowed to happen in one country it would then be used in another until all governments of which the Western powers disapproved were removed from power.[17]

It is apparent from the above discussion that, in Mbeki's assessment of the Zimbabwean problem, issues around democratisation were secondary to the question of sovereignty, the need for stability, and his perception of the threat of regime change by the West in Zimbabwe. As we will see below this sometimes led him into moving too close to Mugabe in the mediation process and opened him up to accusations of favouring the liberation leader and his party during the facilitation, and underplaying or ignoring the centrality of violence as a modality of rule in the Zimbabwean state for much of the 2000s. This position, located around Mbeki's construction of the second stage of the National Democratic Revolution, has been echoed in some of the academic literature on the Zimbabwean crisis, particularly in the the work of Moyo and Yeros. In the publications of the latter, the violence of the authoritarian nationalist state has been interpreted largely within the framework of what they view as 'radicalised states' like Zimbabwe that have 'undergone classic revolutionary situations, which have not yielded revolutionary states'. In this analysis the 'uncivil' popular pressures for land redistribution have been confronted by an array of forces in the donor, NGO and civic sectors which have sought to convert the Zimbabwean crisis into a more 'civilised' good governance agenda, and therefore undermined the radical, redistributive struggles on the land. From this position the struggles around democratisation, human and civic rights have been cast, mistakenly, solely as elitist, Western-driven agendas, and the state-driven violence has been largely downplayed.[18]

It is within this context and framed by the issues outlined above that Mbeki, joined by Nigerian President Obasanjo, made an early attempt in 2002 to mediate a political settlement in Zimbabwe after the violent and contested presidential elections of that year. In response to this attempt the MDC, before the split in the party in 2005,[19] stated its readiness to embark on a process of 'national reconciliation and national healing'. However it noted that such a process should be 'anchored in a sound foundation characterised by an unconditional return to legitimacy' which could only be achieved through fresh presidential elections, under free and fair conditions and supervised 'by the region, the continent and the international community'.[20] ZANU-PF stated, in its submission to the two African presidents, that its legitimacy was not derived primarily from an electoral process but from the 'huge sacrifices which accompanied our rise to statehood' which made the sovereignty of Zimbabwe 'sacred and sacrosanct, a non-negotiable issue we are duty bound to uphold, defend and augment at all times as Zimbabweans'.[21]

Thus the issue of competing conceptions of sovereignty between the parties was a major factor from the time of the emergence of the MDC as a serious challenger for state power in the late 1990s. On the one hand, the MDC, formed in the post-1989 global era of a dominant liberal democratic discourse, based its legitimacy on the sovereignty of the electoral process, constitutionalism and a broad human rights foundation. On the other hand, ZANU-PF, although formally adhering to regular elections, based its legitimacy largely on the legacies of the liberation struggle, a highly problematic redistributive land agenda from 2000, and a dominant ethos of force and coercion which characterised most of the electoral processes in the post-colonial period. These competing discourses continued to run right through the positions of ZANU-PF and, after the 2005 split, the two MDC formations in the period leading to, and in the wording of, the GPA.

The need for a regional mediation in the Zimbabwe situation took on an added urgency after the public beating, arrest and torture of opposition and civic leaders at a peaceful gathering on the 11 March 2007 and the brutal attacks on the MDC structures that followed thereafter.[22] A combination of international pressure and concerned voices in SADC led to an Extra-Ordinary SADC Heads of State summit in Tanzania on 28-29 March 2007. At this summit President Mbeki was mandated to 'continue to facilitate dialogue between the opposition and the Government of Zimbabwe' and report back to the Troika on the progress. The summit also reiterated the appeal to Britain to 'honour its compensation obligations with regard to land reform made at Lancaster House', and appealed for the lifting of all forms of sanctions against Zimbabwe.[23] Thus while SADC rather belatedly took a more active mediation position, it also stated a critical position towards the role of the West in the Zimbabwe problem.

After the Dar es Salaam summit the first meeting in the dialogue process was scheduled for a two-day exchange on 12-13 May 2007. Mbeki sent out a letter to the presidents of the three parties stating that the central objective of the SADC facilitation was to ensure that the 2008 elections were 'conducted in a manner that will make it impossible for any honest person in Zimbabwe to question the legitimacy of their outcomes'. More specifically Mbeki spelt out the major tasks of the facilitation as follows: to endorse the decision to hold parliamentary and presidential elections in 2008; to agree on the steps that must be taken to 'ensure that everybody concerned accepts the results of the elections as being truly representative of the will of the people'; and to agree on the measures that all parties and other social forces must implement and respect to create the necessary climate that will facilitate such acceptance. Mbeki also advised that the leaders of Zimbabwe should communicate the same message to the rest of the world, namely that the 'principal task of the international community is to encourage and support the united effort of the people and the leaders of Zimbabwe and to find a solution to their problems, at all costs avoiding any temptation to divide these people and leaders, regardless of the ways and means that might be used to foment such division'.[24] Thus from the onset, against the background of Mbeki's already discussed analysis of the Zimbabwe problem, he made it clear that the facilitation process would be led by SADC and the Zimbabwean political leaders, and supported but not directed by international players. In this way he hoped to 'begin the process leading to the normalisation of the situation in Zimbabwe',[25] in the face of the 'sanctions' imposed by the EU, the US, Australia and Canada in the 2000s.

Prior to the dialogue process in mid-May, the two MDC formations had sent a joint pre-dialogue statement to Mbeki that was also circulated to ZANU-PF. The document set out fifteen sets of obstacles to the holding of free and fair elections which ranged from the need for electoral and constitutional reforms, to the problems of state violence, state monopolisation of the electronic media and the political abuse of power by traditional leaders.[26] When the delegations of the two MDCs arrived at the South African venue for the talks they were informed that Patrick Chinamasa, ZANU-PF's chief negotiator, had left for Ghana instead of attending the dialogue meeting. The delay caused by Chinamasa's recall from Ghana meant that the planned two-day meeting was reduced to a two-hour session, at which ZANU-PF requested time to respond to the MDC document. The next meeting set for the 3-4 June 2007 was once again delayed because ZANU-PF claimed it needed more time to complete their response to the MDC document. It was finally submitted on 7 June 2007.

The ZANU-PF paper failed to address any of the major issues in MDC document. Instead it spoke largely to the issue of the land question and ZANU-PF's construction of national sovereignty. The document once again confirmed the rupture in the political discourse in Zimbabwe between rights and redistribution issues,[27] stating that in the view of the ruling party,

   ... *the Land Question (and not the so called need for a new Con-*

stitution, alleged human rights violations or alleged lack of the rule of law or a declining economy) is at the centre of the Zimbabwean situation... The Land Question is, pure and simple, a decolonization issue and was at the very heart of armed struggle.[28]

Following the submission of ZANU-PF's document, it was not until the 17-18 June 2007 that the parties finally met for a longer dialogue and agreed on an agenda for the talks. At the suggestion of the SA facilitators it was agreed that the range of issues to be included on the agenda of the talks would be narrowed down to two broad areas, namely a new constitution and the conditions necessary for a free and fair election. Under these areas the agenda included: (i) The Constitution; (ii) Electoral Laws; (iii) Security Legislation (The Public Order and Security Act, POSA); (iv) Communications and Communications Legislation (Broadcasting laws and external radio stations); (v) Political Climate (Demilitarisation of state institutions; hostile rhetoric; use of militia; abuse of state aid and traditional leaders; sanctions; land). At this meeting, the parties also agreed that the modality of the dialogue would involve two processes. In one of these the four lead negotiators would work through the technical aspects of the agenda on their own and then meet regularly with the facilitation team to deal with areas of dispute in agenda items i-iv. In the other process the facilitation team would take the lead on the agenda item dealing with the 'Political Climate'.[29] This meeting was followed by a series of other delays in the dialogue caused largely by ZANU-PF's obstructive behavior, and in early July 2007 the MDCs sent a memorandum to the Facilitator complaining about ZANU-PF's 'serious lack of commitment to the SADC dialogue process'.[30]

With the resumption of talks thereafter the parties made progress on a number of areas. On the constitution a draft was agreed on and signed by the negotiators on 30 September 2007 in Kariba. This document, subsequently referred to as the 'Kariba Draft', soon after became a source of deadlock in terms of its date of implementation. In areas of security, communication and electoral reform some changes were agreed to that would contribute to a more amenable electoral environment in March 2008. However ZANU-PF's gazetting of Amendment 18 in June 2007 caused a major rupture in the dialogue. The Amendment itself included a number of election related measures, including: the harmonisation of presidential and parliamentary elections; provision for Parliament and the senate to jointly sit as an electoral college to choose a new president by a two-thirds majority should the president die, resign, be impeached or become incapacitated in office; an increase of the lower house from 120-210 seats and an increase in the upper house from 66-84 seats.[31] The passing of this Amendment was based on a joint agreement by all the parties to the facilitation. As an MDC report to President Mbeki on this agreement noted:

> We wish to place it on record that at a meeting chaired by your facilitation team on the 18th June 2007 the parties agreed that they would negotiate a draft constitution after which they would appoint a select committee of parliament which would take the draft constitution through a public consultation exercise culminating in the enactment of that constitution before the 2008 election. Furthermore, when the parties negotiated amendments to the Constitution of Zimbabwe Amendment number 18 Bill and its enactment the MDC supported the enactment on the express understanding by the ZANU-PF negotiating team that they would not renege on the enactment of the agreed draft constitution before the 2008 elections. It is also our understanding that our principals Mr. Morgan Tsvangirai and Professor Arthur Mutambara at a meeting with yourself on 15 September 2007 sought and obtained guarantees that ZANU-PF would not be allowed to renege on the agreement to implement a new constitution before the elections.[32]

By the first week of December 2007 it became clear that ZANU-PF had decided to renege on the June agreement. The result was that a deadlock arose in the mediation over 'the date of the election, the timeframe for the implementation of the agreed reforms and the manner, process and timeframe for the making, adoption and implementation of a new constitution'.[33] Mugabe also unilaterally decided that the election would take place in March 2008 and that this decision was not negotiable, despite several attempts to break the deadlock by the SADC facilitator in January 2008. By the time of the SADC Heads of State and Government summit in early February 2008, President Mbeki tried to cover over the cracks in the negotiations, in order to push the process along. In his report to SADC Mbeki congratulated the Zimbabwean parties on reaching 'agreement on all substantive issues' apart from the question of procedure to be followed in enacting the agreed constitution. The MDCs responded angrily to this report and the subsequent SADC communiqué insisting that the issues in the deadlock 'were not matters of procedure but of substance and went to the heart of the matter'.[34] It was clear that once ZANU-PF had dug their heels in on this matter, Mbeki and SADC were prepared to accept this position and move to an election on the basis of the minimal electoral reforms agreed to in Amendment 18 and the Electoral Act. For their part, once SADC had taken this position the two MDCs had little choice but to participate in the March elections.

Despite the obstacles to broader electoral reform caused by ZANU-PF's intransigence the minimum changes brought about by the mediation led to a major shift in Zimbabwean politics. As a result of small but important changes to the system of voting, counting and tallying results at polling stations, opening up the electronic media and freer campaigning space, the two MDC's defeated ZANU-PF in the parliamentary elections, while Morgan Tsvangirai won the first round of the presidential election. The defeat of ZANU-PF was also due to the fractures in ZANU-PF that appeared around the emergence of Simba Makoni's Mavhambo party, which while it did not command a great deal of electoral support, helped to split the ZANU-PF vote, in the context of the ongoing succession battles in the ruling party. For their part the two MDC formations missed the opportunity to increase their lead because of their failure to agree on an electoral pact in January 2008, largely around disagreement over the distribution of parliamentary seats.[35]

The long delays in the announcement of the elections results after the March elections and the massive state-controlled violence that preceded the June Presidential run-off, resulted in universal criticism and non-acceptance of the legitimacy of the latter. Even within SADC, which had throughout the 2000s provided an umbrella of cover for the Mugabe regime against outside criticism, countries like Zambia, Botswana and Tanzania took an increasingly critical stance on ZANU-PF. Additionally, Mbeki's mediation came in for increased criticism from both inside and outside of Zimbabwe. In mid-2008 Tsvangirai stated that the MDC saw Mbeki's role as mediator as 'neither appropriate nor effective', and accused Mbeki of not denouncing the 'well-documented post-election attacks on our people'.[36]

Internationally the US and the UK pushed the Zimbabwe issue onto the UN agenda, supported by the agreement at a G8 meeting in Japan in July 2008 to tighten sanctions against Zimbabwe's ruling elite and to press for the appointment of a Special UN envoy to Zimbabwe.[37] The UN deputy secretary-general Asha Rose Migiro, observed that the situation in Zimbabwe was the 'single greatest challenge in southern Africa' not only because of the terrible humanitarian consequences but also because of the 'dangerous political precedent it sets'.[38] In mid-July 2008 an attempt was made by the UK and the US to pass a UN Security Council Resolution for sanctions against key leaders of the Mugabe regime as well as to impose an arms embargo against the regime. This initiative was vetoed by China and Russia, supported by South Africa. The US Ambassador to the UN expressed his dismay at the SA position observing that it was particularly distressing given the role that international sanctions had played in the democratisation process in SA.[39] US Government spokesman, Sean McCormack, also stated that the SA Government 'has an increasing awareness that the eyes of the world are not only on Zimbabwe, but also on them'.[40]

Moreover, in addition to the criticisms from the Western countries, and dissenting voices in SADC, Mbeki also faced criticism of his 'quiet diplomacy' from the ANC alliance partners, COSATU and the SACP. The latter position was linked to the growing opposition to Mbeki in the ANC that culminated in his removal from the Presidency of the ANC at the Polokwane Congress at the end of 2008. The solidarity of the trade unions against the authoritarian regime in Zimbabwe was clearly demonstrated in April 2008 when the Chinese ship the An Yue Jiang attempted to unload 77 tons of cargo made up of AK-47 ammunition, 1,500 rockets and 3,000 mortar shells, at Durban harbour. Following a court action by the Southern African Litigation Centre to prevent the cargo from being unloaded, the African Trade and Allied Workers Union instructed its members not to handle the cargo. This show of solidarity was backed by other dock workers in the region, as well as by the international workers federations and several international NGOs.

In the face of such criticisms Mbeki was unmoved against what he viewed as the 'regime change projects' of certain forces in South Africa and certain international political players:

> ... the Cosatu and SACP positions on Zimbabwe, seemingly in opposition to the ANC, had much to do with domestic South African (Alliance) politics, and the relevant international alliances, with very little to do relating to any serious effort to resolve the crisis in Zimbabwe.[41]

Nonetheless, by early July 2008, President Mbeki, in the context of this growing pressure, was fighting to keep the mediation on track. However, the dispute over the UN Security Council vote allowed Mbeki to draw on African solidarity again, as African states, having confirmed their support for the mediation at the AU conference Egypt in June 2008, largely stood by what was considered to be the African position of continued negotiations under the SADC process. This position was consistent with the AU insistence on Mugabe's presence at the EU-AU summit in Portugal in December 2007, in the face of the British boycott of the summit because of the Zimbabwean leader's presence. Not long before the summit the then Secretary General of the ANC, Kgalema Motlanthe, released a statement strongly supporting Mugabe and critical of the role of the British in the Zimbabwean crisis:

> The simple truth, therefore, is that SADC, with the full support of the AU, is not only concerned about the situation in Zimbabwe. It is acting on this concern, with the full support and cooperation of the government, the ruling party and the opposition political formations in Zimbabwe. Clearly the British government believes all this means nothing. It is suggesting that it is morally superior to everybody else in the EU and the AU. The question to ask is whence this extraordinary sense of superiority.[42]

The extreme nature of the growing political, economic and humanitarian crisis in Zimbabwe in 2008, exacerbated by the contested June presidential elections, added new urgency to the mediation discussions, and on 21 July a Memorandum of Understanding (MOU) was signed by the three parties. The MOU, characteristic of Mbeki's central concern in the mediation, once again asserted the 'centrality and importance of African institutions in dealing with African problems,'[43] and it was later used in the negotiations 'as the basis for the draft political agreement'.[44]

On Thursday 11 September 2008 the parties completed and signed the Global Political Agreement (GPA) that was later signed at a formal ceremony on Monday 15 September 2008, as the central outcome of the Mbeki-led SADC mediation. The Declaration of Commitment by all parties to the agreement read:

> The parties hereby agree to work together to create a genuine, viable, permanent sustainable and nationally acceptable solution to the Zimbabwe situation, and in particular to implement the ... agreement with the aims of resolving once and for all the current political and economic situations and charting a new political direction for the country.[45]

The agreement was an uneasy compromise between ZANU-PF and the two

MDCs and was the result of a combination of factors: the weakening of both ZANU-PF and the opposition, together with the social forces and civic groups that supported the MDCs; the disastrous economic and humanitarian situation in the country by 2008; pressure from SADC; and growing international isolation of the Mugabe regime. Moreover, while for ZANU-PF the GPA represented an opportunity to climb out of the political and economic rubble it had played such a central role in creating, the MDCs accepted the agreement as their only viable route to state power, in the face of a state still capable and willing to deploy massive repressive power against opposition forces.[46] At the centre of the GPA was the struggle for state power as the competing parties struggled for political spaces and levers in preparation for the election that would be the end result of the mediation and the agreement.

The agreement included provisions for various political and economic reforms that would create the conditions for a generally acceptable election and the 'normalisation' of politics in Zimbabwe. It included broad agreement on: restoration of economic stability and growth; the removal of sanctions; recognition of the 'inevitability and desirability of a comprehensive land reform programme in Zimbabwe'; recognition of the 'fundamental right and duty of the Zimbabwe people to make a constitution by themselves and for themselves'; the promotion of equality, national healing, cohesion and unity; respect for national institutions and events; no external interference in the internal affairs of the country; the right to free political activity; respect for the rule of law and the constitution; freedom of assembly and association; the recognition that state organs and institutions do not belong to any particular political party; the political neutrality of traditional leaders; the establishment of a non-partisan National Youth Training Programme; the provision of humanitarian and food assistance to all who request it regardless of race, ethnicity, gender, political affiliation or religion; the prioritisation of a legislative agenda that would reflect the letter and spirit of the agreement; respect for the security of persons and prevention of violence; freedom of expression and communication. The agreement also set out a framework for government which would be divided between the President, Prime Minister and Cabinet, with the Presidency still a dominant force. Additionally, the Joint Monitoring and Implementation Committee (JOMIC) was established to 'ensure full and proper implementation of the letter and spirit of the Agreement'. All these arrangements were then put into law through Constitutional Amendment No. 19.

It was, however, an agreement that left the coercive arms of the state very much under the control of ZANU-PF, and in that respect represented, in Masunungure's words, 'an asymmetrical distribution of powers and responsibilities in favour of the executive president'.[47] Moreover, the language of the agreement represented an uncomfortable mixture of the contending notions of sovereignty discussed above, with competing narratives of political and civic rights, on the one hand, and redistributive economic demands expressed through the dominant discourse of the liberation struggle on the other, inhabiting an uncomfortable conceptual relationship in the document. It was in short a combined political wish list, but one in which the repressive force of ZANU-PF and its authoritarian construction of sovereignty retained the upper hand. In this respect the agreement was very much in accordance with the regime change concerns of the SADC mediator.

The Challenges of the GPA

Immediately after the GPA was signed disagreements arose over the power-sharing deal, which delayed the coming into being of the Inclusive Government. When the agreement was signed on 11 September an addendum was attached which included the 31 ministries that would have to be divided between the three parties. After the early discussions over these ministries in September it was clear that there were four ministries that were at the heart of the dispute between the parties. These were Finance, Home Affairs, Foreign Affairs and Local Government, and Rural and Urban Development.[48] By early October the dispute had narrowed down to the Ministries of Home Affairs and Finance. While the dispute over this issue was still in play, ZANU-PF unilaterally gazetted what it claimed to be the agreed allocation of ministries to the three parties. This act was part of a trend that marked ZANU-PF's approach throughout the discussion and implementation of the GPA.[49] By the end of 2008 the matters under dispute had expanded to include: the equitable distribution of ministries; the enactment of the law establishing the National Security Council; the appointment of governors and other senior appointments such as the Governor of the Reserve Bank, and the Attorney General; the secession and reversal of all breaches to the Memorandum of Understanding and the GPA; and the enactment of Constitutional Amendment No. 18.[50] By the end of November 2009 the number of outstanding issues had risen to 21 contentious points.

The dispute over the issues delayed the formation of an Inclusive Government until February 2009 when, following renewed pressure from the SADC

Heads of State and Government Summit in Pretoria on 26-27 January 2009, the transitional government began its work.[51] In Tsvangirai's words it was 'time for us to put aside our political differences, to prioritise the welfare of the people in both our policies and actions and to focus on stabilisation, development, progress and democratization'.[52] By this time, in the aftermath of Mbeki's removal from the ANC Presidency at the Polokwane Conference in December 2008, President Zuma had taken over as the Facilitator, accompanied by a new facilitation team. While it appeared, from earlier statements from Zuma, that the new facilitator would take a much more critical stance against Mugabe's recalcitrance, on the whole the Zuma mediation was to remain largely within the paradigm set by Mbeki.

A key factor in this process was that the SADC process received at best a lukewarm response from the EU and the US, largely because the process remained under SADC control and it did not achieve the result they had hoped for, namely the removal of Mugabe. This was unlike the Kofi Annan led process after the disputed election in Kenya in 2008, where the Western countries actively supported the mediation. Once the Inclusive Government got under way it faced several challenges that were major factors impacting on the dynamics of Zimbabwean politics under the GPA. These included: the politics of ZANU-PF and the Zimbabwean state; the politics of the MDCs and the civic movement; SADC, the EU and the US. The following sections will discuss each of these issues in greater depth.

The Politics of ZANU-PF and the Zimbabwean State

Over the last three decades of post-colonial rule in Zimbabwe ZANU-PF has steadily conflated its existence with that of the state leading to its current incarnation as a party/state. In the last decade, in particular, the character of this state has been steadily subject to militarisation in the context of the deepening political and economic crisis in the country, and the growing national and international opposition to the rule of ZANU-PF. This led to two major problems. Firstly the challenge of the succession within ZANU-PF; and secondly the problem of confronting the military factor in Zimbabwean politics, which has grown to be an even larger issue since the early 2000s. From this period, the securocrats increased their leverage over the various organs of the state, the economy and party structures, as well as in the legislature where they contested elections as retired members of the security service. These two factors presented ZANU-PF with the challenge of balancing the requirement of being seen to implement the GPA, while attempting to carry out internal changes that would not threaten its future in the Zimbabwe polity.

The ongoing factional struggles within the party, which have their roots in the longer history of ZANU-PF,[53] were heightened in the period of the GPA. This was as a result of the growing need for a succession plan in the context of an ageing President, the pressure from SADC and the West for a more comprehensive implementation of the agreement, and the risks of running a free and fair election for the future of the party. The sudden death, under very suspicious circumstances, of liberation hero and former military supremo Solomon Mujuru in August 2011, further fuelled speculation on the succession issue in ZANU-PF.[54] However, the seemingly intractable problem of finding a successor to Mugabe who is capable of winning a national election against Morgan Tsvangirai, was once again revealed in an interview given by the President in February 2012 on the occasion of his 88th birthday. Asked whether there were groups in ZANU-PF positioning themselves to succeed him, Mugabe replied confidently:

> Those you cannot avoid. But, they are not as serious. All the people (to say all is too absolute) support that I stand. There is no one who can stand and win at the moment. You have got to groom a candidate. You can't just get someone and put them in the forefront. You must groom a successor.[55]

Yet asked further whether he was grooming such a successor, Mugabe replied: 'Not yet. That will cause much more divisions within the party.' This statement once again captured the problem, in which Mugabe has both generated and used the divisions in his party to perpetuate his supremacy in the party and state. The challenge around this question also surfaced in debates over the constitution. In early February 2012 there was a furore in ZANU-PF over an apparent attempt to include a clause in the constitutional draft document which barred anyone who had already served two five-year terms from standing in future elections.[56] This was clearly aimed at Mugabe and appeared to have the support of all parties in the body driving the constitutional reform process, COPAC. It also confirmed the cross party consensus conveyed in the WikiLeaks documents, that Mugabe should go, but revealed the weakness of developing a political mechanism to carry out this general demand. Responding furiously to this development and with a characteristic *volte face* given his WikiLeaks position supporting the need for Mugabe to step down, ZANU-PF ideologue Jonathan Moyo stated:

> ... we must as a country begin to seriously interrogate the fact that since 1999, constitution-making in Zimbabwe has been corrupted into a convenient but mischievous succession tool within ZANU-PF ranks, and a treacherous regime change instrument within MDC circles and among UK, US and EU interests that have been founding and funding regime change politics in Zimbabwe.[57]

This criticism became part of escalating attempts by Mugabe to unravel the constitutional process and the GPA more generally and move to an early election without a new constitution. In response to comments from South African Foreign Affairs Minister Maite Nkoana-Mashabane in early March 2012, that Zimbabwe could only hold elections after the completion of the constitution-making process as set out in the GPA, Mugabe and other leaders in ZANU-PF reacted strongly to this rather obvious interpretation of the agreement. Mugabe stated:

> The GPA was never meant to be more than two years. The GPA was about ending violence and holding fresh elections without violence and a new constitution. It was never about a new constitution.[58]

Officially the rush by ZANU-PF to a new election was based on the argument that the GPA had become unworkable. However it was more likely that this move was based on concerns over Mugabe's health and the persistent ZANU-PF problem of finding a successor who could win a national election against the opposition MDC formations, particularly the larger MDC led by Morgan Tsvangirai. Combined with this tactic ZANU-PF also carried out a heightened campaign to discredit MDC Morgan Tsvangirai through media campaigns alleging fraud on his part,[59] as well as bad judgement in his personal relations.[60] Additionally, while levels of state violence and intimidation had dropped considerably after the signing of the GPA, various civic groups still reported their concerns in this area. In late 2009 the Zimbabwe Peace Project reported that while the level of violations in the country had declined since the previous year, there were still disturbing incidents of harassment and assaults,[61] while the Zimbabwe Congress of Trade Unions reported a similar decline in human and trade union rights reports in most sectors except the agricultural sector which 'is engulfed in lawless farm invasions'.[62] Similarly the Zimbabwe Human Rights Forum remained concerned with the continued suppression of freedom of expression and association and the disregard of court orders.⁶³

As the jostling over the terms of the GPA continued between the parties, the challenge of the 'outstanding issues' in the agreement and their implementation dragged on in the facilitation process. By November 2009, following the meeting of the SADC Organ Troika Summit in Maputo on the fifth of that month, 29 outstanding issues were identified.⁶⁴ Following this the party Principals reached agreement on 24 issues by mid-June 2010 and the Cabinet then agreed on an implementation matrix for these issues. However, this implementation process was not put into operation, and during this period Tsvangirai expressed his frustration that 'ZANU-PF never intended to implement much of what they signed up for'. By mid-2010, Tsvangirai also stated that 'one of the things that President Mugabe and I do agree on is that ... elections need to happen next year [2011]'.⁶⁵ This position of Tsvangirai and the MDC-T changed in 2011 as it became clear that the conditions for such elections were still not in place.

It became apparent that most of the challenges relating to the outstanding issues were related to ZANU-PF's fears for its future in the event of a comprehensive implementation of the GPA, particularly given the continued problem over succession within the party. In July 2011 the three parties signed on to an Electoral Road Map with timelines dealing with several areas but remained in dispute over other aspects of the agreement. In particular ZANU-PF objected to proposals from the MDCs in the following areas: the staffing of the Zimbabwe Electoral Commission; the role of the security forces in the electoral process; amendments to the Public Order and Security Act (POSA); and the extent of monitoring in the electoral process. In other areas there was agreement, including the removal of sanctions, the completion of the constitutional process, media reform, preparation of a new voter's role, and legislative reforms.⁶⁶ Once again, as with the situation in 2010 after agreement was reached on the outstanding issues and the process of implementation, there was little movement on the Election Road Map. By early 2012 Tsvangirai, as on several previous occasions, expressed his frustration at the slow pace at which the GPA was being implemented. In a letter to Mugabe he sought a reflection on the state of the Inclusive Government and the need to chart a way forward.⁶⁷

Given these challenges the role of the Joint Monitoring and Implementation Committee, set up under Article XX11 of the GPA to 'ensure full and proper implementation of the letter and spirit' of the agreement, became increasingly significant. This body played a key role in providing a platform for continued dialogue between the GPA negotiators. Moreover, after an evaluation in January 2011, JOMIC expanded its activities through the setting up four sub-committees dealing with Operations (violence), Media, Land and Sanctions. It also set up committees, composed of the three parties, in all districts, to ensure a more reliable system of collecting information on violence, human rights abuses and other issues relating to the GPA. Reading through the documents of the JOMIC sub-committees the narrative of the deliberations appears to be aimed at both establishing consensus between the parties, and prefiguring the emergence of a more accountable national state capable of representing all citizens and not just those supporting a particular party. Thus the discussions of this body appeared to focus not only on the immediacy of the GPA challenges but also on the future remaking of the state.[68]

Notwithstanding its potential JOMIC was hampered by an initial lack of resources for its operations, and the undermining of its functions by the 'parallel government' in the security sector. Additionally, in the course of its January 2011 Retreat the members of JOMIC noted some of the major problems affecting the effectiveness of this body. These included: the failure of JOMIC to meet regularly resulting in delays in dealing with GPA issues; the lack of interaction between JOMIC and SADC; and the discord between agreements made in JOMIC and the public positions taken by parties thereafter. It was also noted that there was a disjuncture between discussions on the GPA in cabinet and those in JOMIC:

> ... there is an information gap between JOMIC members who are cabinet ministers and those who are not as some information is discussed during cabinet meetings. It was therefore agreed that the agenda of JOMIC meetings should include government communication to update other members on issues concerning the GPA that would have been discussed in cabinet.[69]

Given the tensions in the government structure of the GPA especially between the powers of the President and the Prime Minister it was unsurprising that such disjunctures emerged not only in the functioning of JOMIC but in the area of policy implementation generally. As with other such agreements the GPA resulted in serious policy gridlock in the area of political reform generally, and more particularly reforms in the electoral, media, and human rights spheres. At the March 2011 summit of the Troika, SADC took a position to assist the functions of JOMIC to move with greater speed by attaching representatives of the three Troika countries to the implementation body. However, by the first quarter of 2012, this SADC decision had not been implemented.

The Challenges of the MDC formations and the Civic Movement

Faced with the enormous task of participating in a political agreement in which it had little control of the coercive arms of the state, and was equally challenged in its lack of experience of statecraft and state power, the MDC formations had to embark on a steep learning curve in order confront the obstructionist tactics of ZANU-PF. One of the major resources which the MDC-T in particular brought to the GPA, was the hope of economic recovery. In this field the MDC-T Minister in charge of this portfolio, Tendai Biti, brought in some key changes such as the dollarisation of the economy, the rapid reduction of the record breaking hyperinflation and the curbing of the quasi-fiscal activities of the Reserve Bank Governor Gideon Gono, which initially sparked some optimism around the potential for growth. In his first budget speech Minister Biti, while acknowledging the challenges of external factors such as drought and sanctions in inhibiting growth in the economy, placed much greater emphasis on internal policy factors. As the Zimbabwe Congress of Trade Unions noted, the budget statement 'broke ranks with the "populist" approach that resulted in the implementation of half-hearted and wrong-headed interventions'.[70]

However, the short-term measures taken to alleviate the debilitating economic situation in the country faced longer-term problems. First, the Inclusive Government faced enormous debt problems with public and publically guaranteed debt amounting to US$6.9 billion or 157% of GDP.[71] Moreover, while the short-term effects of the dollarisation process resulted in a large reduction in inflation, the longer-term challenges included the loss of the central bank's function of 'lender of last resort', and an independent monetary and exchange rate policy.[72] While Biti negotiated massive humanitarian assistance from the EU and the US to deal with immediate problems in health and education, in particular, his push for a 'normalisation' of relations with the international financial institutions was hindered by the continued problems in the implementation of the GPA and the imperatives of the 'targeted measures' imposed by the West. This situation confined donor funding to the humanitarian field, largely channeled away from the central government structures, while avoiding any broader development funding.

The form of this donor funding caused tensions within the GPA as ZANU-PF viewed it as an attempt to channel funds in ways that benefitted the social ministries run by the MDC formations. This in turn exacerbated the challenges around putting in place better procedures to account for the funds from the Chiadzwa diamond fields over which the ruling party had taken control from 2006, raising continuing questions about how the Zimbabwe Mining Development Corporation managed the revenues.[73] Thus while ZANU-PF went along formally with the MDC's attempts to 'normalise' relations with the West the party pursued its own more partisan economic strategies around the diamond revenues while extending this fight to the minerals sector more generally. This initiative was part of a renewed indigenisation policy embarked on in 2010. Following the Indigenous and Economic Empowerment Act 2007, the Government introduced the Indigenous and Economic Empowerment (General) Regulations in 2010, amid dispute over the interpretation and timing of this issue within the Inclusive Government. The regulations stated that every business entity with an asset value of above US$500,000 must within five years cede a controlling interest of not less than 51% of shares to indigenous Zimbabweans unless a lesser share or longer period within which to achieve indigenisation is justified.[74]

The indigenisation debate began in earnest in the mid-1990s during the economic structural adjustment period, when emerging business groupings such as the Indigenous Business Development Centre (IBDC) and the Affirmative Action Group (AAG) were formed to lobby the state for cheaper credit and broad preferential treatment in order to be able enter the private sector on more competitive terms against the white monopoly in this area.[75] These groups had close ties with the ruling party and state and their ideas grew in influence in the late 1990s. However their programme was subsumed under the land seizures of the 2000s. By 2011 this indigenisation strategy was firmly linked to ZANU-PF's anti-sanctions campaign, with both forming the central part of its campaign message as it prepared for new elections. The message was spelt out in a pamphlet issued at this time:

> The story of Zimbabwe sanctions has its roots firmly in the West's selfish desire to deny Zimbabweans the right to be in charge of their economy and destiny. It is about making sure that we are not in control of our own resources, particularly land. It is about making us continue to wallow in colonialism-induced poverty. It is about blocking people's empowerment so that whites remain in charge, remotely controlling our economy.[76]

Thus a major part of the MDC's policy battle in the Inclusive Government was the fight to control the threat of ZANU-PF's appropriation of national resources under the politics of indigenisation and the language of sovereignty. This appropriation has taken place under what has been described as a 'centralised structure of rent management that is oriented to the short term' in which economic decisions are taken 'with a view to buying off opposition and ensuring temporary regime survival'.[77] However, this characterisation does not fully capture the complexity of the political economy that has emerged since the land reform of the 2000s. As a survey of recent research on the land question has observed, it is clear that the land structure inherited from the settler colonial past, namely the 'dualist' pattern of a large, white capitalist sector and African smallholder reserves has been fundamentally changed. The dominant form of agriculture is now 'small-scale, relies mainly but not exclusively on household labour, and produces for domestic consumption as well as the market'.[78] This 're-peasantisation' as Sam Moyo[79] refers to it, has created its own 'entrepreneurial dynamism' and 'productive potential' resulting in new areas of economic activity with novel marketing and value chains.[80] However it is also clear that as Scoones et al have noted:

> Only with land viewed as a source of livelihood and redistributed economic wealth, and not as a political weapon or source of patronage, will the real potentials of Zimbabwe's land reform be fully realised.[81]

Confronted with this combination of ZANU-PF's authoritarian nationalism, patronage politics, and colonial redress the MDCs have since their formation struggled to develop a political language that would straddle all these challenges.[82] Emerging in the post-1989 era of global politics but drawing on a longer history of struggles for labour, civic and human rights from the colonial period, the MDC political vision was dominated by a liberal democratic and human rights agenda that was constantly confronted with the dilemma of challenging ZANU-PF's anti-democratic political practices while being unable to respond robustly to its message of colonial redress. This is a common feature of human-rights-driven organisations in the contemporary era where commitment to the latter often seeks to postpone large-scale redistribution.[83] This dilemma continued in the period of the GPA, during which the economic vista of both MDCs never rose beyond their long-term commitment to liberalised economic policies.

The MDCs also had to deal with the challenge of entering an Inclusive Government, not only with limited knowledge of the state, but also with the ongoing need to establish organisational capacity and democratic accountability in their structures in the face of the pervasive threat of harassment and repression by ZANU-PF. These factors in addition to ethnic fissures led to differences in strategy that caused the split in the MDC in 2005.[84] Moreover, in the aftermath of the state-led political violence of the 2008 presidential election re-run, the party structures of the MDC-T in particular were severely disrupted, reinforcing the problem of organisational capacity within the opposition. This challenge was highlighted in a report on the MDC-T 2011 Congress:

> *MDC has weak party structures that do not effectively participate in key party processes which raises questions over their ability to participate in key national processes. This probably is an indicator as to why participation has been low during the COPAC processes, national elections and mass actions.*[85]

This report also noted the existence of factionalism and violence in the party. This factionalism had 'strong but divisive regional and ethnic undertones',[86] that also expressed itself in the criticisms of Tsvangirai's leadership in the WikiLeaks revelations. If the common lament amongst Mugabe's lieutenants was that he should step down immediately, Tsvangirai's critics within his party complained about his lack of decisiveness and penchant for surrounding himself with bad advisors.[87] Such factors impacted on the MDC-T's ability to operate more effectively within the GPA.

If the MDC-T faced enormous challenges, those of the small MDC formation were formidable. Using its balance of power in the GPA to influence Parliament and negotiations over the GPA, this formation forged 'temporary alliances with the MDC-T and ZANU-PF, on issues of strategic interest to itself'.[88] While this strategy kept the small formation in the political game, it alienated it further from MDC-T dominated civic groups, as well as opening it up to resignations and a destructive leadership battle that resulted in a change of presidency, but with the former president retaining his position as a Principal under the GPA with the connivance of both Mugabe and Tsvangirai. This lack of a consistent working relationship between the two MDCs, which proved so counter-productive in the 2008 elections, once again worked to the advantage of ZANU-PF. The result of this ongoing division between the two MDCs was that the smaller formation decided to concentrate its energies on building a regional base in the Matabeleland, Bulawayo and Midlands provinces in an attempt to capitalise on the long-term sets of grievances around state violence and developmental neglect that were experienced in these areas.

With regard to civil society most of the civic organisations in the country continued to focus on the state violations of the bodies of victims and the monitoring of political reforms rather than the structural legacies of Zimbabwe's political economy. Thus the rupture in the country's rights/redistribution discourse was carried over into the GPA period, when the battles over 'outstanding issues' were formulated in terms of one side or the other of this contested political language. From the onset, the human rights organisations expressed grave reservations about the capacity of the GPA to deliver on the mechanisms that would stop the rights abuses of the state, and put in place the legal and institutional mechanisms required to ensure the cessation of such politically driven violence. The critical position of the civic groups was to a large extent based on their marginalisation from the mediation process, with all parties to the process sceptical of the role of the civic bodies and the probable delays that this would cause to the mediation. From this perspective the seminal issues of constitutional reform, respect for the rule of law, electoral reform, freedom of organisation and expression, and security sector transformation remained the most abiding demands of the major civil society groups allied to the MDC-T. Other civic grouping with close relations to ZANU-PF, such as the war veterans movement, placed greater emphasis on the righting of colonial structural legacies, such as land question and the indigenisation of national resources, however problematically formulated. The enmity of these discourses found no respite under the GPA.[89]

SADC, the EU and the US

For much of the 2000s SADC provided Mugabe and ZANU-PF with regional solidarity against what was constructed as an attack on Zimbabwean sovereignty by the West, and an attempt to enforce a regime change agenda. 'Restrictive measures' were imposed by the EU, US, Australia and Canada in the 2000s on the assets and international travel of individuals in ZANU-PF accused of human rights abuses, and business restrictions were placed on companies associated with ZANU-PF. However these 'restrictive measures' impacted more broadly than on the specific individuals and companies they were intended to punish and have had a more widespread affect on the flow of development assistance to the country. As part of these measures, the conditions stipulated for their removal included: respect for human rights and the rule of law; freedom of the media; an end to political violence; a commitment to 'equitable, legal and transparent land reform'; and the subordination of the military and police services to civilian government.[90]

An assessment carried out by the EU in 2011 on the effects of the sanctions concluded that, while they 'succeeded in fostering opposition to Mugabe within his own ranks,' they were in large measure a failure for two reasons. Firstly, the 'infelicitous coincidence' that the measures were imposed at the same time as an acute economic crisis in Zimbabwe 'allowed the government to present economic hardship as a result of Western sanctions'. Secondly, the report noted that the differences in approach to the Zimbabwe question by South Africa and the EU undermined the sanctions regime. More specifically, while South Africa brokered the GPA on behalf of SADC, the EU followed a more '"maximalist" logic which regards Mugabe and the ZANU-PF as illegitimate and demands their removal from power'. The result was that the EU offered 'half-hearted' support to the GNU.[91] An assessment of Canadian sanctions on Zimbabwe in 2009 reached a similar conclusion, namely that Canadian policy offered little in the way of incentives to the Government of Zimbabwe. Moreover while Canada's measures were motivated by democratic governance and human rights norms, they were a *de facto* demonstration of a 'policy preference for regime change'.[92]

Whatever the efficacy of the sanctions measures in bringing attention to the human rights abuses of the Mugabe regime for much of the post-2000 period during which SADC played down this issue, the effects of the measures became increasingly counter-productive after the signing of the GPA. In the words of a high-level EU official after a visit to Zimbabwe in September 2011, 'there seems to be a general agreement that the measures are not effective in achieving their objective at this point'.[93] An indication of the slowly changing position of the EU on this issue was the removal of an additional 51 individuals and 20 entities from the visa ban and asset freeze in February 2012, leaving 112 individuals and eleven entities still on the list. According to the EU this decision was made in recognition of the developments under the GPA and to 'encourage further progress'. Moreover, the restrictions on development assistance were extended for six months 'with a view to begin preparation for enhanced co-operation as and when these Measures can be lifted'. In terms of this co-operation, by early 2012 the EU had already spent close to US$1 billion on assistance to the Inclusive Government in the areas of health and education.[94] In March the Australian Government followed the trend and removed 82 individuals from its financial and travel sanctions list.[95] In effect both these moves indicated a realisation that there had to be some movement on this question, while also showing the reluctance to let go of the strategy of sanctions as a tool of leverage.[96] This change of tone was also apparent in the position of the US Ambassador to Zimbabwe, Charles Ray, if not in the policy of his government. At a public presentation in July 2011 Ray observed:

> Some of us – on both sides – cut off communication at exactly the time we needed to be communicating more. As we reduced our interactions, nuance became the first casualty. We adopted more absolutist vocabulary ... Over time, parts of the bilateral relationship showed signs of distress. Through our actions and public statements, we seemed to actively cultivate a loss of confidence between each other ... at the government-to-government level both sides made mis-steps and both sides are deserving of a share of the blame for the degraded state of the formal bilateral relationship.[97]

The SADC position, in line with Article IV of the GPA, was to push for the lifting of sanctions. In April 2011 the regional body dispatched a delegation made up of representatives from Namibia, Zambia, South Africa and the SADC Secretariat to engage the EU, UK and the US on the sanctions issue. In their discussions, SADC found some flexibility on the part of the EU and the UK to review the issue based on a 'substantive road map with clear benchmarks'. The most obstinate voice in these deliberations was that of US State Department Secretary of State for African Affairs, Johnnie Carson, who 'stated categorically that the US State Department is not convinced that there was meaningful progress on the ground in Zimbabwe'.[98]

The task of the SADC delegation was made more difficult by the fact that representatives of the EU, UK and the US attempted to justify their stubborn hold on the sanctions position on the basis of the mixed messages they had received from different political parties in the Inclusive Government and representatives of civil society. The SADC report noted that their efforts to shift the sanctions policy were

> ... not helped by the fact that some Zimbabwean leaders and some NGOs from Zimbabwe have called for continued imposition of sanctions on Zimbabwe until all the provisions of the GPA are fully implemented.[99]

It is not surprising that such mixed messages from the MDCs and the civics persisted into the period of the GPA, as both grouping had supported the sanctions for much of the 2000s when the position of SADC appeared to condone the human rights abuses of the Mugabe regime in the name of regional sovereignty. While this appeal to the 'universalism' of the human rights agenda kept pushing at the limits of ZANU-PF's authoritarian nationalist politics, it also attracted criticisms that it was an extension of Western constructions of the human rights agenda, which often undermined the framework of international rights and legitimised the right to a regime change agenda.

Conclusion

The GPA and its many challenges was the product of a convergence of factors, namely: the unwillingness of a party of liberation to accept electoral defeat; the inability of the opposition to claim state power due to the militarisation of the ruling party's response to defeat; a clash of different notions of state sovereignty in which the electoral wishes of the Zimbabwean citizenry were subordinated to selective nationalist claims of the ruling party; and the role of SADC in facilitating an agreement that attempted to balance the need for regional sovereignty against outside interference with the legitimate electoral demands of the Zimbabwean electorate. The result of this complex mix of ingredients was a brew that placed a short term halt on the rapid political and economic decline in the country and opened up some space for new political arrangements, while also providing an authoritarian regime with opportunities to regain lost ground. The period of the Inclusive Government generated a new set of dynamics that made it impossible for ZANU-PF to return to the *status quo ante*, while also exposing the strengths and weaknesses of the former opposition parties as they took part in unequally shared state power.

As Zimbabweans await the next election there is renewed anxiety about whether it will lead to the generally acceptable result that was intended by the facilitation and the GPA. The ongoing contestations over outstanding issues in the GPA and their implementation, the ever-present threat of ZANU-PF coercion and violence in the context of the succession battles, the weaknesses that have been exposed in the politics of the MDCs, and the disagreements between SADC and the West over the implementation of the GPA, do not augur well for the future. Given this configuration of forces and the improbability of one party emerging with a sufficient majority as well as regional and international legitimacy to rule the country on its own, it is difficult to foresee an alternative to another form of GNU in the near future.

In 2006 the Zimbabwean poet Chris Magadza wrote a scathing poem on

'Quiet Diplomacy' expressing the frustration that many Zimbabweans felt over the process. In his words, *Blow upon blow / To the deafening applause / of the African Union / We silently bear the pain / in the amphitheatre / of quiet diplomacy.*[100] The imprint of quiet diplomacy proved to be more complex and ambiguous than Magadza's sense of exasperation, but few would doubt the pervasiveness of this sort of feeling amongst Zimbabweans throughout the period of the GPA.

Endnotes

I would like to thank former President of SA, Thabo Mbeki for his frank and useful comments on my draft paper, both at a conference organised by Mahmood Mamdani in Makerere in January 2012 and in subsequent email correspondence. I would also like to thank to thank Isaac Maphosa, David Moore and Jocelyn Alexander for their comments.

1 I. Scoones, N. Marongwe, B. Mavedzenge, F. Murimbarimba, J. Mahenehene, and C. Sukume, *Zimbabwe's Land Reform: Myths and Realities* (Harare: Weaver Press, Johannesburg: Jacana Media, 2010).

2 A. Carl LeVan, 'Power Sharing and Inclusive politics in Uncertain democracies', *Governance: An International Journal of Policy, Administration and Institutions,* 24 (1), 2011, pp. 31-53; Ian S. Spears, 'Understanding inclusive peace agreements in Africa: the problems of power sharing', *Third World Quarterly,* 21 (1), 2000, pp. 105-118; See also the Special Issue of *Africa Spectrum,* 44, (3), 2009, on 'Power Sharing in Africa'.

3 N. Cheeseman and B. M. Tendi, 'Power-sharing in comparative perspective: the dynamics of "unity government" in Kenya and Zimbabwe', *Journal of Modern African Studies,* 48 (2), 2010, pp. 203-229.

4 Derek Matyszak, *Law, Politics and Zimbabwe's 'Unity' Government* (Harare, Konrad-Adenauer-Stiftung, 2010) p. 69.

5 Richard Saunders, 'Zimbabwe: Liberation nationalism – old and born-again', *Review of African Political Economy,* 38 (127), 2011, p. 130. Such analysis has been reflected in the many reports by the International Crisis Group (ICG) on the GPA. See for example, ICG, 'Resistance and Denial: Zimbabwe's Stalled Reform Agenda' (Johannesburg/Brussels, 2011.)

6 Norma Kriger, 'ZANU-PF politics under Zimbabwe's Power-Sharing Government,' *Journal of Contemporary African Studies,* 30 (1), 2012, p. 9.

7 James Muzondidya, 'Zimbabwe's failed transition? An analysis of the challenges and complexities in Zimbabwe's transition to democracy in the post-2000 period', in Tim Murithi and Aquilina Mawadza (eds), *Zimbabwe in Transition: A View from Within* (Johannesburg: Jacana Media, 2011.)

8 For my earlier thoughts on the GPA see Brian Raftopoulos, 'The GPA as a "passive revolution": Notes on contemporary politics in Zimbabwe', *The Round Table*, 99 (411), 2010, pp.705-18. In attempting to understand the difficulties of the Zimbabwe situation Stephen Chan, while characterising the GPA as 'a grand, complex and clumsy compromise which prioritised inclusion over democratic processes', also warns that those who criticise and condemn Mbeki must ask 'What would any of us in Mbeki's stead have done, or been able to do?' Stephen Chan, *Old Treacheries, New Deceits: Insights into Southern African Politics* (Johannesburg and Cape Town: Jonathan Ball Publishers, 2011) pp. 210-11. See also several reports by the Solidarity Peace Trust including: *Walking a thin line – The political and humanitarian challenges facing Zimbabwe's GPA leadership and its ordinary citizens*, Johannesburg, 30 June 2009; *What Options for Zimbabwe?* Johannesburg, 31 March 2010; *The Hard Road to Reform*, Johannesburg, 13 April 2011.

9 For a *longue durée* understanding of Zimbabwean history and politics see Brian Raftopoulos and Alois Mlambo (eds), *Becoming Zimbabwe*, op. cit.

10 Ian Phimister and Brian Raftopoulos, 'Mugabe, Mbeki and the politics of anti-imperialism', *Review of African Political Economy*, 101, 2004, pp. 385-400; Sabelo Ndlovu-Gatsheni, 'Making sense of Mugabeism in Local and Global politics: "So Blair, keep your England and let me keep my Zimbabwe"', *Third World Quarterly*, 30 (6), 2009, pp. 1139-1158. This section draws heavily from Raftopoulos, 'The GPA as a "Passive Revolution"', op cit.

11 Linda Freeman, 'South Africa's Zimbabwe Policy: Unraveling the Contradictions', *Journal of Contemporary African Studies*, 23 (2), 2005, pp. 147-72; Adam Habib, 'South Africa's foreign policy: hegemonic aspirations, neoliberal orientations, and global transformations', *South African Journal of International Affairs*, 16 (2), 2009, pp. 143-59; Chris Lansberg, *The Quiet Diplomacy of Liberation: International Politics and South Africa's Transition*, (Johannesburg: Jacana Media, 2004); Martin Adelman, 'Quiet Diplomacy: The reasons behind Mbeki's Zimbabwe policy', *Africa Spectrum*, 39 (2), 2004, pp. 249-276.

12 Meeting between the author, when he was Chair of the Crisis in Zimbabwe Coalition, and Frank Chikane, Secretary to the SA Cabinet in Cape Town, 16-17 April 2003.

13 'The Mbeki-Mugabe papers: What Mbeki told Mugabe – A discussion document', *New Agenda*, 30, Second Quarter, 2008, pp. 56-72. This document 'prepared to facilitate discussions between the ANC and ZANU-PF ... was an official ANC

document, adopted at a formal meeting of the ANC National Executive Committee'. Email communication from Thabo Mbeki 13 April 2012.

14 Blessing-Miles Tendi, *Making History in Mugabe's Zimbabwe* (Oxford, Peter Lang, 2010), Chapter 4. On this argument Mbeki notes that: 'At no point' was the ANC engagement with the Zimbabwe question 'informed by the consideration that in 1990 Zimbabwe had postponed acting on the land question, thus to favour the South African transformation process, even though it is very true that the Zimbabwe Government did take this important decision'. Email communication from Thabo Mbeki, 13 April 2012.

15 David Moore, 'A Decade of Disquieting Diplomacy: South Africa, Zimbabwe and the Ideology of the National Democratic Revolution, 1999-2009', History Compass, 8 (8), 2010, pp.752-767. Similarly Matyszak characterises the policy of 'quiet diplomcy' largely as a 'refusal to address and , by extension, to condemn, human rights abuses and crimes against humanity perpetrated by the Mugabe regime and its supporters, no matter how egregious'. See *Law, Politics and Zimbabwe's 'Unity' Government*, op cit. Mbeki argues that the above document 'focused on the strategic challenge of the National Democratic Revolution in Zimbabwe to sustain and entrench democratic practice', arguing this was fundamental to addressing even the country's socio-economic challenges. Email communication from Thabo Mbeki, 13 April 2012.

16 Stephen Chan offers a more nuanced assessment of this issue in his *Old Treacheries, New Deceits,* op cit.

17 Frank Chikane, *Eight Days on September, The Removal of Thabo Mbeki (*Johannesburg: Picador Africa, 2012), pp. 96-7.

18 Sam Moyo and Paris Yeros, 'Land Occupations and Land Reform in Zimbabwe: Towards the National Democratic Revolution', in Sam Moyo and Paris Yeros (eds), *Reclaiming the Land: The Resurgence of Rural Movements in Africa, Asia and Latin America* (London: Zed Books, Cape Town: David Philip, 2005); Sam Moyo and Paris Yeros, 'After Zimbabwe: State, Nation and Region in Africa', in Sam Moyo and Paris Yeros (eds), *Reclaiming the Nation: The Return of the National Question in Africa, Asia and Latin America* (London: Pluto Press, 2011).

19 In late 2005 the MDC split ostensibly over the issue of participation in the senate elections of that year. However there were more long-term organisational problems in the party that gave rise to the rupture. These included issues around accountability of the leadership, the existence of a 'kitchen cabinet' in the party, ethnic conflicts, differences around strategy and the intra-party violence. The split led to two MDC formations, the larger led by Morgan Tsvangirai and the smaller by Arthur Mutambara. The negative impact of the split on the democratic forces in the country are still being felt.

20 Morgan Tsvangirai, 'A Brief for President Olusegun Obesanjo, Republic of

Nigeria and President Thabo Mbeki, Republic of South Africa', 2002. This position was restated by the two MDC formations in 2006 when both sent out a call for a renewed political dialogue based on the need for a new constitutional dispensation. See MDC-T, 'Resolution of the Zimbabwean Crisis: Signposts to Peace, Democracy and Legitimacy, Reconstruction and National Healing', Harare, May 2006; MDC, 'Discussion document on the need for political dialogue to resolve the crisis in Zimbabwe', Harare, October 2006.

21 Patrick Chinamasa, 'Opening remarks by Patrick Chinamasa, head of the ZANU-PF team to the ZANU-PF-MDC dialogue', Parliament Building, Harare, 8 April 2002.

22 Solidarity Peace Trust, 'Destructive Engagement: Violence, Mediation and Politics in Zimbabwe', Johannesburg, 2007.

23 Communique: 2007 Extra-Ordinary SADC Summit of State and Government, 28-29 March 2007, Dar-es Salaam.

24 Letter from Thabo Mbeki to Morgan Tsvangirai, Arthur Mutambara, c.c. President Mugabe, 4 April 2007.

25 Ibid.

26 MDC Submission to the South African President Thabo Mbeki: SADC appointed Mediator on Zimbabwe, 'Conditions for free and fair elections in Zimbabwe. A pre-dialogue statement', 11 April 2007.

27 For an extensive discussion of this issue see Erin McCandless, *Polarisation and Transformation in Zimbabwe: Social Movements, Strategy Dilemmas and Change* (New York: Lexington Books, 2011).

28 SADC Initiated Dialogue: Government of Zimbabwe/ZANU-PF Position paper, 1 June 2007. For a more general discussion of this ZANU-PF discourse see Terence Ranger, 'Historiography, patriotic history and the history of the nation: The Struggle for the past in Zimbabwe', *Journal of Southern African Studies*, 30 (2), 2004, pp. 215-34; and Blessing-Miles Tendi, *Making History in Mugabe's Zimbabwe*.

29 Zimbabwe Institute, 'SADC Dialogue Report', Cape Town, 2009.

30 MDC 'Memorandum to the South African Government on the apparent lack of commitment by ZANU-PF to the SADC sponsored Zimbabwe Dialogue Process', July 2007.

31 International Crisis Group, 'Zimbabwe: A Regional Solution?' *Africa Report*, 132, 18 September 2007, Johannesburg and Brussels.

32 MDC Negotiating Team's 'Statement to the Facilitator his Excellency the President of the Republic of South Africa, President Thabo Mbeki, on the deadlock between the MDC and the Government of Zimbabwe/ZanuPF', 14 December 2007.

33 MDC Press Statement on the failed SADC Dialogue on the Crisis in Zimbabwe, 21 February 2008.

34 Ibid.
35 David Coltart, a member of the smaller MDC formation, expressed his frustration over the continued inability of the two MDCs to agree on an election pact: 'Firstly, as far back as April 2007 the MDC-M... agreed that it would support the sole opposition candidacy of Morgan Tsvangirai. Secondly, it was the MDC-T which rejected the agreement reached by the two teams of negotiators in May 2007. Thirdly, in January 2008 the MDC-M agreed again to the sole candidacy of Morgan Tsvangirai. Once again it was the MDC-T which rejected the agreement reached this time by the leadership of the two political entities on spurious grounds related to the Parliamentary election, which has always been secondary to the all-important presidential election ....It was only after the rejection of the agreement on 5 February that Simba Makoni announced his candidacy.' David Coltart, 'A perspective on the talks and the election of the speaker: 3 September 2008', Bulawayo, 3 September 2008.
36 Wally Mbhele and Dominic Mahlangu, 'If you go on like this, there will be no country left', *Sunday Times*, 1 June 2008.
37 Peter Fabricius, 'Slap in the face for Mbeki as G8 calls for UN envoy to mediate in Zimbabwe', *Cape Times*, 9 July 2008.
38 'Low key support for Mugabe at AU', *Business Day*, 8 July 2008.
39 Joe Lauria, 'UN Zim vote sours US-SA relations', *The Sunday Independent*, 13 July 2008.
40 Rowan Philip and Dominic Mahlangu, 'Only God will remove me', *Sunday Times*, 22 June 2008.
41 Email communication from Thabo Mbeki, 13 April 2012.
42 Kgalema Motlanthe, 'The EU-Africa summit must go ahead with Mugabe', newzimbabwe.com Accessed on 18/12/07.
43 Memorandum of Understanding between ZANU-PF and the two MDC formations, Harare, 21 July 2008.
44 Zimbabwe Institute, ' SADC Dialogue Report', Cape Town, 2009.
45 Global Political Agreement, 15 September 2008, (Ministry of Constitutional Affairs, Government of Zimbabwe, 2009), p. 3.
46 Brian Raftopoulos, 'What prospects for Zimbabwe's GNU?' *Amandla*, Issue No.7, April/May 2009, p. 28; Solidarity Peace Trust, *Walking a thin line: The political and Humanitarian challenges facing Zimbabwe's GPA leadership – and its ordinary citizens.* Johannesburg, 30 June 2009.
47 Eldred Masunungure, 'Zimbabwe's Power-Sharing Agreement'. Paper prepared for a Workshop on 'The Consequences of Political Inclusion in Africa,' American University, Washington DC, 24-25 April 2009.
48 A useful report on the initial discussions around the division of these ministries can be found in MDC-M, 'Report to SADC on the dispute relating to the allocation

of Ministries under the Zimbabwe Power Sharing Agreement', n.d. This document records the changes in position of the various parties over this issue, revealing the obstructive behaviour of ZANU-PF as well as the equivocation of the MDC-T. It also reveals the rather Panglossian hopes of the MDC-M, which because of its electoral weakness placed the most faith in the future of the GPA. In commenting on the allocation of ministries, this party stated: 'We hold the view that the most important issue is delivering a better life to the people of Zimbabwe. As a result we do not lay great stress on the glamorous Ministries which ZANU-PF and the MDC-T have been fighting over. Seeking to control the coercive apparatus of the state such as the police, the army, the intelligence organizations and the traditional leaders assumes that the inclusive government should and will continue to behave in an antidemocratic and coercive manner.' To its credit, throughout much of the mediation and the ongoing discussions on the GPA the smaller MDC formation used its little leverage to try to push for reconciliatory positions.

49 See Matyszak, *Law Politics and Zimbabwe's 'Unity' Government*, for more on this.

50 MDC (T) Response to SADC Position paper. www.zimonline.co.za/Article. aspx?Articled=4131 Accessed on 27/01/09. See also the discussion of the early months of the GPA in Solidarity Peace Trust, *'Walking a thin line'*.

51 Communiqué, Extraordinary Summit of the SADC Heads of State and Government, Presidential Guest House, Pretoria, Republic of South Africa, 26-27 January 2009.

52 Statement by the Leader of the Movement for Democratic Change, President Morgan Tsvangirai, on the Resolutions of the Party's National Council Meeting, Harare, 30 January 2009.

53 Zimbabwe Institute, 'The Dynamics of ZANU-PF Politics in the Post-Tsholotsho Phase', Cape Town, March 2006; Wilfred Mhanda, *Dzino, Memories of a Freedom Fighter* (Harare: Weaver Press, 2011).

54 Dumisani Muleya and Faith Zaba, 'Mujuru allies cry "murder most foul"'. www. theindependent.co.zw/local/32126-mujuru-allies-cry-murder-most-foul.htm Accessed on 22/08/11.

55 'The President @ 88', Interview with Nomsa Nkala, *The Sunday Mail*, 19 February, 2012.

56 Farai Mutsaka and Thelma Chikwanha, 'ZANU-PF officials in Mugabe ouster plot'. www.thezimbabwemail.com/zimbabwe/10561-zanu-pf-offcials-in-mugabe-ouster-pl Accessed on 15/02/12. Caesar Zvayi, 'Outrage over the draft constitution', www.herald.co.zw/index.php?view=article&catid=37%Atop-stories&id=33653%3 Accessed on 10/02/12.

57 Jonathan Moyo, 'Copac's first draft: No acceptable Zim constitutional vision',

The Sunday Mail, 19 February 2012. For Moyo's WikiLeaks comments see 'Jonathan Moyo on Mugabe succession, US policy', *Zimbabwe Independent*, 16 September 2011. Commenting on the WikiLeaks saga, Ibbo Mandaza observed: 'As the WikiLeaks revelations testify, almost everyone in Zimbabwe, not to mention ZANU-PF itself, wherein, from the Vice Presidents, throughout the politburo and central committee, and even among ordinary functionaries, the call, albeit in whispers, has been that Mugabe must go, not now but yesterday.' *Zimbabwe Independent*, 16 September 2011.

58 'Constitution was never about writing a new constitution – Mugabe',. www.radiovop.com/index.php/national-news/8439-gpa-was-never-about-writing-a-n Accessed on 13/03/12.

59 Tsvangirai and his nephew Hebson Makuvise were accused of misappropriating US$1.5 million in public funds meant to buy a house for the Prime Minister in the up-market Highlands suburb in Harare. Dumisani Muleya and Faith Zaba, 'Tsvangirai fraud scandal deepens', www.theindependent.co.zw/local/32034-tsvangirai-fraud-scandal-deepens.html Accessed on 12/08/11.

60 'Statement by Morgan Tsvangirai terminating his customary marriage to Lorcadia Karimatsenga Tembo'. www.newzimbabwe.com/news/printVersion.aspx?newsID=6612 Accessed on 1/12/11. Commenting on the relationship, Tsvangirai stated: 'I have become a spectator in this relationship and things are happening too fast, on camera and without my knowledge. This has led me to conclude that there is a greater and thicker plot around this issue which has undermined my confidence in this relationship.'

61 Zimbabwe Peace Project Report, Harare, 25 September 2009, p. 3.

62 Zimbabwe Congress of Trade Unions, 'Report of Human and Trade Unions Rights Violations 2009', 22 January 2010, p. 16.

63 Zimbabwe Human Rights Forum, 'Statement on the occasion of the First Anniversary of the Government of National Unity', Harare, 13 February 2010. See also the Civil Society Monitoring Mechanism (CISOMM), 'Annual Review of the performance of the inclusive government of Zimbabwe 2009/10', Harare, 13 February 2010.

64 Final Report of the Negotiators on the Post-Maputo Inter-party Dialogue. April 2010; Movement for Democratic Change, *Conditions for a Sustainable Election in Zimbabwe (CoSEZ)*, Harare, 2012.

65 Address by the Prime Minister of the Republic of Zimbabwe, the Right Honourable Morgan Tsvangirai to the Southern African Liason Office, Pretoria, 27 May 2010.

66 Zimbabwe Election Road Map with Timelines. 6 July 2011. Unrealistically the timelines for completion of the road map were set for completion within 2011. In

light of the terms of the GPA and the various agreements on the outstanding issues and the Election Road Map, particularly on the need for constitutional reform, it is disingenuous to say the least, for Mugabe and other ZANU-PF spokespersons to make the claim that the GPA did not stipulate the need for a new constitution before the next election.

67 Memorandum to President Robert Mugabe from the Rt. Honourable Prime Minister, Morgan Tsvangirai, 2 February 2012. www.thezimbabwemail.com/zimbabwe/10466-coalition-on-brink-of-collapse%3A Accessed on 07/02/12.

68 See the following JOMIC sub-committee reports: Operations sub-committee report Jan-April 2011; Operations sub-committee report 24 May 2011; Co-Chairs Update Report 30 May 2011; Lands sub-committee report Jan-April 2011; Media sub-committee report Jan-April 2011; Media sub-committee report 24 May 2011.

69 Report on the JOMIC Retreat, 14-16 January 2011, Nyanga, Zimbabwe.

70 G. Kanyenze, T. Kondo, P. Chitambara and J. Martens, *Beyond the Enclave: towards the pro-poor and inclusive development strategy for Zimbabwe,* (Harare: Weaver Press, Harare, 2011) p 47.

71 International Monetary Fund, 'Zimbabwe: Debt Sustainability Analysis', Washington DC, 29 April 2010.

72 Kanyenze et al., op cit p. 51.

73 Global Witness, 'Return of the Blood Diamond: The deadly race to control Zimbabwe's new-found mineral wealth', London, 2010; Richard Saunders, 'Geologies of Power: Blood Diamonds, Security Politics and Zimbabwe's Troubled Transition', in M. Clarke and C. Bassett (eds), *Legacies of Liberation: postcolonial struggles for a democratic Southern Africa,* (Toronto: Fernwood, Johannesburg: HSRC Press), forthcoming 2012.

74 For a legal discussion of the legislation see D. Matyszak, 'Everything you ever wanted to know (and then some) about Zimbabwe's Indigenisation and Economic Empowerment legislation but (quite rightly) were too afraid to ask', Research and Advocacy Unit (RAU), Harare, 2010.

75 B. Raftopoulos and D. Compagnon, 'Indigenisation and Neo-Authoritarian Politics in Zimbabwe', in S. Darnoff and L. Laakso (eds), *Twenty Years of Politics in Zimbabwe* (London: Palgrave, 2003).

76 ZANU-PF, 'Sanctions are real: They are not targeted', March 2011. See discussion of the indigenization/sanctions messaging in 2011 in Solidarity Peace Trust, 'The Hard Road to Reform', Johannesburg, 13 April 2011.

77 M. Dawson and T. Kelsall, 'Anti-developmental patrimonialism in Zimbabwe', Working Paper 19, African Power and Politics Programme (APPP), Overseas Development Institute, June 2011, p. 26. An abridged version of this paper appears as M. Dawson and T. Kelsall, 'Anti-development patrimonialism in Zimbabwe', in the

Special issue of the *Journal of Contemporary African Studies: Progress in Zimbabwe,* 30 (1), January 2012.

78 L. Cliffe, J. Alexander, B. Cousins, and R. Gaidzanwa, 'An overview of Fast Track Land Reform in Zimbabwe: editorial introduction', *Journal of Peasant Studies,* 38 (5), 2011, p. 923, (Special Issue on Zimbabwean Land Reform).

79 Sam Moyo, 'Three Decades of agrarian reform in Zimbabwe', *Journal of Peasant Studies,* 38 (3), 2011, p. 513.

80 I. Scoones, N. Marongwe, B. Mavedzenge, F. Murimbarimba, J. Mahenehene and C. Sukume, 'Zimbabwe's land reform: challenging the myths', *Journal of Peasant Studies,* op.cit., p. 986.

81 Ibid p. 991.

82 B. Raftopoulos, 'The Zimbabwean crisis and the challenges for the left', *Journal of Southern African Studies,* 32 (2), 2006, pp. 203-219.

83 R. Meister, *After Evil: A Politics of Human Rights* (New York: Columbia University Press, 2011).

84 B. Raftopoulos, 'Reflections on Democratic Politics in Zimbabwe: The Politics of the MDC', in B. Raftopoulos and K. Alexander (eds), *Reflections on Democratic Politics in Zimbabwe,* Institute for Justice and Reconciliation, Cape Town, 2006.

85 P. Zamchiya, 'A Report on the Movement for Democratic Change Congress held from 28-30 April 2011', Harare 2011, p. 20.

86 Zimbabwe Institute, 'Zimbabwe Situational Analysis: A Review of the Political Landscape after two years of Inclusive Government', Policy Brief, No.1, February 2011, p. 13.

87 'MDC-T top brass mocks Tsvangirai,' www.herald.co.zw/index.php?view=article &catid=37%3Atopstories&id=20349% Accessed on 06/09/11.

88 Zimbabwe Institute, op cit p.11. For an insightful analysis of the challenges faced by the two MDC formations in the GPA negotiations, see Thys Hoekman, 'The Politics of Negotiation: Opposition and Power-Sharing in Zimbabwe' (M.Phil Thesis, University of Oxford, 2012.)

89 E. McCandless, *Polarisation and Transformation*; also see D. Moore and B. Raftopoulos, 'Zimbabwe's democracy of diminished expectations', in S. Chiumbu and M. Musemwa, *Crisis! What Crisis? The Multiple Dimensions of the Zimbabwean Crisis* (Cape Town: HSRC Press, 2012).

90 J. MacDermott, *Breaking the Mould in Zimbabwe – Pragmatic Engagement at a Critical Juncture.* FOI, Swedish Defense Research Agency, 2009, Stockholm.

91 European Union, Directorate-General for External Policies of the Union, *Impact of Sanctions and Isolation measures with North Korea, Burma/Myanmar, Iran and Zimbabwe as case studies,* Brussels, 2011.

92 Heather Cameron, 'Sanctioning Zimbabwe: Comparing the European Union

and Canadian Approaches', MA Public Policy Dissertation, King's College, University of London, 2009.

93 Restreint UE.FM EAS COREU, To all Coreu Urgent, GF SP/EAS/1337/11, 160911 1414Z, Acronym COAFR, Subject COAFR-Zimbabwe-MD Westcott's visit September 12-13, 2011.

94 European Union, 'Declaration by the High Representative, Catherine Ashton, on behalf of the European Union on Zimbabwe', Brussels, 17 February 2012.

95 Media Release: The Hon Dr. Craig Emerson MP, Acting Minister for Foreign Affairs, Minister of Trade, 5 March 2012. http://foreignminister.gov.au/releases/2012/ce_mr_120305 Accessed on 08/03/2012.

96 The same ambiguity could be read in the report of the International Crisis Group at this time: 'Zimbabwe's Sanctions Standoff', Johannesburg/Brussels, 6 February 2012.

97 Ambassador Charles Ray, 'The Future of U.S.-Zimbabwe Relations', Sapes Trust Dialogue, 28 July 2011.

98 SADC, 'Report of the SADC Senior Officials Mission to Britain, the United States of America, and the European Union Headquarters', 26 April – 2 May 2011. SADC/EOA/2/2011/5.

99 Ibid.

100 Chris Magadza, 'Quiet Diplomacy', http://www.poetryinternationalweb.net/pi/site/poem/item/6552/auto/QUIET-DIPLOMACY Accessed on 25/07/12.

CHAPTER 2

The Opposition Dilemma in Zimbabwe: A Critical Review of the Politics of the Movement for Democratic Change Parties under the GPA Government Framework, 2009-2012

JAMES MUZONDIDYA

Introduction

The chapter seeks to analyse the changes and continuities in the politics of the two MDC parties (the MDC led by Morgan Tsvangirai, MDC-T, and the MDC led by Welshman Ncube, MDC-N) within the context of the Global Political Agreement (GPA) or Interparty Political Agreement government.[1] It specifically tries to understand how the GPA environment has shaped the political dynamics of these two parties and how they have tried to influence Zimbabwe's political and economic trajectory within the space and opportunities provided by the GPA. The analysis focuses on the following:

- The motives and imperatives for the two political parties' involvement in the GPA, focusing on both the internal and external forces that shaped their involvement.
- The evolving political strategies of the two parties over the last four years of the GPA.

- The opportunities and gains made by the respective parties within the GPA.
- The two parties' growth/development in the last few years of the GPA and prospects for their future growth.
- The internal and external constraints and challenges encountered by the two parties within the GPA framework. The latter includes dealing with the problems of the transition from opposition to government (learning the art of statecraft); addressing the Zimbabwe population's social and economic expectations within an environment of limited economic growth or external support; managing the relationship between the two MDCs within and beyond government, and with an impatient civic society, external donors and partners; as well as dealing with ZANU-PF's intransigency, profligacy and unilateralism.

Historical Background: Contending Perspectives around the GPA

The politics or political behaviour of the two MDC parties over the last four years of the interparty government cannot be explained without understanding the context informing their entry into the GPA; and the internal and external dynamics which influenced the two parties to sign the agreement with ZANU-PF on 15 September 2008, so becoming part of the inclusive government in February 2009. However, if the agreement followed five months of incertitude, it was also preceded by years of intense political combat between ZANU-PF and the MDC parties, violence and repression, decay of the national infrastructure and institutions of governance, serious economic and social decay characterised by hyperinflation, an unaffordable cost of living, the erosion of educational and health services, and the high prevalence of epidemics such as cholera, typhoid, tuberculosis, and other HIV-AIDS-related infections. Nonetheless, the GPA per se was prompted primarily by the political stalemate that occurred among Zimbabwe's political parties following the disputed results of the March 2008 harmonised elections and the violent presidential run-off of June 2008. The dispute over these results not only created a serious political deadlock that put Zimbabwe on the verge of a civil war but also sparked an unprecedented economic disaster that worsened the plight of the population, especially the rural peasants and urban workers.

By the time the three key political parties agreed to sign the GPA, they had each run out of political and economic options. First, ZANU-PF had exhausted its capacity to continue governing on its own because of what Masunungure and others have described as 'a debilitating double crisis: a *crisis of legitimacy*, and a *crisis of efficacy*'.[2] The former, a result of the erosion of popular electoral support; its 'electoral victories' and 'right to rule' being challenged by allegations of electoral fraud and the deployment of violence during elections since 2000.[3] The latter, the crisis of efficacy, being a result of the ZANU-PF government's failure to deliver valued public goods and services in the country's rapidly deteriorating economic environment.[4] In addition, by 2007-08, ZANU-PF was left with very few economic resources to maintain its rule through patronage. Furthermore, the violence in the run-up to the controversial presidential runoff of June 2008 had seriously undermined the party's credibility within the region.[5] With its popular legitimacy greatly eroded both within the country and outside, ZANU-PF could only realistically continue to rule through its control over coercive power i.e. the state security apparatus and paramilitary forces, and this could not be sustainable in the long run.

The MDC formations, as Brian Raftopoulos has noted, went into the GPA government due to a combination of factors. These included the parties' realisation of their inability to translate their victory in the 2008 and 2000 elections into state power in the face of ZANU-PF's control of the coercive arms of the state; the rising human cost of state repression and violence against the parties' structures in the countryside; the structural erosion and political exhaustion of its support base, particularly in urban areas; and the growing anxiety about the success of Western pressure in resolving the Zimbabwe Crisis.[6] The MDC-T in particular had been gaining in popular support over the years of economic and political crisis but had not been able to translate that popular support into state power. While it had marginally won the March 2008 election,[7] it had no means to take over control of government because of the securocrats' resistance to its takeover. The MDC-N had won only ten of the contested 210 parliamentary seats and could not realistically hope to form a government on its own.[8] It was more concerned about the two dominant parties' unilateralism, especially the MDC-T's attempts to sideline it from the post-2008 political negotiation processes. It therefore welcomed the 'power-sharing deal' as its best chance to salvage its leverage in parliament where it held the balance of power.[9] Given the political deadlock in the country and the worsening of the economic and humanitarian crisis, the establishment of a power-sharing government was the most pragmatic solution for all the parties involved.

Contrary to the perception of most analysts who have described it as a coalition government,[10] Zimbabwe's power-sharing government was never meant to be a coalition government.[11] Coalition governments are formed in times of crises such as wars or moments of political deadlock. Zimbabwe's GPA government was indeed formed at a time of political and economic paralysis. But what distinguishes it from more typical coalition governments is that while there was an agreement for power sharing among Zimbabwe's three parties, there was never a framework or agreement for co-operation in governance once the GPA had been signed.[12]

The three political parties that signed the GPA, and the other internal and external actors involved in the whole settlement process, including the Southern African and Development Community (SADC), the African Union (AU), the European Union and the government of the United States, were all motivated by different, and often conflicting, motives and imperatives. President Thabo Mbeki who facilitated the political agreement between Zimbabwe's adversarial parties viewed the GPA as a transitional agreement that had to serve two main purposes.[13] The first was to be a transitional political arrangement to prevent Zimbabwe, which was then on the brink of political and economic collapse, from sliding towards a major economic and political disaster that would affect the whole region.[14] The second was to establish an agreed political framework in which Zimbabwe's conflicting parties could further negotiate the modalities of future political contestation, i.e. rules of the political game. This, in the SADC leadership's view, was to be done via a new constitutional and electoral framework to be established within the GPA's initial two-year time frame.[15] The purpose of the GPA, in this sense, was to facilitate peace, and then stabilise the country politically and economically before another election, which would then, presumably, resolve the key question of political legitimacy among the conflicting parties.[16]

Zimbabwe's political parties, on the other hand, viewed the GPA in rather different terms. For ZANU-PF, which only reluctantly agreed to share power with the MDCs under domestic, regional and international pressure, the GPA provided an opportunity to regroup and reconsolidate its hegemonic grip over power, which had been weakened over the previous few years of political struggle with the MDC, and badly shaken by the March 2008 results. It basically viewed the GPA as an opportunity to achieve the required space to rebuild and strengthen the party without giving too much ground.[17] The two MDC formations by and large regarded the interparty government as a strategic entry point from which to gain valuable experience in governance, to get a hand on the levers of state power, and to restructure and reform institutions of governance in a way that created space for democratisation and free and fair elections. The MDC-T in particular, and some of its international backers, viewed the GPA as an instrument for the transfer of hegemonic power from ZANU-PF to MDC-T.[18]

The GPA is signed. (L-R front row) D.P. Arthur Mutambara, President Robert Mugabe, Prime Minister Morgan Tsvangirai and President Thabo Mbeki.

The three parties which signed the GPA thus understood the GPA government as some form of ceasefire mechanism, following exhausting years of the inconclusive battle for power (2000-08). For all parties, the GPA government was never about political reconciliation or unity although they often referred to the new government as a 'unity government' or 'inclusive government'. From day one, the GPA was more about how the three parties could each use that space to rebuild and consolidate their power both inside and outside government.

The GPA Economy and Party Politics

The political economy of the GPA government, incorporating especially the various changes over the last three years, has fundamentally shaped the balance of power in the country and the strategic options available to Zimbabwe's political parties. First and foremost, the introduction of the GPA government and the dollarisation of the economy brought some economic stability. This gave rise to infrastructural development and relative improvement in the delivery of social services and the socio-economic welfare of the people. These gave some relief to the majority of Zimbabweans who were still suffering from the negative effects of almost a decade of a debilitating economic and political crisis, one that had intensified after the controversial June 2008 presidential election. This sense of economic relief has continued to be shared by many Zimbabweans, even though the economy has not much improved since the early economic stability and growth of 2009, which followed the formation of the GPA government.[19]

The relative improvement in the economic and social conditions of the country has had far-reaching political implications. Anecdotal evidence from newspaper reports and opinion polls suggest that the two MDCs, especially MDC-T which has always been viewed by the public as more able to make a difference than the relatively smaller unit led by Welshman Ncube, initially gained considerable political capital from the relative economic progress made under GPA.[20] Having endured years of economic debility under ZANU-PF's hegemonic control, a number of people credited the introduction of the MDC into government with many of the economic reforms and changes occurring in the country. ZANU-PF's propaganda has tried to project the improvements as products of ZANU-PF's policy initiatives, but not many discerning Zimbabweans have been won over by this rhetoric. Thus, politically, the MDC-T benefited from the economic and infrastructural developments of the first few years of GPA government.[21]

However, the economy has ironically turned out to be the Achilles' heel of the opposition movement in Zimbabwe. First, the economic stability created the breathing space that ZANU-PF needed to deal with issues other than the fire-fighting strategies of the rapid economic decline during the period pre-2009. Second, the economic stability that followed dollarisation helped many business ventures, including party officials' business ventures and ZANU-PF's many investment companies, to stabilise and recover. To a certain extent, the dollarisation also helped ZANU-PF officials, and their companies, to rely on the dollarised domestic market to accumulate and build up foreign currency reserves, rather than relying on external sources. In this way, dollarisation helped embargoed ZANU-PF companies not only to recover but to deal with the economic restrictions imposed by sanctions by creating a viable domestic market upon which they can now rely.²²

The partial recovery of business and the economy has helped ZANU-PF and its leadership to regain its financial muscle, which was much needed to bolster the party's organisational strength and its patronage system. At the same time, ZANU-PF's political strength has also been boosted by the growing importance of diamond mining at Chiadzwa and Marange mines whose revenue has largely gone into ZANU-PF and its leadership's coffers rather than to the government.²³

While ZANU-PF seems to have benefited most from the economy's partial recovery, the same cannot be said for the GPA government and the opposition parties whose popular mobilisation capacity has been negatively affected by the limited growth in the economy. The GPA government's capacity to grow the economy and to introduce economic and social reforms has remained constrained by political uncertainty and sanctions, which have both negatively affected its ability to attract international finance and investment.²⁴ The continued existence of US and EU targeted sanctions has specifically frustrated the GPA government's efforts to revive and grow the domestic economy. As the Minister of Finance, Tendai Biti, recently explained in response to the US government's decision to extend sanctions to Marange Resources and Mbada diamond companies, the decision would negatively affect his 2012 budgetary plan to raise $600 million from diamond sales' revenue for capital development and other government programmes aimed at reviving the economy and rebuilding crumbling infrastructure.²⁵

The GPA government's capacity to address the myriad of economic and social challenges confronting the country have also been negatively affected by the limited bilateral support to Zimbabwe by the international community. Sceptical about the stability and future of the GPA, many of Zimbabwe's traditional European development partners have been reluctant to increase development assistance to support the country's recovery and reconstruction. They have opted to focus on short-term humanitarian assistance under the Humanitarian Plus scheme rather than longer-term financial assistance.²⁶ The lack of adequate economic support for the country's economic recovery has resulted in a partial recovery or 'arrested development'.

The 'arrested development' that has occurred under the economy's partial recovery has resulted in a 'crisis of expectations' among a number of Zimbabweans. Having welcomed the economic and social progress that took place as a positive sign of the opposition parties' ability to govern and to turn things around, a growing number of people have been expressing frustration with the limited nature of changes that the GPA government has been able to bring about.[27] Others have been particularly frustrated by the inability of the opposition to deal with the challenges confronting the country and their inability to improve service delivery in those areas where they have had greater control, such as urban councils.

Civil servants protest their wages.

The ability of the opposition to deliver social and economic changes has indeed often been frustrated by ZANU-PF's continued dominant control over the state and the economy.[28] In many of the urban areas under the control of the MDC parties, for instance, ZANU-PF leaders have organised their party supporters, particularly the unemployed youths, to take over council properties and revenue-generating projects. In Harare, ZANU-PF activists have not only taken over market stalls, bus termini, parking areas and Council land but have also redirected council revenue towards themselves by either collecting council fees themselves or charging 'protection fees' to people who want to operate on those areas they have taken over.[29] The result of all this has been the disruption of council services and loss of revenue by urban councils, and this has seriously affected their ability to address the difficulties confronting the urban constituencies. But, in the eyes of a growing number of Zimbabweans who do not fully understand the intricacies of GPA power struggles, the MDC-controlled councils' failures to address their social problems and the GPA government's inability to provide people with jobs and other economic opportunities is an indication of the inability of the opposition parties to govern, rather than ZANU-PF whose record of failure is well documented.

At the same time, ZANU-PF has also sought to gain political advantage against the opposition MDC parties by launching a propaganda crusade aimed at projecting all the failures of the GPA government as a reflection of the 'MDC's inability to govern'. The MDC parties have been publicly accused by ZANU-PF of 'failing to award civil servants salary increases', 'being reluctant to support farmers and the revival of agriculture' and 'frustrating government efforts to resuscitate the closed industries in Bulawayo and other parts of the country' at a time when the government is struggling to raise enough money to pay for many of the basic services like health care and salaries.[30] Having allocated the MDC parties social cluster ministries during the power-sharing negotiations, ZANU-PF has over the last four years opportunistically managed to turn around and use that against the MDC formations. However, for the undiscerning members of the public whose access to sources of alternative information is limited, it is difficult to tell the truth from the propaganda and a significant number of people's political opinions are shaped by what they read in the national media. As a result, there has been some growing disenchantment with the opposition MDC parties among those who had given them the benefit of the doubt before their entry into government.[31]

The Battle for the Control of the State

Since its formation in February 2009, the GPA has been the site of intense contestation for the control of the state between ZANU-PF, which viewed the GPA framework as a period to regroup and reconsolidate its hegemonic grip over power, and the two MDC formations, which by and large regarded the interparty government as a strategic entry point to valuable experience, and an opportunity to restructure the state to pave way for their assumption of government through free and fair elections. The political strategy of the two MDCs from the onset of GPA government was to facilitate a democratic transfer of power through institutional reforms in the crucial areas of the security sector, electoral laws and the constitution.[32] Though differing in terms of tactics, the MDC formations' overall strategy was to embark on a gradual transfer of power from ZANU-PF's hegemonic control. They intended to do this through political and economic reforms facilitated by the ongoing constitution-making process, and parliamentary and policy reforms in those ministries controlled by the two parties.

The two MDCs have indeed tried to use the existing political space within the GPA framework to open up the state to greater levels of accountability by pushing through some important political and legislative reforms since their entry into government.[33] These include the Reserve Bank Amendment Act, successfully introduced in Parliament in 2009 by the Minister of Finance and MDC Secretary General, Tendai Biti, to restrict the powers of the Reserve Bank Governor over monetary policy; the Mineral Exploration Corporation Bill, initiated by the same Minister to bring transparency and accountability in the mining and marketing of diamonds and other precious minerals; and the Public Order and Security Act (Amendment) Bill, introduced into the House of Assembly by the MDC-T Chief Whip, Innocent Gonese, in 2009 as a Private Members' Bill, in a bid to remove the current Act's restrictions on freedom of speech, movement, association and assembly.[34]

The MDC formations have also tried to use the opening up of political space under the GPA to demand more transparency and accountability from the state and government parastatals. For example, the two parties' MPs have increasingly questioned government ministers, including those representing ZANU-PF, on a number of public interest issues, such as the awarding of irregular tenders and mining licences as well as lack of transparency in certain financial transactions.[35] Utilising their representation on portfolio committees, the two parties have also sought to enforce transparency in government by setting up committees of inquiry to investigate ministries and parastatals suspected of corruption.[36] At the same time, the two parties have managed to use many other negotiating forums in the GPA government, such as the Joint Monitoring and Implementation Committee (JOMIC), the GPA Negotiators meetings, Cabinet meetings and the weekly GPA Principals Meeting, to push through reforms in various sectors of the economy, politics, the media, and security. The legislative and political reforms undertaken in the last four years have all helped to open up new spaces for democratic reform in the political and governance structures of the country. In addition, through their involvement in the ongoing constitutional reform process being spearheaded by the Zimbabwe Constitution Select Committee (COPAC), the two parties have also managed to push for some substantial political and social reforms in their negotiations with their ZANU-PF counterparts.

ZANU-PF Hegemony and Resistance to Change

Notwithstanding the above progress, the ability of the two MDC parties to influence policy change within the GPA government has remained limited, mainly due to three key factors: the skewed nature of the GPA itself; ZANU-PF's resistance to suggested changes; and the opposition parties' internal weaknesses, which have affected their ability to take advantage of the few opportunities that have occurred. First and foremost, as analysts have correctly observed, Zimbabwe's GPA was lopsided; it gave ZANU-PF more substantive power.[37] Overall, the power-sharing agreement was drafted to leave President Mugabe with undiluted executive powers, so allowing him the space to act unilaterally on issues of interest to himself and his party. Taking advantage of this weakness, Mugabe has used his executive powers over the last three years to make decisions on governance and policy issues, such as the appointment of senior government officials and enactment of legislation, without consulting his MDC partner leaders.[38] In addition to the above, the division of power within the GPA virtually gave ZANU-PF the 'hard levers' of state power through control of both the bureaucracy and influential government portfolios, such as Defence, Security, Local Government, Mining, Land, Agriculture and Transport. At the other hand, the two MDC parties' control over government was weak from the beginning because they held the 'soft levers' of state power in the form of service ministries such as Education, Health, Labour and Social Welfare.[39] With their limited control of government, the two MDC parties have found it very difficult to make significant progress in policy changes.

Second, the ability of the opposition parties to use their leverage during this phase has been restricted because ZANU-PF is not interested in any reforms that would loosen its hold on power.[40] While agreeing to some of the reforms negotiated in the GPA, ZANU-PF was bent on using them and the new institutions to legitimise itself and push its own agenda. The Zimbabwe Electoral Commission (ZEC), for instance, appeared to be broadly representative but was, in fact, still dominated by ZANU-PF through their control of its secretariat and support staff.[41] In addition, ZEC was starved of both material resources and manpower to carry out its tasks, and this has ensured that the partisan Registrar General's office remains in control of the election processes, from voter registration to the counting of the votes.[42] The same applies to other GPA commissions like the Media Commission whose commissioners were drawn from a variety of stakeholders but which remains dominated by a ZANU-PF bureaucracy. The Human Rights Commission has not only been deliberately starved of resources and a legal framework, but has also been cleverly used to give an impression of legitimacy to the GPA process. It exists on paper only.[43] All this has been part of a deliberate, calculated strategy by ZANU-PF to retain power.

Since the signing of the GPA, the ZANU-PF-led government has also done little to remove the restrictive media framework. Repressive media legislation remains intact and there have been no moves to liberalise the airwaves or the print media.[44] The result of this tight control is that the majority of the public are still reliant on the heavily censored, government-controlled media and have no access to alternative forms of information. The ability of Zimbabwean citizens to make informed choices has therefore continued to be inhibited by a lack of diverse sources of information.

The ZANU-PF strategy, consistent with its hegemonic political culture, has been to engage in cosmetic political and economic reforms that will not result in furthering democracy or result in a loss of its historic monopoly over power.[45] The slowdown of the constitutional reform process and the delays in the implementation of aspects of the GPA have all formed part of the broad ZANU-PF strategy of retarding political reform. Indeed, over the last four years, ZANU-PF has kept the strategic doors to its power, such as the security sector and the mining and agricultural industries, firmly closed.

Second, and more importantly, ZANU-PF has managed to frustrate the two MDC parties' attempts to influence policy within the framework of the GPA by creating a parallel, informal government controlled by ZANU-PF securocrats which coalesces around the President's Office and the Joint Operations Command. This parallel structure has not only managed to sideline the leadership of the two MDCs from decision-making processes, but has also sidelined some ZANU-PF leaders in government by directing government policy outside the authority of the formal cabinet.[46]

The failure to get ZANU-PF co-operation on a number of agreements and reforms has resulted in political frustration among leaders and supporters of the two MDCs.[47] At the same time, the inability of the parties to steer rapid change in the economy and politics of the country has led to disenchantment among some of their supporters and sympathisers. All these developments, coupled with reported cases of corruption among some of the parties' elected officials, have affected their popularity among members of the public.[48]

Strategic and Organisational Weaknesses within the MDC Formations

Much more significantly, the MDC parties' political effectiveness in influencing GPA processes has been influenced by their respective organisational weaknesses, manifested in the lack of cohesiveness, discipline, effective strategy and limited leadership capacity.[49] From the onset of the GPA government, the MDC parties' participation was constrained by their lack of governing experience and weak leadership capacity. As the MDC-T Treasurer, Roy Bennett, reportedly acknowledged in his private conversation with the US Ambassador to Zimbabwe, Charles Ray, in 2010, the party lacked people with experience in administration and the few who had it were overstretched.[50]

From its establishment in 1999, the MDC had focused on resisting ZANU-PF dictatorship and the onslaught on its membership and structures, rather than growing the party's administrative capacity. In addition, the MDC had always struggled to attract and retain Zimbabwe's intellectuals and elites within its leadership structures.[51] This has ultimately affected its capacity to engage with the sophisticated art of governance, particularly within the contested and treacherous terrain of GPA government where they have had to deal with ZANU-PF, a party with incumbent experience. The lack of leadership capacity in both parties has not only been evident in the way they have struggled to manage some of the administrative/bureaucratic issues but also in the competency levels of some of the people deployed by these parties to represent them.[52] As political analyst and former government bureaucrat, Ibbo Mandaza, has noted with respect to the MDC-T's experience in the GPA government over the last few years, 'Tsvangirai and his party... have been exposed as organisationally vacuous, far too short on managerial capacity and unable to sustain the "Reform Agenda" that had been more implicit than explicit within the opposition movement.'[53] The party's limited administrative experience has also caused bungling on a number of bureaucratic issues.[54] On the other hand, the lack of leadership capacity in the Ncube-led MDC has resulted in the overburdening of its few capable leaders. A good example is the party's Secretary General, Priscilla Misihairabwi-Mushonga, whose list of responsibilities include representing the party in Cabinet, JOMIC, the GPA Negotiation Team and the Cabinet Re-engagement Team with Europe.

The two MDC's failure to use GPA opportunities has also been caused by the lack of effective strategy. While ZANU-PF has been more strategic in using the GPA space to rebuild and reposition itself, the two MDCs have not done so. Even a cursory glance of the terms of the agreement, for instance, reveals that the GPA is lopsided in favour of ZANU-PF and that its negotiators were much more careful and strategic in their choice of wording.[55] Similarly, it is also clear that the MDCs, especially the MDC-T, has not been strategic in the ongoing GPA negotiations over the problems in its implementation. The list of issues the MDC-T has pushed for include 'soft power' issues, such as the appointment of deputy ministers and senior civil servants, which would not substantially change the balance of power even if ZANU-PF were to make concessions. ZANU-PF, on the other hand, has stuck to 'hard power' issues such as travel restrictions on its leaders and economic sanctions, both of which affect the party's capacity to operate effectively.[56]

In addition, while the two MDCs have indeed utilised spaces like parliament to advance their political interests, they have not done so effectively, nor have they utilised a wide range of opportunities available within the GPA environment to push for democratisation.[57] The number of reforms pushed through in Private Members' bills, for instance, has been limited.[58] More crucially, the parties have not taken effective measures to empower some of the GPA's institutions of democratic reform and accountability, such as the Anti-Corruption Commission, Human Rights Commission, JOMIC and the Organ on National Reconciliation, Healing and Integration, which could have given them more leveraging powers if they were fully operational.[59] Nor have they taken their opportunity in government to show the electorate that they have innovative ideas for dealing with the country's political and economic challenges. The MDC-T, in particular, which controls all urban councils and eleven rural district councils in the country, has not effectively used that space to demonstrate its governance capacity. As a result, the party has not been able to win new votes through its performance.

The two MDCs' effectiveness in influencing Zimbabwe's political progress and economic recovery under the GPA framework has particularly been affected by the progressive decline in their organisational strength, which is primarily the result of the intraparty and interparty squabbling. The political relations between the leadership of the two parties has remained acrimonious since the 2005 split, and the breakdown of the February 2008 interparty dialogue aimed at establishing an electoral pact before the March 2008 elections. As a result, the two parties have often worked to undermine each other, even in instances when it would be more strategic for them to co-operate. Because of their mutual mistrust, the two parties have failed to pull together on matters of mutual interest and long-term strategic interest.[60] A good example of this is the breakdown of the regular GPA Principals meeting, which were important in resolving some of the problems in the GPA government. The decision by the MDC-T President Tsvangirai to continue supporting Arthur Mutambara's claims to the posts of Deputy Prime Minister and President of the MDC-N, after his defeat by Welshman Ncube in the party's January 2011 elections, has effectively rendered the Principals Meeting an academic exercise because Mutambara does not have the political legitimacy to represent the MDC-N in those meetings.[61]

The legal challenge to the election of the Sixth Parliament's Speaker, which almost led to the dethronement of MDC-T's Lovemore Moyo as Speaker of the Zimbabwe Parliament in April 2011, also demonstrates how the interparty rivalry between the two MDCs has cost the two parties in terms of political leverage.[62] The challenge was brought by former independent MP, Jonathan Moyo, who has now rejoined ZANU-PF, and supported by the MDC-N's Moses Mzila Ndlovu, Patrick Dube and Siyabonga Ncube. Though sharing little common political cause with either Moyo or ZANU-PF, the MDC-N MPs supported the challenge in order to get back at the MDC-T for its failure to support their nominated candidate, Paul Themba Nyathi, for the same post. During the election rerun, the MDC-T's candidate narrowly avoided electoral defeat by the ZANU-PF candidate after some of the MDC-N MPs decided to defy their party leadership's directive to abstain from voting rather than voting for the MDC-T or ZANU-PF, which had both continued to snub it over the issue of Mutambara.[63]

While the interparty struggles between the two MDCs have negatively affected their ability to engage with the GPA processes, the intraparty struggles within both parties have seriously affected both their organisational growth within the GPA framework and prospects for future growth. For instance, the Ncube-led MDC, which won ten seats in the March 2008 parliamentary elections and has used its strength in Zimbabwe's hung parliament to influence policy decisions in both parliament and negotiations over the GPA, now has only seven seats as a result of both intraparty and interparty struggles.[64] This followed the expulsion of three of its MPs for allegedly taking financial bribes from the MDC-T in order to undermine their own party. Nonetheless, their dismissal has reduced the MDC-N's voting strength because no by-elections have taken place to replace them.

In addition, the MDC-N's capacity to shape political processes within the GPA framework was fundamentally shaken after its Congress of January 2011, which resulted in some significant changes in its leadership structures.[65] Since then, the MDC-N has tried to reposition and rebrand itself while modifying its mobilisation strategy. Realising its limitations in building a powerful national base in Zimbabwe's two-party political system and ethnicised/regionalised politics, the party has focused more on consolidating its support base in the south-western provinces of Matabeleland, Bulawayo and Midlands where it has traditionally attracted a larger following since the 2005 split.[66] Its efforts to build a powerful regional support base as its launch-pad to a broader national mobilisation campaign has received an unplanned boost due to the seeming reluctance of both President Mugabe and Prime Minister Tsvangirai to appoint Welshman Ncube, as the party's Political Principal and Deputy Prime Minister in the GPA government. The political bickering over this issue has generated intense national debate about the marginalisation of Ndebeles, and their home provinces of Matabeleland in Zimbabwe's economy and politics. It has also helped the party to gain regional political sympathy from those who feel that the MDC-N and its new leader are being unfairly treated on account of their ethnicity. The fact that both President Mugabe and Prime Minister Tsvangirai have decided to close ranks in supporting the Shona-speaking Mutambara has added credence to the perception of ethnic favouritism.[67]

While the MDC-N's repositioning and rebranding might have gained it political support in Matabeleland, the same process might have cost it support in the Shona-speaking parts of the country where it has increasingly been viewed as a regional party, with a regional support base and a 'regional agenda'.[68] This perception of the MDC-N has been entrenched by accusations and counter-accusations about tribalism, which followed the replacement of the Shona-speaking Mutambara from the presidency of the party by the Ndebele-speaking Ncube.[69] Within the context of Zimbabwe's highly ethnicised politics, the perception of MDC-N as a regional party has negatively affected its capacity to mobilise voters around its ideas in the Shona-speaking areas of the country and some residents of the ethnically cosmopolitan urban centres of Bulawayo and Gweru.[70] The internal divisions within the party over the removal of Mutambara from the party presidency and the subsequent dismissal of some of the party's leaders, including the National Chairperson of the party (Joubert Mudzumwe), the National Chairperson of the Women's Assembly (Hilda Sibanda), the National Chairperson of the Youth Assembly (Constantine Chipadza), the party's National Director of Information and Publicity (Maxwell Zimuto), Secretary for Education (Tsitsi Dangarembga) and Secretary for Economic Affairs (Morgan Changamire) further weakened the leadership structure of the party.

The MDC-T has not been spared from intraparty struggles that have confronted the MDC-N. Many of the cracks in the united MDC, around issues of internal democracy, accountability and use of violence, which resulted in the 2005 split, have continued to haunt the MDC-T throughout the GPA phase. The intraparty struggles of the MDC-T actually worsened after the signing of the GPA when both party activists and donors began to position themselves for greater influence in government. These internecine struggles grew more intense as the party began to restructure itself in preparation for its electoral congress of May 2011.[71] Some of the highlights of this political infighting expressed themselves in violence involving party officials and youths.[72] The struggles also resulted in the reassigning of the administrative duties of the Secretary General, Tendai Biti, to the Deputy Secretary General, Tapiwa Mashakada, and the suspension of some officials of the party, particularly those suspected to be close to Biti.[73]

The intraparty struggles within the MDC-T have divided the party into two main factions. They comprise one organising around Secretary General Biti who has been accused of being involved in 'plotting a leadership coup against Tsvangirai'.[74] Biti and his supporters, who include the Chairman of the influential Harare Province, Paul Madzore, have been accused of trying to stuff the provincial leadership structures with his loyalists to ensure that he emerges as the winner in the future battle for party leadership.[75] Biti's leadership ambitions have been reportedly supported by some sympathisers within the business and intellectual circles as well as some Western donor countries who believe that Biti, unlike Tsvangirai, has the intellectual and political acumen to match Mugabe and his successors within ZANU PF.[76]

Biti's leadership ambitions have been challenged by a group mobilising around Tsvangirai and his political confidant, Ian Makone, who is also believed to harbour ambitions to succeed Tsvangirai.[77] Tsvangirai's backers within the factional politics of the party reportedly include the current Organising Secretary of the party and former youth leader, Nelson Chamisa – allegedly another key player in the race to succeed Tsvangirai.[78]

The MDC-T's organisational strength in the countryside has been undermined by the struggles for leadership in all the provinces where it has a strong presence. These include Midlands, Manicaland, Masvingo and the party's political bedrock of Matabeleland, where it has historically been assured of the majority on account of Matabeleland's protest politics that are rooted in the region's disillusionment with ZANU-PF's failure to address both the legacy of the Gukurahundi massacres and the economic marginalisation of the region.[79] The Bulawayo province of the party has specifically been rocked by serious infighting and internal factionalism that have affected the party's organisational capacity,[80] while the party's supporters in other parts of Matabeleland have increasingly criticised it for insensitivity to the problems of the region and failure to come out with a clear justice and reconciliation framework that deals with the legacy of Gukurahundi.

As in the past, ethnic and regional divisions within the party have continued to undermine its organisational strength and performance during the GPA period. In the period leading to the 2011 congress, for instance, MDC-T's ability to work as an organised movement with one voice was greatly undermined by the creation of political factions based on ethnic and regional lines. The ethnic dimensions of MDC-T politics have largely expressed themselves as Karanga-Manyika/Zezuru struggles and Ndebele-Shona intraparty divisions. The former have resulted in the creation of what some political observers have described as the 'Karanga Axis of Power' within the MDC – a factional grouping of MDC-T leaders originating from the provinces of Masvingo and Midlands mobilising around a Karanga political identity.[81] These factional leaders have tried to carve out political space for themselves in the party by mobilising around Karanga perceptions of marginalisation from national and party politics by both Zezuru and Manyika leaders.[82]

The internal divisions within the MDC-T have become so serious that, whilst not necessarily resulting in another split as in 2005, they have negatively affected the party's effectiveness in the GPA government and will negatively affect its electoral performances if they are not resolved in a timely way.[83] They have also resulted in the absence of a coherent strategy to guide the party in its dealings with GPA processes. This has become evident in the conflicting messages on certain issues, which have emanated from the Prime

Minister's Office, controlled by a close group of party bureaucrats headed by Tsvangirai's long-term political confidante and principal advisor in government, Ian Makone, and the Party headquarters, under the direction of Secretary General Biti.[84] The lack of an agreed strategy has weakened the MDC-T's bargaining power and positioning within the GPA and given ZANU-PF ample opportunity to exploit the MDC-T's lack of coherence and consistency. Most importantly, the divisions are occurring at a crucial time in the party's history when it not only needs to prove its political worthiness to citizens while in government but also needs to unite its best brains and energy against a resurgent ZANU-PF.

The organisational and mobilising capacity of the two MDCs during the last few years of the GPA has also been negatively affected by growing cases of corruption and abuse of public office by some of their officials, especially those of the relatively stronger MDC-T, which has more ministers in government and controls all the country's urban councils and eleven rural district councils. A number of the MDC-T's ward councillors and mayors have been implicated in cases of corruption that range from illegal transfers of council land and properties to themselves, relatives and friends to soliciting bribes from residents desperate for housing stands and houses.[85] Some of the high-profile cases of corruption involving the MDC-T representatives in local administration include the Chitungwiza land scandal which resulted in the party firing all its 23 councillors in 2010; the mismanagement and looting of Council land and resources by councillors in Bindura; the Kwekwe audit report findings of 2010 which unearthed serious financial irregularities involving the under-banking of collected revenue and the Marondera corruption case which resulted in the suspension of the mayor by his party in March 2012 for receiving kickbacks from companies and individuals in return for tenders.[86] The corruption among the party's representatives in local authorities, MDC parliamentarians and government officials, as the MDC leadership itself has admitted, has the potential to cost the party dearly during the next elections.[87]

The MDC-T President Tsvangirai's recent personal problems around allegations of womanising and corruption have contributed to the negative public image of the MDC-T[88] and invited public criticism and condemnation by both critics and supporters alike. Critics have argued that the reports about Tsvangirai's controversial love life reflect badly on his sense of personal judgment as well as his moral authority and capacity as a national leader.[89] At the same time, the reports about corruption implicating him and his close relatives have led to questions being raised about his morality and commitment to managing the national economy transparently. ZANU-PF has capitalised on these internal weaknesses and constantly sought to gain political mileage by giving the cases of corruption and the MDC-T leader's controversial love life maximum coverage in the state media.[90]

In addition to the above, the opposition parties' capacity to organise and mobilise the masses in the last four years of the GPA government has been negatively affected by the continued weakening of two of their key traditional constituencies of support, labour and civics. Labour has specifically remained very weak under the GPA economy, mainly because of the continued informalisation of the economy, the high unemployment rate (estimated at more than 80%) and the vulnerability of employed workers in a weak and fragile economy.[91] This continued informalisation of labour, as Raftopoulos has correctly argued, has 'severely eroded the structural basis for labour and opposition mobilisation in a more informally constituted economy, in which the discipline and modalities of formal organisation built up by a once formidable labour movement have been lost to the different rhythms of survivalist opportunism endemic in the more precarious conditions of informal livelihoods.'[92] At the same time, the labour movement's capacity to mobilise the few workers still in formal employment has been greatly weakened by the factionalism and split in the main labour organisation, the Zimbabwe Congress of Trade Unions (ZCTU) over leadership and management of the organisation.[93]

In addition, the civic movement has been in gradual decline since the birth of the MDC, which increasingly overshadowed it after 1999. It continued to weaken within the GPA environment when a number of civil society leaders, who had remained within the movement after the post-2000 departure of other experienced civic leaders and activists, were incorporated into the structures of the government by the two MDC parties at the formation of the GPA government. The Global Political Agreement also destabilised the civic movement in the sense that it came at a time when civics least expected it to happen and it took time to adjust to the new dynamics and develop appropriate responses.[94] As a result, civic society responses to the GPA environment have not only been uncoordinated but fragmented.

Internal divisions and polarisation along factional party political lines, and limited leadership capacity, mainly due to the departure of experienced leaders and activists into government, politics and the diaspora have also contributed to the current weak state of the civil society movement.[95] Another serious weakness in Zimbabwe's civic movement over the last few years has been its incapacity to mobilise the masses. Progressively elitist in their leadership and composition, and dependent increasingly on external donors rather than internal membership for survival, most civil society organisations have failed to link their agendas to the day-to-day struggles of the people or establish an organic linkage with the masses.[96] Their capacity to mobilise people for action or build mass support among both the struggling rural and urban populations of Zimbabwe have thus progressively declined over the years, especially after 2009 when the MDC parties with whom they had formed a close political partnership had become part of the government.

Conclusion

The GPA environment has presented the MDC parties with an opportunity to grow and mature as political parties through learning the art of governance, the space to mobilise the nation around their agenda through demonstrating their leadership capacity and to shape the transition to democracy through gradual reforms. The two parties have indeed managed to influence a number of processes and developments in the country throughout the last four years of the GPA government. They have, however, also missed a number of opportunities to shape the political and economic direction of the country due to a combination of both internal and external constraints.

ZANU-PF has, in fact, been more shrewd in its engagement with the transition process than its political opponents, including both political parties and civics as well as international opponents such as the US and EU countries. It has been effectively using the transition arrangement to regroup and reorganise, and it is now better organised than it was in 2008. It has thus been winning the battle for control of the state against the MDC and has been winning its propaganda war against the West over the issue of sanctions and regime change within the region. As a result, it is now reasserting itself as the dominant political party in the country. ZANU-PF assertiveness is evident in the way it has been making unilateral government decisions, without consulting its partners in the GPA government, proscribing space for the MDC to organise, and harassing MDC officials, including senior MDC officials, in parliament and government.

ENDNOTES

1 The MDC party that is led by Professor Welshman Ncube is formally called the MDC, but for purposes of convenience and clarity this chapter will refer to it as MDC-N. The breakaway faction of the same party that is led by Arthur Mutambara is referred to in this chapter as MDC-M.

2 E. Masunungure, 'Zimbabwe's Power Sharing Agreement', paper prepared for a Workshop on The Consequences of Political Inclusion in Africa, American University, Washington, DC April, 24-25, 2009; D. Matsyzak, *Law, Politics and Zimbabwe's 'Unity' Government* (Harare: Konrad Adenauer Stftung and Research and Advocacy Unity), pp. 94-95.

3 See ibid; B. Raftopoulos, 'The Global Political Agreement as a "Passive Revolution"': Notes on Contemporary Politics in Zimbabwe', *The Roundtable*, 99: 411, 2010, p. 707.

4 Masunungure, 'Zimbabwe's Power Sharing Agreement'.

5 See D. Matsyzak, *Zimbabwe's 'Unity' Government,* pp. 94-95.

6 Raftopoulos, 'The Global Political Agreement as a "Passive Revolution"', p. 708.

7 See Zimbabwe Electoral Commission (ZEC), 2008. Report of the 2008 General Elections (Harare: ZEC); Zimbabwe Electoral Support Network (ZESN), 2008. Report on the Zimbabwe March 29 2008 Harmonised Elections and 27 June Presidential Run-Off (Harare: ZESN).

8 The MDC-T won 99 seats in parliament against Zanu PF's 97 seats, while the MDC won 10 seats.

9 See B. Raftopoulos, 'Elections, Mediation and Deadlock in Zimbabwe', ARI, 119/2008. www.realinstitutoelcano.org/wps/.../Content?...2008.

10 M. Bratton, 'Zimbabwe: Power Sharing Deal under Stress', *USIS Peace Brief*, 66, November 3, 2010.

11 A coalition government includes members of different political parties who co-operate to form a government. Coalition governments are usually formed when a single party cannot command enough seats in parliament to form a government and then two parties or several parties who can work together group to form a governing majority. The idea is to give a government the high degree of perceived political legitimacy it desires whilst also playing a role in diminishing internal political strife.

12 Priscilla Misihairabwi-Mushonga (MDC Negotiator and Minister of Regional and International Integration), Presentation at the Institute of Justice and Reconciliation Policy Advisory Seminar – Zimbabwe's Government of National Unity: A two-year Appraisal, Cape Town, 10 March 2011.

13 See B. Raftopoulos chapter in this book for more detailed discussion on Mbeki mediation strategy on the Zimbabwe Crisis.

14 See T. Murithi and A. Mawadza, 'Voices from Pan-African Society on Zimbabwe: South Africa, The African Union and SADC', in T. Murithi and A. Mawadza, (eds), *Zimbabwe in Transition: A View from Within* (Johannesburg: Jacana Media, 2011), pp. 294-296.

15 See Global Political Agreement 15 September 2008, Articles vi, x, xvii & xxiii; B. Raftopoulos, 'The Global Political Agreement as a "Passive Revolution"', pp 710-713; A.S. Mlambo and B. Raftopoulos, 'The Regional Dimension of Zimbabwe's Multilayered Crisis: an Analysis' (Conference on Election Processes, Liberation Movements and Democratic Change in Africa, Maputo, 8-11 April 2010), pp. 8-10.

16 Ibid; Masunungure, 'Zimbabwe's Power Sharing Agreement'; Murithi and Mawadza, 'Voices from Pan-African Society on Zimbabwe', pp. 294-296.

17 Matyszak, *Zimbabwe's Unity Government*, pp. 98-102.

18 See Morgan Tsvangirai iterview with Debora Pata, 3rd Degree Programme on etv (SA), August 2008, cited in Matyszak, *Law, Politics and Zimbabwe's Unity Government*, p. 95.

19 'Urban Poverty: A social time bomb', *The Standard*, 1 August 2009; 'Sombre birthday for ailing GNU', *The Standard*, 6 February 2010; 'Value of shares traded on ZSE falls 7,6%', *The Business Herald*, 2 March 2010; Civil Society Monitoring Mechanism (CISOMM), *Annual Review of the Performance of the Inclusive Government of Zimbabwe, February 2009-February 2010*, 11 February 2010; Priscilla Misihairabwi-Mushonga (MDC Negotiator and Minister of Regional and International Integration), Tapiwa Mashakada (Minister of Trade and Investment Promotion), Presentation at the Institute of Justice and Reconciliation Policy Advisory Seminar-Zimbabwe's Government of National Unity: A two-year Appraisal, Cape Town, 10 March 2011.

20 'Two thirds Zimbabweans still want GNU to succeed', www.zimdiaspora.com, 11 February 2010; 'Zimbabweans not ready for elections, yet', www.zimonline, 24 February 2010.

21 See M. Bratton and Masunungure, *The Anatomy of Political Predation: Leaders, Elites and Coalitions in Zimbabwe, 1980-2010*. Development Leadership Program, Research Paper 9, January 2011, pp. 40-41.

22 Zimbabwe Institute, 'Zimbabwe Situational Analysis: A Review of the Political Landscape after Two Years of Inclusive Government', ZI Policy Brief, No.1, February 2011.

23 'ZANU PF loyalists exposed as diamond directors', *SW Radio Africa*, 14 February 2012. www.swradioafrica.com/.../**zanu-pf**-loyalists-exposed-as-**diam**; 'Biti says diamond revenue is going to a parallel government', *The Insider*, 17 May 2012. www.insiderzim.com/stories/3954.html; 'Diamond looting sucks in minister' *Daily News*, 26 June 2011.

24 See Zimbabwe Institute, 'Revisiting "Targeted Sanctions": Policy Options for Resolving the Sanctions Deadlock in Zimbabwe, ZI Policy Brief No. 1, January 2012; 'Biti attacks US government', *Sunday Mail*, 15 January 2012.
25 'Biti attacks US government', *Sunday Mail*, 15 January 2012.
26 African Development Bank, *Zimbabwe: Country Brief*, January 2010, p. 6; L. Ploch, *The Transitional Government and Implications for US Policy*, Congressional Research Service, October 2011, pp.5-6.
27 'Sombre birthday for ailing GNU', *The Standard*, 6 February 2010.
28 N. Kriger, 'ZANU PF politics under Zimbabwe's 'Power Sharing' government', *Journal of Contemporary African Studies*, 30 (1), 2012, pp. 11-26.
29 Precious Shumba, 'Uncovering the Chipangano gang in Mbare', www.nehandaradiocom 2 November 2011; 'ZPF's violent Chipangano Gang running "Parallel Council" in Harare', *SW Radio Africa*, 28 March 2012; 'Savanhu linked to Chipagano', *Zimbabwe Independent*, 11 November 2011; 'Councillors demand Masunda's Eviction', *Daily News*, 1 September 2011; 'Mayor's Easy Park decision may backfire', *Daily News*, 7 January 2012; 'Zanu PF blocks Mbare project', *Daily News*, 14 July 2011; 'How Chipangano stalled fuel project', *Daily News on Sunday*, 26 February 2012.
30 See 'Giving Me Chance to talk about Missing Diamonds', *Newsday*, 16 March 2011; 'No diamonds money for civil service pay rise: Biti', *The Standard*, 7 February 2011; 'Civil servants vs Biti', *The Herald*, 26 March 2011.
31 See 'Sombre birthday for ailing GNU', *The Standard*, 6 February 2010.
32 Discussion with MDC-N and MDC-T officials, 3 July 2011.
33 Mlambo and Raftopoulos, 'The Regional dimension of Zimbabwe's multilayered crisis', p.11; Raftopoulos, 'The GPA as a "Passive Revolution"'.
34 'Reserve Bank of Zimbabwe Amendment Bill', www.zimtreasury.org; 'Government considers new diamond act', *The Herald*, 16 July 2010; 'New diamond act on cards', *Daily News*, 26 June 2011; R. Saunders, 'Briefing Note: Mining and Crisis' (Netherlands Institute for Southern Africa, June 2007); 'MDC-T Chief Whip Innocent Gonese on POSA amendments', *The Zimbabwean*, 7 October 2010; 'Senate shoots down POSA Amendment Bill', *The Herald*, 1 August 2011.
35 See 'Zimbabwe Parliamentary Committee presses mining firm for answers on diamonds', www.voanews.com/zimbabwe. 8 March 2010; 'Air Zimbabwe boss to appear before Parliamentary Committee', www.intozimbabwe.com. 10 April 2011; 'Coltart says he had nothing to do with tender for textbooks', www.swradioafrica.com. 21 March 2012.
36 See 'Report of Portfolio Committee on Transport and Infrastructural Development conducted an inquiry into the operations of Air Zimbabwe Holdings and the Civil Aviation Authority of Zimbabwe' (Parliament of Zimbabwe, 2010); 'Second

Report of The Portfolio Committee on State Enterprises and Parastals Management on Supply of Water Treatment Chemicals by Chemplex Corporation on Harare City Council' (Parliament of Zimbabwe, December 16, 2010).
37 Matsyzak, *Law, Politics and Zimbabwe's 'Unity' Government*, pp. 66-86; Masunungure, 'Zimbabwe's Power Sharing Agreement'; N. Cheeseman and B. Tendi. 'Power-sharing in comparative perspective: The dynamics of "unity government" in Kenya and Zimbabwe', *Journal of Modern African Studies* 48 (2), 2010, pp. 203–29.
38 'PM fumes over CIO boss', *Financial Gazette*, 22 July 2011; 'Tsvangirai slams Mugabe power grab', *Zimbabwe Independent*, 8 October 2010; 'Mugabe unilaterally appoints Judges as MDC cry foul', *SW Radio Africa*, 21 May 2010. www.swradioafrica.com/.../judgeinpocket210510.htm.
39 For a detailed discussion on the balance of power in the GPA Government, see A. Magaisa, '2 Years on: The Balance of Power in Zimbabwe', newzimbabwe.com. 10 February 2011; Magaisa, 'Part 2: Balance of Power in Zimbabwe after 2 Years of GNU', newzibabwe.com. 15 February 2011. See also Nathaniel Manheru, 'GPA: When it will not die', *The Herald*, 12 February 2011.
40 See 'ZANU PF strategy to frustrate the MDC-T working', *Zimbabwe Independent*, 3 February 2012.
41 P. Ruhanya, 'Case against Zimbabwe Electoral Commission', *The Standard*, 12 February 2012.
42 'Zimbabwe Electoral Commission broke', www.zimdaily.com. 17 July 2011; Crisis Coalition, 'Further electoral reforms required', www.crisis.org. 9 February 2012.
43 The Commission currently has no legal mandate to operate mainly because the Ministry of Justice and Legal Affairs took too long to finalise the Human Rights Commission Bill, which is supposed to give the Commission its legal mandate to start work.
44 Civil Society Monitoring Mechanism (CISSOM), *Six Month Shadow Report on the Performance of the Inclusive Government of Zimbabwe* (Harare: CISSOM, 2010), pp. 31-36.
45 For more detailed discussion about the history of ZANU-PF hegemony, see M. Sithole and J. Makumbe, 'Elections in Zimbabwe: The ZANU-PF hegemony and its incipient decline', *African Journal of Political Science*, 2 (1), 1997; W. Ncube 'Constitutionalism, democracy and political practice in Zimbabwe', in I. Mandaza and L. Sachikonye, eds, *The One Party State and Democracy: The Zimbabwe Debate* (Harare: Sapes Books, 1991); L. Sachikonye, *When a State Turns on its Citizens: 60 Years of Institutionalised Violence in Zimbabwe* (Johannesburg: Jacana Media, 2011), pp. 1-44.
46 For a more comprehensive discussion about this parallel government as well as ZANU PF's strategic use of informal structures and networks of power to govern,

see Zimbabwe Institute, 'Zimbabwe Situational Analysis: A Review of the Political Landscape after Two Years of Inclusive Government' (ZI Policy Brief, No.1, February 2011); N. Kriger, 'ZANU PF politics under Zimbabwe's "Power Sharing" Government', *Journal of Contemporary African Studies*, 30 (1), 2012, pp. 11-26; K. Chitiyo, 'The Case for Security Sector Reform in Zimbabwe' (Occasional Paper, Royal United Service Institute, September 2009), pp. 4-36; J. Muzondidya '"Our Guns are Our Votes": The Political-Military Alliance in Zimbabwean Politics and Prospects for Democratic Transition' (AEGIS 3rd European Conference on African Studies, Leipzig, 4-7 June 2009).

47 See 'Tsvangirai petitions SADC', *Financial Gazette*, 21 November 2011; 'Biti lambasts parallel government structures', *Newsday*, 23 November 2011; 'Zanu PF running parallel government', *SW Radio Africa*, 13 January 2012. http://www.swradioafrica.com.

48 'Commission to probe corruption in MDC-T', *Zimbabwe Independent*, 18 February 2010; 'Councillors take corruption to extremes', *Financial Gazette*, 11-17 March 2010.

49 Many of these problems have been troubling the organisation from its very formation in 1999. See B. Raftopoulos, 'Reflections on opposition politics in Zimbabwe: the politics of the Movement for Democratic Change (MDC)', in B. Raftopoulos and K. Alexander (Eds), *Reflections on Democratic Politics in Zimbabwe* (Cape Town: Institute for Justice and Reconciliation, 2006); B. Raftopoulos, 'The Spell of Indecision in Zimbabwean Politics', *Solidarity Peace Trust*, 18 December 2011; D. Nkomo, 'Weaknesses limiting MDC-T effectiveness', *Zimbabwe Independent*, 14 January 2011; N. Ncube, 'Is MDC-T Still a Viable brand', *Financial Gazette*, 23 March 2012; 'Ibbo Mandaza Blasts MDC-T', *The Herald*, 31 January 2011.

50 See 'MDC-T weakness is in governing, not campaigning: Bennett', *The Zimbabwean*, 28 March 2012. Also see 'US Ambassador says MDC lacks vision', *The Insider*, 22 March 2012. www.insiderzim.com/.../2240-us-ambassador-says-mdc-lacks

51 The reasons for this failure are varied and many. The internal reasons include the anti-intellectualism of some of the party's leaders, especially those from the trade union movement, and the lack of traction in the party's underdeveloped policies. The external reasons include the repressive political environment of Zimbabwe and the attendant high political risk of involvement in opposition politics which tended to keep those with careers and economic interests to protect away.

52 M. Bratton and E. Masunungure, *The Anatomy of Political Predation: Leaders, Elites and Coalitions in Zimbabwe, 1980-2010* (Developmental Leadership Programme, Research Paper 9, January 2011), pp. 38-40.

53 Ibbo Mandaza, '2012 elections or Another GNU', *Zimbabwe Independent*, 17 February 2012.

54 The MDC-T's list of administrative bungles include the direct appointment of officials to the Prime Minister's Office by the party, rather than through the Public Services Commission, and Prime Minister Tsvangirai's blunder in the signing of the Bilateral Protection Agreement with South Korea. See Nathaniel Manheru, 'PM: From East without wisdom', *The Herald*, 12 June 2010; 'More divisions in Government as Mugabe undermines Tsvangirai', *SW Radio Africa*, 10 June 2010.

55 T. Mafukidze 'MDC spurned chance for judicial reform', *Zimbabwe Independent*, 10 June 2010; Matsyzak, *Zimbabwe's 'Unity' Government*.

56 See Nathaniel Manheru, '2011: The year sanctions will go!' *The Herald*, 7 January 2011; Manheru, 'Anti-Sanctions Campaign: The day the lion knew how to draw', *The Herald*, 4 March 2011; Manheru, 'Sanctions: Political Gain, Civilian Pain', *The Herald*, 11 June 2011.

57 Action Aid, 'A Gathering Storm: Zimbabwe's Final Hope for Reform' (November 2010), p. 10.

58 From the time the GPA was inaugurated in February 2009 to the end of 2011, the MDC parties' MPs had tabled only one Private Member's Bill – The Public Order and Security Act Amendment Bill, which was introduced in Parliament by the MDC-T Chief Whip, Innocent Gonese, in December 2010. The only other two Private Member's Bills initiated by MPs from these parties to date were only introduced into parliament at the beginning of 2012. These are the Criminal Procedure and Evidence Act Amendment Bill, tabled by Gonese in March 2012, and the Urban Councils Act Amendment Bill, tabled by MDC-T Member of Parliament for Buhera Central, Tungwara Matimba, in February 2012. See John Makamure, 'Polarised debate on legislation weaken parliament', *Newsday*, 6 April 2012; 'Gonese seeks to repeal sections of the CPEA', *Daily News*, 30 March 2012; Veritas Bill Watch 46 of 31 December 2010.

59 All these institutions are currently being funded by private donors and the two parties have done little to ensure that they are capacitated through the provision of adequate human and material resources.

60 See Raftopoulos, 'Elections, Mediation and Deadlock in Zimbabwe', ARI, 119/2008. www.realinstitutoelcano.org/wps/Content?...2008.; Raftopoulos 'The GPA as a "Passive Revolution"'.

61 Tsvangirai and his party's decision seems to be calculated at frustrating Welshman Ncube's ascendancy to the position of Deputy Prime Minister. See Priscilla Misihairabwi-Mushonga, 'The Method in the Madness', *Newsday*, 21 December 2011.

62 Lovemore Moyo's election was nullified at the end of March 2011, after the Supreme Court ruled that his initial election in 2008 was unprocedural.

63 Interview with MDC-N official, March 201; Nathaniel Manheru, 'ZANU PF: Keeping the eye off the ball', *The Herald*, 2 April 2011.

64 The MDC-N politics has been characterised by the forging of temporary alliances with both the MDC-T and ZANU-PF on issues of strategic interest to itself. This strategy has left the party unpopular with opposition supporters, especially MDC-T supporters, and some international donors sympathetic to the opposition who view it as engaging in divisive politics and helping ZANU-PF to strengthen its bargaining power over the opposition.

65 The Congress resulted in the election of Professor Welshman Ncube, the party's former Secretary General, as the new President of the party, replacing Arthur Mutambara who had grown unpopular in the party because of his unilateralism and populist politics. The other significant changes were the election of Priscilla Misihairabwi-Mushonga to the position of Secretary General and Qhubani Moyo, the former Organizing Secretary for Youth, to the position of National Organising Secretary.

66 See Zimbabwe Electoral Support Network (ZESN), *Report on the 2005 Zimbabwe Election* (Harare: ZESN, 2005); ZESN, *Report on the Zimbabwe March 29 2008 Harmonised Elections and 27 June Presidential Run-Off* (Harare: ZESN, 2008); Zimbabwe Electoral Commission (ZEC), *Report of the 2008 General Elections* (Harare: ZEC, 2008.).

67 See 'MDC accuses Mugabe of tribalism', *Newsday*, 30 January 2011; 'Mugabe, Tsvangirai plot against Ncube', *The Standard*, 25 December 2011; 'Ncube hits back at Mugabe, Tsvangirai', *The Standard*, 19 February 2012; 'MDC-T reshuffle sidelines Matabeleland politicians – Analysts', www.newzimbabwe.com, 25 June 2010; 'MDC-T in dilemma as Matabeleland demand proportional representation', *The Standard*, 30 January 2011.

68 Edwin Ndlovu, 'Tribalism bane of Zim Politics' *Financial Gazette*, 6 January 2011; Conway Tutani, 'Prejudice: The overreadiness to overread', *Newsday*, 2 March 2012. 'Dumisani Nkomo, 'Odds heavily stacked against ZAPU', *Zimbabwe Independent*, 3 February 2011; 'MDC Council expels Mutambara', *Zimbabwe Independent*, 11 February 2011.

69 'Tribal revolt fears after Mutambara ousted', *The Zimbabwe Mail*, 15 January 2011. www.thezimbabwemail.com; 'MDC demotes robotics scientist Mutambara from Deputy Prime Minister', *The Herald*, 24 January 2011.

70 The MDC performed fairly well in the rural provinces of Matabeleland South and North in the 2008 elections, securing 10 of the possible seats, but failed to win a single seat in Bulawayo. The MDC loss in Bulawayo could be explained by factors such as the popularity of the MDC-T in urban areas. However, the significant influence of the 'Shona vote' in the Bulawayo results cannot be overlooked, given that the 2005 split in the MDC was perceived by many Zimbabweans as a Ndebele-Shona split. Bulawayo, unlike the largely rural provinces of Matabeleland, which are populated by Ndebeles, is a more cosmopolitan city populated by a significantly high

number of Shona labour migrants who have replaced their Matabeleland counterparts trekking to South Africa over the last decade of the economic crisis. See Solidarity Peace Trust, *Gone to Egoli: Economic Survival Strategies in Matabeleland* (Solidarity Peace Trust, 30 June 2009), pp. 10-14; Deborah Potts, 'Internal Migration in Zimbabwe: The Impact of Livelihood Destruction in Rural and Urban Areas', in J. Crush and D. Tevera (eds), *Zimbabwe's Exodus: Crisis, Migration, Survival* (Cape Town: Southern Africa Migration Programme, 2010) pp. 93-94; Khumbulani Maphosa, 'Ndebele-Shona relations recipe for disaster', *Newsday*, 23 November 2011.

71 'Battle lines drawn as MDC Congress Looms', *The Standard*, 2 January 2011; 'MDC-T dismisses reports of in-fighting and factionalism', *SW Radio Africa* (London), 30 April 2010.

72 The violence within the MDC is reminiscent of the violence among party members around the period of the party's split into two opposing factions in 2005. See MDC, 'Zhou Commission of Inquiry into the Mabvuku Incident' (Unpublished internal MDC Report, 2006); Movement for Democratic Change, 'Commission of Inquiry into Disturbances at Party Headquarters' (Compiled by Dr Tichaona Mudzingwa, Hon. Giles Mutsekwa and Hon. Moses Mzila-Ndlovu), Draft Report December 2004.

73 'More heads roll as MDC-T rift widens', *The Herald*, 14 June 2010; 'MDC-T clips Biti's wings', *The Herald*, 24 May 2010; 'Heads roll at MDC-T', *The Herald*, 17 May 2010.

74 See Nathaniel Manheru, 'Tsvangirai: The growl of a disembodied politician', *The Saturday Herald*, 5 May 2012; 'Factionalism rocks MDC-T', *The Sunday Mail*, 21 April 2012.

75 See 'MDC faction wants congress deferred', *Zimbabwe Independent*, 17 June 2010; 'Factionalism rocks MDC-T', *Sunday Mail*, 21 April 2012.

76 One of the widely acknowledged weaknesses of Tsvangirai, as a leader of the opposition, is his failure to be an intellectual match of Mugabe and his lieutenants. As a result, he has been outmatched in his debates with Mugabe and this has cost the party many battles. See 'How Biti escaped cabinet dismissal', *Zimbabwe Independent*, 25 June 2010; 'West wants Tsvangirai out, says Madhuku', *Sunday Mail*, 28 April 2012; Nathaniel Manheru, 'Tsvangirai: The growl of a disembodied politician', *The Saturday Herald*, 5 May 2012.

77 Ian Makone has been associated with an influential group of leaders within the MDC-T, referred to as the 'Kitchen Cabinet', who have been accused of manipulating decision-making processes within the party through exploiting their close personal relationships with Tsvangirai. This kitchen cabinet has not only been blamed for the current infighting within the party but also for the infighting which resulted in the 2005 split. See Raftopoulos, 2005; 'ZANU PF exploits latest MDC Rift', *Mail and Guardian*, 14 May 2010.

78 See 'Chamisa vs Mudzuri', *Newsday*, 17 January 2011; 'Knives out for Mudzuri', *Zimbabwe Mail*, 22 January 2011; 'Factionalism rocks MDC-T', *Sunday Mail*, 21 April 2012.

79 See 'Factionalism threatens to tear the MDC-T apart in Midlands', *Financial Gazette*, 27 January 2012; 'MDC-T suspends legislators over factionalism', *The Herald*, 30 April 2012; 'Factionalism rocks MDC-T in Bulawayo', *Financial Gazette*, 23 March 2012; 'Chamisa reads Riot Act to warring MDC-T factions', *Newsday*, 1 August 2011.

80 'MDC-T riddled with factionalism', *The Sunday News*, 19 November 2010; 'Battle for MDC-T posts hots up', *The Herald*, 5 February 2011; 'PM must rein in Gorden Moyo', *Zimbabwe Independent*, 25 February 2011.

81 Some of the prominent names that have been associated with this 'Karanga Axis' of power include the former Organising Secretary, Elias Mudzuri; former Women's Assembly president and current Minister of Public Service, Lucia Matibenga; current Organising Secretary and Cabinet Minister, Nelson Chamisa; Deputy Secretary General and Minister of Trade and Investment, Tapiwa Mashakada; and the late Minister of Public Service, Elphas Mukonoweshuro. See 'MDC Faction Wants Congress Deferred', *Zimbabwe Independent*, 17 June 2010; 'Knives out for Mudzuri', *Zimbabwe Mail*, 22 January 2011. For detailed discussion of the roots and dynamics of Karanga political ethnicity in Zimbabwean politics, see J. Muzondidya and S. Ndlovu-Gatsheni, 'Echoing silences: Ethnicity in postcolonial Zimbabwe, 1980-2007', *African Journal of Conflict Resolution*, 27 (2), 2007, pp. 275-97; M. Sithole, *Zimbabwe: Struggles within the struggle*, (Harare: Rujeko Publishers, 1999).

82 Tsvangirai and Makone are both from Manicaland, while Biti is from Mashonaland province. See 'Knives out for Mudzuri', *Zimbabwe Mail*, 22 January 2011; 'Chamisa vs Mudzuri', *Newsday*, 17 January 2011.

83 See 'MDC-T fights factionalism before Congress', *Zimbabwe Independent*, 18 February 2011.

84 See 'PM hits hard times', *Financial Gazette*, 17 May 2012; 'Tsvangirai, Biti on collision course?', *Financial Gazette*, 6 May 2010.

85 See 'MDC-T probes councils', *Financial Gazette*, 27 April 2012; Violet Gonda, 'Interview: MDC-T denies corruption, defends record', *SW Radio Africa*, 12 February 2012. Available at www.newzimbabwe.com.

86 The Chitungwiza councillors were accused of subdividing open space and land reserved for public amenities, such as schools and recreational facilities, into residential stands which they sold to individuals for between US$4,000 and US$5,000. They officially receipted only $500, and pocketed the difference. See 'Rampant Corruption at Chitungwiza City Council', *Sunday Mail*, 4 February 2012; 'Chitungwiza corruption saga takes new twist', *Financial Gazette*, 19 February 2010; 'Welshman

castigates Bulawayo city fathers', *Bulawayo24 News*, 30 April 2012; 'Bindura corruption exposed', *ZBC News*, 13 February 2012. www.zbc.co.zw/.../16485-bindura-corruption-exposed-.html.

87 See 'MDC-T must deal decisively with corrupt councillors', *Newsday*, 19 December 2012; 'MDC Probes Corrupt Councillors', *Daily News*, 24 April 2012; 'Daggers out for corrupt MDC-T councillors', *Newsday*, 23 March 2012.

88 See 'Tsvangirai impregnates 23-year old Bulawayo girl', 24 November 2011. www.zimdiaspora.com/index.php?...**tsvangirai**...; 'Tsvangirai terminates relationship with Locadia 12 days after performing Customary Rites', *The Herald*, 1 December 2011; 'Tsvangirai in a fix over new fiancee'', *The Standard*, 21 April 2012; 'Tsvangirai under US$1.5m Probe', *Zimbabwe Independent*, 5 August 2011.

89 See 'Tsvangirai's controversial love-life makes him unfit to lead Zimbabwe', *Bulawayo24 News*, 8 May 2012. Available at http://bulwayo24.com; Tendai Moyo, 'Tsvangirai's escapades: Where are the women's groups?', *The Herald*, 5 December 2011; Jonathan Moyo, 'Morgan's Open-zip and Shut-mind approaches', *The Sunday Mail*, 4 December 2011.

90 See 'Chombo cracks whip on graft: Appoints 5 member revival team for Chitungwiza', *The Herald*, 27 January 2011.

91 J. Muzondidya, 'Zimbabwe 2010-2014: Context Analysis for Oxfam Zimbabwe's Five Year Strategic Planning', Consultancy for Oxfam International, February-March 2010.

92 Raftopoulos, 'The GPA as a "Passive Revolution"', p. 708.

93 The infighting within the ZCTU between the organisation's former Secretary General, Wellington Chibebe, and President, Lovemore Matombo, over the leadership and management of the organisation has greatly weakened both the ZCTU and its affiliate organisations who have now organised themselves into two factions competing for the control of the labour movement. See 'Infighting in Labour Unions Blights Workers Day', *The Herald*, 2 May 2012; 'Matombo attacks MDC', *Daily News*, 2 May 2012; 'Workers Bear Brunt of Trade Union Strife' *Zimbabwe Independent*, 3 May 2012.

94 Cephas Zinhumwe (Chief Executive Officer, National Association of Non-Governmental Organisations), 'Civil Society Perspectives on the Constitution' (Multi-Stakeholders' Regional Exchange Workshop on Constitutional Reforms: Harare, 4-5 July 2011); Macdonald Lewanika (National Coordinator, Crisis Coalition in Zimbabwe) Presentation at the Institute of Justice and Reconciliation Policy Advisory Seminar – Zimbabwe's Government of National Unity: A two-year Appraisal, Cape Town, 10 March 2011.

95 See J. Muzondidya 'Zimbabwe's Failed Transition? An Analysis of the Challenges and Complexities in Zimbabwe's Transition to Democracy in the post-2000

period', in T. Murithi and A. Mawadza, eds, *Zimbabwe in Transition: Conversations from Within* (Johannesburg: Jacana Media, 2011) pp. 29-30; L. Sachikonye, 'The State of the Civics in Zimbabwe' Consultancy Report prepared for the Zimbabwe Institute, February 2008; E. Masunungure, 'Zimbabwe: Country Context', Paper presented at Oxfam Planning, Harare, 9 November 2009.

96 Muzondidya, 'Zimbabwe's Failed Transition', p. 29; K. Zigomo, 'A Community-Based Approach to Sustainable Development: The Role of Civil Society in Rebuilding Zimbabwe', 2 April 2012, Solidarity Peace Trust: http://www.solidaritypeacetrust.org/1159/community-based-approach-to-sustainable-development/

CHAPTER 3

ZANU-PF and the Government of National Unity 2009-12[1]

GERALD CHIKOZHO MAZARIRE

The Road to the GPA: Competing Narratives

The possibility of a Government of National Unity (GNU) bringing together ZANU-PF and the MDC had existed since 2002 when the Commonwealth Heads of Government tried to get Robert Mugabe and Morgan Tsvangirai talking together in a diplomatic move that culminated in a summit on Zimbabwe in Abuja in September of that year. This initiative took place against the backdrop of the disputed 2002 presidential election and the on-going spate of violence that gripped the country. It was spearheaded by eminent persons from South Africa, Nigeria and Australia. The talks collapsed when ZANU-PF pulled out after Tsvangirai persisted with a lawsuit contesting Mugabe's win.[2]

Already the patterns that shaped the interests represented in the Global Political Agreement (GPA), signed six years later between the same actors, had become visible. First, the central role of South Africa in negotiating the outcome; second, the personal attitudes of the key protagonists in the conflict i.e. Mugabe and Tsvangirai, the interests they represented, and the immediate circumstances shaping the negotiations. For Mugabe and ZANU-PF, this meant defending the sovereignty of the country, and the gains of the liberation struggle, from Western forces of regime change, while playing a balancing act between regional acceptance and growing international illegitimacy. For Tsvangirai and the MDC, the discussions represented a difficult moment of triumph in the struggle to dislodge Mugabe and a fossilised ZANU-PF autocracy. This was not withstanding international sympathy for the MDC and Tsvangirai; regional support for them being ambivalent. Neither side was willing to concede defeat. Several later initiatives by Zimbabwean businessmen and churches also failed to achieve a breakthrough despite making some inroads.

In his recent biography, Morgan Tsvangirai identifies 2004 as a turning point in the stalemate. It was then that Thabo Mbeki, the South African president who had been involved indirectly since 2000, assumed an active role in formulating a strategy to bring stability to Zimbabwe rather than ensuring a lasting democracy in the country.[3] Briefly, Tsvangirai's thesis is that by 2004 Mbeki believed that both Mugabe and Tsvangirai had become liabilities to Zimbabwean politics and business, and had to be replaced by reformist forces within ZANU-PF and the MDC. With the support of some Western embassies in Harare as well as 'ambitious politicians' in ZANU-PF and some 'wily and power-hungry politicians' in the MDC, Mbeki contrived a plan that was to initiate a simultaneous split in both the MDC and ZANU-PF. In 2004, ZANU-PF saw attempts by a faction led by Mnangagwa to position itself for the takeover of the party by going for the vice-presidency, a position previously held by the late Simon Muzenda. The result was the 'Tsholotsho Declaration' of 18 November 2004 that endorsed Mnangagwa for this office. This initiative was, however, punished by the suspension of six provincial chairpersons from ZANU-PF and the demotion of Mnangagwa in both the party and Cabinet. Mnangagwa subsequently lost the vice-presidency to Mujuru in circumstances that are detailed below.

Within the MDC, Welshman Ncube and senior members of the party from Matabeleland made significant strides not only to remove Tsvangirai from power but to move the administrative apparatus of the party to Bulawayo. Subsequent squabbles resulted in lack of co-ordination and the poor showing of the MDC in the 2005 parliamentary elections where it won 41 seats from the 57 of 2000. In October, the split was eventually achieved in the MDC when Welshman Ncube and the pro-Senate group broke away. Mbeki's solution to the Zimbabwean crisis, according to Tsvangirayi, was to merge this group with the Mnangagwa faction in ZANU-PF, but when the latter was thwarted by Mugabe, and the Ncube group was 'heavily trounced' by ZANU-PF in the Senate elections, Mbeki was forced into a retreat. The MDC March 2006 Congress not only suspended the Ncube faction but emerged with a revamped MDC that put in place the groundwork for its impressive performance in the highly contested 2008 parliamentary and presidential elections. The Ncube faction, at a loss for leadership, settled for Arthur Mutambara but once again performed poorly in the elections.[4]

Mbeki resurfaced in the June 2008 election results, which remained unknown to the world for five weeks. According to Tsvangirai, he flagged the option of a run-off before the results were officially announced. Tsvangirai thus believes that he was party to a conspiracy by the military to keep Mugabe in power by 'manipulating the votes to create grounds for a run-off' which they would supervise. While Mugabe proceeded in a one-man presidential run-off, at Mbeki's behest, he conceded to inter-party dialogue and the first face-to-face meeting with Tsvangirai at the Rainbow Towers Hotel. Mugabe continued to behave like 'a generous giver of power which he could none the less withdraw at will' hoping for an arrangement like the 1987 ZAPU/ZANU Unity Accord, argues Tsvangirai. In the meantime Mbeki hurriedly concluded the Memorandum of Agreement in order to attend to a crisis at home that led, in September 2008, to his own ouster from the leadership of the ANC and the South African presidency. However, the mounting crisis and violence in Zimbabwe led SADC leaders and the new South African government, under interim President Kgalema Motlanthe, to seek 'a solution, no matter how defective it might be at the beginning.'[5]

Tsvangirai's attack on Mbeki has been challenged of late, particularly for lack of clarity on the Mbeki MDC-M conspiracy. Although generally seen as an unfair broker, Mbeki has been credited for coming out with a miracle agreement that was acceptable to two intransigent parties. A study of Mbeki's mediation strategies has submitted that they were based on 'agenda setting', informed by his historic links with ZANU-PF and Robert Mugabe as well as his perceived Pan-African sympathies for both which courted antagonism from the MDC-T. It agrees with the view that Mbeki sought a quick solution to the Zimbabwean crisis because of his own troubles at home but adds the urgency of the 2010 World Cup and rising concerns with Zimbabwean immigration into South Africa that resulted in the xenophobic attacks in the same year.[6]

SADC intervention enabled discussions to begin the preparation of the Kariba Draft constitution, but Mbeki convinced the MDC to support the constitutional amendments in Parliament with assurances that elections would only be held when the draft was in place. This allowed Mugabe to declare early elections and Mbeki to gain diplomatic mileage from them.[7] Mbeki's genius as a mediator is lauded; he brought in the MDC-M, a party not directly involved in the conflict (because it did not contest the presidential election), as an interlocutor, which changed the direction of the negotiations in favour of whom they sided with, a strategy that quickened the negotiating process. He introduced negotiating rules such as media silence and the exclusion of civic forces, which although it weakened the MDC's negotiating clout, it allowed ZANU-PF and Mugabe to make some concessions without feeling humiliated in public, while allowing them to feel they were in control. Articles were negotiated individually and signed under the rule that subsequent changes were disallowed, which again helped to speed up the process. Finally, Mbeki persuaded negotiators to postpone some important matters until the GPA had been signed, arguing that the MDC could make the necessary changes from within, after joining government. This left it vulnerable to pressures from the public and SADC as well as those who wanted a quick solution to the crisis.[8]

The ZANU-PF position abounds in many versions by its various spinners, the most inclusive summary being that given by Jonathan Moyo. He maintains that despite the divisions fermenting in the party in 2004, ZANU-PF managed to command a two-thirds majority in Parliament following the 2005 parliamentary elections. It was, however, unable to translate this into a meaningful or useful victory because of the divisions within the party, so the *de facto* administration of the party was transferred to the Reserve Bank of Zimbabwe (RBZ) under Gideon Gono following the total collapse of the Zimbabwe dollar. The MDC only achieved a new lease of life after the 7 March 2007 'Tsvangirai incident',[9] when SADC convened an extraordinary summit in Dar es Salaam on 29 March 2007. Moyo (and ZANU-PF)'s reading of the leaked US diplomatic cables show that the US worked with the MDC-T on a three-pronged strategy to isolate Mugabe from ZANU-PF, SADC, and the Security Sector. While it succeeded with first two, it failed to win over the latter by the time of the harmonised 2008 elections. The reaction of the US and the West to the first round of the presidential elections was to encourage Tsvangirai to form a government without a run-off which prompted 'nationalist forces' within ZANU-PF who had fallen out with Mugabe to regroup and support his re-election in order to avert 'regime change'.[10] The US strategy was further compromised by the MDC-T's about-turn when they argued that 'Mugabe was part of the solution rather than part of the problem' and would rather have him stay (by delaying the election) rather than go.

The implications of this reading are critical for explaining ZANU's attitude within the inclusive government, i.e. that sanctions are inextricably linked to the US/Western/MDC strategy; that an early election is as necessary as it is overdue, and with it, all the outstanding issues in the GPA will be rendered irrelevant; and, more importantly, that the security sector stands firm against the regime-change agenda and therefore no reform of it is necessary. This chapter will seek to trace the strategies used by ZANU-PF to achieve these and other goals. It will attempt to situate the discussion in the broader historical context, which informed the party's thinking over time, and show how these beliefs translated into actions throughout the tenure of the GNU.

While taking cognisance of the view that ZANU-PF is neither a static, homogenous nor monolithic organisation, the chapter acknowledges that it strove to protect particular interests informed by its own past. This objective was aggravated by the fact that its principal opponent – and bedfellow within the GNU – the MDC-T did not share the same perspectives and disagreed with the approach, while ZANU-PF wanted to package its past in order to justify its interests. For instance, Prime Minister Morgan Tsvangirai responded to Defence Minister's Emmerson Mnangagwa's call to military officers to prioritise their role to defend the country from 'regime change' by saying, 'That statement is irresponsible. Regime change took place in 2008'.[11] This battle of perspectives has translated into one of power where ZANU-PF strives to demonstrate to its partners that it still wields state power while simultaneously struggling to assert such power within itself as a party. The following is an attempt to document the mechanisms ZANU-PF has deployed in order to maintain unbridled power within the GNU despite going into the arrangement in its weakest state.

The Problem of the Military in ZANU's Failed Transition from Liberation Movement to Political Party

Most commentators on ZANU-PF's conduct in the GNU locate its power in its control of Zimbabwe's security forces, and this has largely framed the debate on 'securocrats' and increased the calls for Security Sector Reform (SSR). Since 2002, Zimbabwe's service chiefs have openly expressed their support for the ZANU-PF's presidential candidate Robert Mugabe, while concomitantly threatening to thwart a Tsvangirai victory. In addition, most senior members of the security forces have retired to become active members of the party. During the tenure of the GNU, a new development has seen their retirement into the party's strategic commissariat department, a move widely interpreted as a military takeover of the party. In 2010, for example, two recently retired service chiefs, Air Vice-Marshall Henry Muchena and a former CIO Director Sidney Nyanhungo, undertook vigorous reorientation meetings with ZANU-PF structures at a time when an increasing number of serving and retired military intelligence officials have openly declared their interest to contest the forthcoming elections.[12]

The centrality of the commissariat department within ZANU-PF dates back to the liberation struggle, particularly after 1977, when the party was reorganised under Robert Mugabe. ZANU saw it as its organ for political work amongst its fighting forces; it subscribed to the view that an ideologically impoverished cadre was inadequate to the task of holding a gun for the purpose of liberating his/her country. Under Mayor Urimbo the department made tremendous efforts to fulfil this task because, since 1978, it had become the internal propaganda organ of the party, and one that usefully served its leadership.[13]

Several scholars, however, locate the legacy of 'securocracy' in ZANU-PF's failed transition from a liberation movement managing fighters to mobilise the masses into a political party in a multi-party democracy. Others trace the problem to a failed demobilisation and reintegration programme for ex-fighters, arguing that the latter have come to haunt the party and the state forcing both to offer concessions in the quest for legitimacy and self-preservation. This welfarist argument suggests a collusion of interests between marginalised ex-fighters and desperate ZANU-PF politicians. All these perspectives on the unfinished business of the liberation struggle seek to explain why ZANU-PF continues to function as if it were still fighting this war.

Norma Kriger's study of what she terms Zimbabwe's 'Guerilla Veterans' located the problem in the post-independence integration exercise's attempt to create an apolitical army, which would foster regime stability in the face of attempts by the various guerrilla leaders in the Joint Operations Command (JOC) to protect their own senior commanders from merit tests. In the end Kriger lauds the tactical efficiency of the British supervisory team in working 'in and down' ensuring that the guerrilla leaders were satisfied that their best men had been well placed.[14] The British team played an active political role in the quest for regime stability. In short, they created a multi-partisan army.

Kriger's argument is echoed in other studies that attempt to account for the disturbances that followed the integration exercise pitting ex-ZANLA against ex-ZIPRA forces in events that eventually led to the *Gukurahundi* conflict. The 'tactical efficiency' of the supervising mission is said to have translated to a 'tactical elimination' of ex-ZIPRA forces by a predominantly ZANLA Zimbabwe National Army (ZNA), an allegation that researchers like Abiodun Alao query given that ZANLA had more guerrillas than ZIPRA.[15] Eliakim Sibanda, nonetheless, vigorously pursued the 'elimination' argument submitting that by 1983 the army was integrated 2:1 in favour of ZANLA, and that there was a deliberate effort to undermine those ZIPRA members trained in intelligence and the air force.[16] After the crackdown, Sibanda alleges that Mugabe promoted Jevan Maseko to Lt.-General to appease the Ndebele, while continuing to appoint 'well qualified' ex-ZIPRA commanders to marginal roles in the army with the exception of Brigadiers Ben Mathe and Charles Grey.[17] Sabelo Ndlovu-Gatsheni, who has also made reference to forced demobilisation of ZIPRA cadres from the ZNA at the height of the *Gukurahundi* conflict, does not pursue the fate of former ZIPRA after the Unity Accord. Indeed, this matter occupies no space in his four-pronged critique of the faults of 1987 Unity Agreement explaining why it has failed to restore cordial civil-military relations in Zimbabwe.[18] Martin Rupiya, a former exponent of the 'welfarist' argument, traces the problem of ZANU-PF securocracy to a later period of Zimbabwe's independence, when increased civilian institutional weaknesses have warranted intervention by elements from the armed forces as lack of delivery has translated into political problems for the ruling party. This saw the appointment of Service chiefs to positions of responsibility in key government positions such as Electoral Supervisory Commission, the National Oil Company of Zimbabwe and the Grain Marketing Board from 2002 onwards on the basis of a long tradition of familiarity and service during the liberation struggle based on mutual trust. Rupiya predicted, however, that any change in the make-up of institutions where these appointments were made would result in a crisis.[19]

A study by the Zimbabwe Institute on the Zimbabwean military suggests that the problem of securocrats is also a product of a 'buy-in' by Rhodesian securocrats into the problematic 1979 Lancaster House Agreement, which brought ZANU-PF into power in 1980, and allowed some of the Rhodesian security personnel to continue serving the new government. ZANU-PF, however, maintained a 'party-military' nexus which helped to stabilise the state and shield the government from any military takeover.[20] Although acknowledging that the military men have always had a significant say in party politics, this report goes on to say that the military itself was not deeply entrenched in the day-to-day running of the country until the late 1990s when Mugabe had to seek its protection against rising discontent amongst the masses and within the party.

This study, whose major weakness is that it draws heavily from only one newspaper source, makes a number of implicit assumptions. First, that the Zimbabwean military was at one point interested in being an impartial professional force, a point Kriger's study (cited above) refutes; second – a point emphasised by most exponents of SSR – that the standard procedure of appointing senior commissioned officers (from the rank of major) in the army is, but should not be, a political exercise. Both assertions are as misleading for ZANU-PF as they are for all liberation movements of Eastern Bloc inspiration. First, despite the integration exercise, all former combatants in Zimbabwe were recruited by individual and often hostile political parties: ZAPU, ZANU, FROLIZI and to some extent the UANC. It was under these parties that they were trained and deployed. Attempts by the trained cadres to unite or transform themselves into professional armies without allegiance to any party either disintegrated or were ruthlessly thwarted, as indeed happened to the Zimbabwe Liberation Army (ZLA) in 1975 and the Zimbabwe People's Army (ZIPA) in 1976. ZANU-PF has frequently forwarded this argument in rejecting SSR.

The other critical point to note is that the military structure of Zimbabwe's guerrilla armies was modelled along the lines of modern Eastern (and Western) conventional armies. ZANLA and ZIPRA were organised under a 'High Command', which loosely translated to a Joint Operations Committee (JOC) under a Chief of Defence. He was the modern equivalent of a four-star general presiding over a three-star lieutenant general (Chief of Operations), four, two-star major generals (responsible for the Political Commissariat, Security and Intelligence, Logistics and Supplies, Training and Medicine) and a controlled number of single-star brigadier generals (deputies in these and other offices as deemed necessary). The second tier was the 'General Staff' composed of senior officers or the equivalent of commissioned officers under colonels (Provincial Commanders), lieutenant-colonels (Sectorial Commanders) and majors (Detachment Commanders). The third tier was junior commissioned officers: captains (Platoon Commanders) and lieutenants (Section Commanders) who presided over non-comissioned officers in sections of eight men/women who replicated the four offices as above. The 1980-81 integration exercise did little to change the structure of this model. If anything, this was the British Military Advisory Training Team's easiest task; they simply reproduced it. The only difference was that this command structure had to be spread evenly across the entire security sector of the new Zimbabwean state, including the air force, police, Central Intelligence Organisation and prison services. Talks of problems with ranking and seniority in the two guerrilla armies by the British integration officers were both condescending and patronising; but Norma Kriger's study seems to accept these uncritically.

Most studies on the 1980 transition and reintegration exercise have failed to take into account the strategic intention of the demobilisation of Zimbabwe's guerrilla armies, particularly ZANLA. They have paid undue attention to the welfare aspect of this exercise viewing the ex-combatant as a victim of the process, if not a pleasure-seeking hooligan who squanders his demobilisation pay-out. They ignore the fact that both ZIPRA and ZANLA had evolved internal mechanisms of retiring and redeploying cadres into areas of civilian responsibilities in anticipation of establishing administrations during the war in the 'liberated zones'. This was an in-built demobilisation strategy based on the fundatmental principle that 'once a soldier, always a soldier' so that even in their civilian responsibilities, these cadres could be recalled when the need arose. In 1978 ZIPRA re-assigned its senior army commanders such as Akim Ndlovu, Mbulawa Noko, Report Phelekezela Mphoko, Cephas Cele, Sam Moyo, Elliot Masengo and Gordon Munyanyi to diplomatic responsibilities while a new breed of commanders under Lookout Masuku (Commander) was unveiled. These included Ambrose Mutinhiri (Deputy Commander) Gevan Maseko (Chief of Staff) Ananias Gwenzi (Military Intelligence), Gedi Ndlovu, Eddie Sigoge (Personnel) David Thondlana (Training), Mike Grey (Operations) and Sekuru Patrick (National Security).[21]

ZANLA did the same, recalling several provincial commanders and reassigning them to the Chimoio military headquarters or sending them on external missions. They included Rex Tichafa, Anderson Mhuru, Perence Shiri,

Dominic Chinenge (Constantine Chiwenga), Bornwell Masawi, Edzai Mabhunu, Henry Muchena, Freddie Matanga and Harry Tanganeropa. ZANLA used its profile of military victories in 1978 to explore possibilities of relations with Soviet proxies such as Romania where it sent its first set of cadres to be trained as policemen. It sent missions to the Arab world who were successful in sourcing funding from Syria and support from the Palestine Liberation Organisation. In 1979 ZANU struck a relationship with Lt.-Col. Mengistu Haile Mariam which established the basis for training Zimbabwean pilots in Ethiopia after 1980. Manpower Planning was a strategy formulated by ZANU in anticipation of independence, which preoccupied ZANU's technocrats at its political headquarters in Maputo, and became a critical part of Mugabe's new government. Not every cadre was planned to remain in the army, yet the party owned every cadre deployed elsewhere because it had nurtured them. At independence there was some continuity: many senior army commanders who did not continue in the army, became ambassadors and governors including Mark Dube (Joshua Misihairambwi) and Gevan Maseko. Other commanders were spread across the security sector, in the air force (Josiah Tungamirayi), CIO (Eddison Shirihuru), police (Steven Chocha/Augustine Chihuri) and other paramilitary units such as the prison service, the Department of National Parks and Wildlife and the Zimbabwe People's Militia. Some of ZANLA's best soldiers in the rank and file were seconded to municipal police units across the country. Technocrats became permanent secretaries and senior civil servants or were appointed to head parastatals. Ministers were drawn from party officials. While the ZNA has gained a lot of skilled manpower in various areas and recruited commissioned officers in the post-independence period, very few have ascended to critical appointments in government or to the ranks of colonel and above without liberation war credentials. The Crisis Coalition Group's 2011 compilation of appointments of former military, CIO and police officers to ministerial, governor, MP, parastatal or commission responsibilities by Mugabe simply confirms a systematic policy of appointments and succession that has been in existence since at least 1978.[22] The problem of securocracy is traceable to this source and this is a point that ZANU-PF has articulated so well throughout the entire tenure of the GNU. Looked at more closely, it is not only a ZANU-PF problem, it is a national problem bound to haunt Zimbabwe until the entire liberation generation has faded away, a feature that informs the problem of war veterans as well.

Fellow Travellers or Permanent Allies? The ZANU-PF War Veterans Alliance and the GPA

The relationship between ZANU-PF and the war veterans has also excited considerable interest. The general tendency has been to see the two movements as virtually inextricable. Recent scholarship has, however, overturned this rather simplistic perspective emphasising that the relationship is more complex because they are neither monolithic nor homogeneous organisations. They represent various and sometimes competing interests within and between each other culminating in what could be termed a 'love-hate' relationship. It is useful to appreciate the reaction to and conduct of both ZANU-PF and the war veterans in the GPA through this lens. In her recent book, Erin McCandless has shown that the Zimbabwe National Liberation War Veterans Association (ZN-LWVA) has generally operated in a manner consistent with its constitutional aims as an organisation founded in 1989. Although mindful of the fact that they had organised themselves in different ways before they split into various factions, McCandless's research has also demonstrated that the war veterans' movement has cleavages along the lines of rural/urban, class, race, ethnicity and gender. She also identifies three characteristics of the war veterans' relationship with ZANU-PF, namely, vanguard of the party capable of disciplining it and holding it to account; a parent-child relationship as the movement was 'born out of ZANU-PF'; and, finally, as the party or Mugabe's militia, to be unleashed as and when the party faces a crisis.[23] These distinctions do not overlook the fact that the senior sections of the movement have been co-opted into the party while the grassroots, in their pursuit of various interests, have invariably doubled as the party's storm troopers. Indeed, after the 2000 land occupations, ZANU-PF officially incorporated the ZNLWVA as a taskforce of its Central Committee while symbolically moving government responsibility for the war veterans from the Ministry of Social Welfare to that of Defence.[24] The war veterans have generally played these multiple roles throughout the post-2000 period in a way that has allowed ZANU-PF to entrench its hegemony. An illustrative case is their disruptions of local authorities perceived to be sympathetic to the MDC. In Matabeleland and Midlands provinces, JoAnn McGregor shows that from February 2001, war veterans closed rural district council offices and schools, fired or suspended officials and subjected them to their approval through 'vetting'. They accused the officials of corruption and maladministration, but more importantly, of being MDC. In the process ZA-

NU-PF paid scant attention to what was going on, although these disruptions effectively allowed it to reassert its control at the local level, which it had lost to the MDC in the 2000 elections. The activities of the war veterans in these two provinces alone, however, exposed inherent divisions in the movement consistent with McCandless's typology.[25]

The role of the war veterans can increasingly be seen through this lens throughout the tenure of the GNU. In July 2009 nearly 4,000 delegates gathered at the Harare International Conference Centre to design and appoint committees to gather information from the people to find out what they wanted in the new constitution. The meeting was marred by booing and disorder: one of the more spectacular incidents was the hurling of the Speaker of Parliament, Lovemore Moyo, from the podium as he was sprayed with water by ZANU-PF delegates.[26] Later, it was learnt that the majority of these hecklers were war veterans led by Joseph Chinotimba and Jabulani Sibanda, some of whom broke into song, 'Zvikaramba tinoita zva June' (a song threatening a repeat of the violence unleashed on MDC supporters in June 2008).[27]

A COPAC outreach meeting

When the actual COPAC outreach work began, several disruptive incidents were recorded for which both ZANU-PF elements and war veterans were deemed responsible. At Chikonohono township in Mashonaland West, suspected ZANU-PF youths chased villagers from a meeting in the presence of the former governor, Jonathan Samkange, and some ZANU-PF and MDC officials, barely two weeks after the team began its countrywide meetings. The youth demanded the presence of uniformed police at these meetings.[28] This trend spread throughout the country with some cases of assault of villagers and MDC party functionaries happening in full view of the police. As the entire COPAC exercise proceeded, war veterans maintained a heavy presence at the meetings, interfering with the drafting exercise. In January 2012, COPAC was forced to tighten its own security after war veterans stormed a private retreat session in Vumba and disrupted a COPAC media-civic society briefing in Harare, alleging that the drafters were ignoring the views of the people.[29]

In October 2010, war veterans' leader, Jabulani Sibanda, arrived in Masvingo Province to launch 'Operation Kubudirana Pachena' (operation coming out in the open) an exercise aimed ostensibly at educating people across the province 'about how Zimbabwe attained its independence and the continued threats posed to the country by neo-colonial aggressors'. ZANU-PF performed dismally there during the March 2008 harmonised election: the province has 26 parliamentary constituencies and the MDC-T, which had one seat prior to the election, won 13 seats previously under the control of ZANU.[30] There is reason to believe Jabulani Sibanda's mission was to re-educate the Masvingo rural electorate ZANU-PF-style on the consequences of voting for the opposition in the following elections. It also served to 'educate' the people on the 'appropriate' submissions to the draft constitution as the COPAC outreach exercise was taking place simultaneously. A countrywide initiative by ZANU-PF and the war veterans targeted directly at the COPAC exercise was to be later christened 'Operation Chimumumu' (be mute: do not express your views to COPAC).[31]

Sibanda's operation in Masvingo not only forced people to his meetings but he was quoted on occasions threatening villagers if they did not vote for ZANU-PF. Addressing a meeting at Zvehuru Primary school, Sibanda threatened that war veterans would 'roast livers' of all the 'sell-outs' who voted for the MDC.[32] By June 2011, however, his controversial operation had already sown divisions within ZANU-PF itself as provincial party stalwarts felt that his activities would surely cost the party their much needed votes. In any case, Sibanda had camped in Masvingo for almost a year and was seen to be effectively pushing a campaign agenda serving specific factions within the party. His tendency to 'field' candidates riled party members who felt that he was overstepping his mandate and defeating the purpose of an official party primary election exercise. The party's Provincial Co-ordinating Committee was forced to pass a resolution ordering Sibanda to immediately cease his activities and leave the province.[33] Explaining the decision, ZANU-PF Masvingo Provincial Chairman, Lovemore Matuke, stated:

> We felt that he had overstayed in Masvingo judging by what he was doing and considering that he was in Masvingo since October last year and wanted to be here until August this year, it means that he wanted to spend a year here and Zanu-PF has ten political provinces so it means that for him to cover all the other provinces he would need ten years, so we felt that it will be better if he goes to other provinces.[34]

Interestingly, the war veterans' body overruled this resolution claiming that Sibanda's activities were outside the domain of the party's provincial leadership as he was in Masvingo on the instruction of the ZNLWVA, an affiliate of ZANU-PF, answerable directly to President Mugabe. The Masvingo War Veterans' Provincial Chairman, Retired Colonel Jefta Rupuvu, remarked:

> We are an affiliate of Zanu-PF and we have our own leadership structure [that] goes all the way to President Mugabe, who is our patron. We do not take instructions from the Zanu-PF provincial executive or politburo members but we have total allegiance to our patron who is President Mugabe.[35]

This statement summarises the complex relationship war veterans have always had with ZANU-PF, while playing the role of vanguard by launching their own operation to re-educate the masses on safeguarding the gains of liberation, they would not submit themselves to party structures, at least at the grassroots level, but have a hotline, and be answerable only, to the patron. Meanwhile, Jabulani Sibanda preached the role of his movement as one of a militia front for ZANU-PF. It should be noted that at this point Sibanda had not been readmitted to ZANU-PF following his suspension in 2004 after the Tsholotsho *indaba*.

War veterans took their disruptions further as they packaged their vanguard role of safeguarding the interests of the nation from external threats. They featured prominently in sessions of the public hearings of the Human Rights Bill using the strategy across the provinces of demanding that the readings be done in local languages since language itself was an essential human right. Two incidents in Mutare and Masvingo occurred where hearings were disrupted because the Bill was read in English. The main public hearing of the Bill in

Parliament on 23 July 2011 was abandoned after war veterans and ZANU-PF supporters started assaulting MDC MPs and journalists accusing them of not singing the national anthem.[36] Brian Tshuma, the MDC-T Hwange Central legislator was beaten up together with five other journalists in the Senate Chamber where the hearing was scheduled. ZANU-PF members had allegedly gathered at Parliament building as early as 7 a.m. and when the commotion began they were chanting their party slogans and singing anti-Tsvangirai songs.[37] The Bill had been one of the requirements of the Election Road Map demanded by SADC and it was supposed to have been passed in the second session of Parliament which expired in July 2010. It was only passed in June 2011 after a tumultuous affair. The road map, the electoral and human rights bills as well as the new constitution were the only outstanding GPA issues and the role of the war veterans in all this is as ambiguous as it is complex. ZANU-PF on its own, however, cannot claim overall patronage over the war veterans.

One of the rowdy ZANU protesters being escorted out of parliament.

ZANU's Strategies as Negotiator and Partner in the GPA
THE HARDLINERS AND ENTRENCHED POSITIONS

Tsvangirai has recently offered a telling summary of the Mugabe negotiating strategy:

> ... I recall telling my family in 1999 that, from my experience of dealing with Mugabe while I was the ZCTU Secretary General,

> the man detested difficult conversations. One of his strengths was his technique of calculated procrastination; he could delay the discussion until it began to flow his way. Perhaps there was something to be learnt from this but at the same time it meant he approached any dialogue in bad faith. With hindsight I could see that what Mugabe did when challenged and cornered was to drag things out to wear down an opponent before making insincere concessions. Mugabe always saw disagreement, no matter how miniscule, as conflict. He would never accede to a generally preferred position in our meetings with him. An outcome should satisfy his desired outcome first, before he could make slight shifts – but then, only slight – to portray him as a generous giver. To me Mugabe was a leader who would readily burn down a house rather than live in it with a colleague or compatriot who had differences with him....[38]

Tsvangirai's assessment confirms how much Mugabe, a person with a great deal of experience in political negotiations since the 1976 Geneva Conference, learned from his predecessor, Ian Smith. The latter's remark, 'I have a country to run', made to the Chairperson of the Geneva Conference reflects the same casual, almost dismissive, 'business as usual' approach adopted by Mugabe during the GPA negotiations. During the Geneva negotiations Smith embarked on strategies to weaken his opponents such as bombing ZANU's Chimoio training camp; similarly, during the Lancaster House negotiations in 1979, he bombed Nyadzonia and the ZIPRA camps in Zambia. Throughout the talks, he remained adamant that he would not negotiate with 'terrorists' but only with 'moderate blacks'. Mugabe, likewise, refused to negotiate with the MDC 'western stooges' on an equal footing.

In the negotiations with ZAPU after the civil war in Matabeleland, ZANU moved a step further to incorporate the role of hardliners in the talks. While continuously viewing ZAPU as a dissident movement, it used hardliners like Maurice Nyagumbo, the longest serving of all Zimbawe's political prisoners, and a senior minister in the ZANU-PF Cabinet, who had also spearheaded Mugabe's assault on Nkomo during Gukurahundi; Emmerson Mnangagwa, ZANU's chief of Intelligence and Mugabe's personal assistant in the party during the struggle; and Eddison Zvobgo, a lawyer who had also played a significant part in ZANU-PF's propaganda machinery, including the portrayal of Mugabe as an invincible leader. The ZAPU team was led by Joseph Msika,

John Nkomo and Naison Ndlovu. Nyagumbo chaired each of the six meetings held by the negotiating committee while Mugabe chaired all the eight meetings of the presidents of the negotiating parties. When it mattered, other ZANU hardliners were 'smuggled' into the negotiating team, notably Herbert Ushewokunze, a socialist ideologue, whose commitment to a one-party state was unquestioned. Nyagumbo made it explicitly clear that the terms of the negotiations were simply the absorption of ZAPU into ZANU; the name of the party and its leadership were not negotiable.[39] Indeed Joseph Msika and his group raised their concerns with these preconditions and more than two years of negotiations wore them down to the point that Nyagumbo and ZANU really appeared as if they were doing ZAPU a favour. In the end, ZAPU became more concerned with keeping ZANU interested in the negotiations and started to give in to all of their demands one by one: first; the name of the party; second, its logo, and then a laundry list of other matters including the punctuation of the party's acronym!

As in the case of Tsvangirai and the MDCs, most of the ZAPU demands did not become part of the agreement and could only be entertained after ZAPU had conformed and signed the agreement. In her interesting comparison of the 1987 Unity Accord and the 2008 GPA, Shari Eppel notes that the Unity Agreement was a surrender arrangement whose sole and intended purpose was to terminate the existence of ZAPU while the GPA was a power-sharing agreement meant to facilitate a transitional arrangement in which an enabling environment for free and fair elections would be created.[40] The MDC was in a much stronger position than ZAPU was in 1987. In 2008-09, she argues, there was a wider coverage of events in Zimbabwe in the public media, on the internet, on cellphones and within a wider circulation of private newspapers not toeing the ZANU line. Certainly Mugabe is no longer the popular statesman that he was in the 1980s; if anything, he has become the object of international rebuke. Regional bodies such as SADC and the AU have been directly involved while the presence of a powerful neighbour has facilitated its intervention as a mediator.

Negotiations between the MDCs and ZANU-PF have continued to be an important feature of the GNU throughout its life to date and ZANU has continued to use a more or less similar strategy to the one it used against ZAPU between 1985 and 1987. Perceived ZANU-PF hardliners were seconded to the negotiating team in the form of Nicholas Goche, a former state security minister and Patrick Chinamasa, a legal expert with lots of experience as a legal minister and the country's former Attorney General. More importantly, Chinamasa proved his mettle as a hard nut to crack when he handled the Finance Ministry in Mugabe's so-called 'war cabinet' in the crisis leading to the GPA. More recently, Emmerson Mnangagwa and Jonathan Moyo have been 'smuggled' into the negotiations when the two negotiators seem to weaken or give in to particular pressures.

Like in 1987, ZANU went into the negotiations with entrenched, non-negotiable positions and with the comparative advantage that it was negotiating from the political high ground as a party in power. It is an irony that the 'outstanding issues' of the GPA were matters left out in the quick quest for a settlement and it seemed somewhat absurd to anticipate a solution to them when they were in themselves the real source of ZANU's power in the whole arrangement. As will become apparent below, it is also something of a miracle that ZANU-PF has been able to compromise on some of its entrenched positions. Let us turn to some of its strategies for maintaining the political higher ground.

THE PURSUIT OF HARD POWER

ZANU-PF's display of power is traceable to its ability to lose an election and stay in power. Starting with the delays in announcing the outcome of the March 2008 Presidential Election as opposed to the efficiency and speed with which the winner of the 27 June Presidential run-off was announced, ZANU was already at work to make sure that whatever arrangement would obtain thereafter should find them securely in position. Contrary to the view that ZANU-PF's arbitrary exercise of power and its assertiveness stem from increased confidence in the political and economic situation obtaining since the formation of the GNU, ZANU has always been determined to be a triumphant loser.[41] In fact, as far as the economy is concerned, ZANU-PF proffers the thesis that it was not the GPA that normalised it but the introduction of the multi-currency regime by ZANU-PF Finance Minister, Patrick Chinamasa, in 2009.[42]

While the circumstances surrounding the outcome of the actual agreement have already been discussed, it is important to point out that the agreement is itself vague about 'power'. While it stated that Tsvangirai would share executive authority with Mugabe, the nature of this executive authority is nowhere indicated in the agreement or the constitution.[43] Mugabe remained effectively in control of all the important arms of government; and all legislative amendments to key areas, such as repressive laws, depended on his signature or a two-thirds majority in Parliament, neither of which was in any way possible. In addition, the agreement assigns responsibilities to the principals in their individual capacities rather than to their offices with the assumption that this was a short-term interim arrangement. Not only has this led to academic arguments over changes inspired by developments within individual political parties but has allowed Mugabe and ZANU-PF to inherit the Mbeki strategy of using the MDC-M as interlocutor against Tsvangirai and MDC-T.

According to Derek Matyszak, the ZANU-PF strategy to maintain power in the agreement was informed by the desire to contain alarm within its ranks that it had lost to the MDC-T. It therefore did much to demonstrate that nothing had changed.[44] Mugabe rode roughshod over limitations imposed on him by the GPA in a move that made concessions to the divisions within ZANU-PF as a party rather than to other signatories of the GPA. He appointed, for example, 41 ministers instead of the 31 provided for in the agreement. Of these 21 were ZANU-PF nominees while the remainder were shared between the MDC formations. Although it is a common belief that the MDCs were given, 'empty' or 'junior' ministries or those related to infrastructure or service delivery, Tsvangirai submits a different argument based on his experience in government since the GPA. In his opinion, these ministries became the real source of the MDC power because of the measurable outcomes from the ministers' individual performance, influences and alliances. ZANU-PF, he argues, misunderstood the role that social ministries, which dealt with people's daily lives, played in enhancing political power. To them controlling the security meant power 'but security without sound national economic performance means nothing'.[45] This argument cannot however be pushed too far given how the MDC ministers have argued amongst themselves over the responsibilities of their ministries and how Mugabe neutralised the delivery ability of MDC ministries by appointing all the permanent secretaries. ZANU-PF also made every effort to move strategic elements in any ministry controlled by the MDC to one or other under its control. Finance Minister Tendai Biti once quarrelled with the late former minister of Social Welfare, Professor Elphas Mukonoweshuro, on civil servants' salaries. Meanwhile, while state parastatals fall under the MDC-T portfolio, nearly all of them are controlled by boards run by security personnel or ZANU-PF sympathisers. The Ministry of Transport and Communication, a ZANU-PF portfolio, is in charge of key parastatals such as Air Zimbabwe and the National Railways of Zimbabwe. It took over responsibility of administering the strategic telecommunication sector from the Ministry of Information and Technology, an MDC portfolio, while the Ministry of Information and Publicity under ZANU-PF controls all state media. Where ZANU-PF has elected to share power, such as in the case of Home Affairs, individual presidential appointments are semi-autonomous institutions in themselves, such as the Commissioner of Police or the Registrar General which, until the passing of the new Electoral Act, has been in charge of the voter's roll. Tsvangirai has also failed to rein in any errant ZANU-PF ministers who violate his directives or orders, notably, the Minister of Information, Webster Shamu, Local Government Minister, Ignatius Chombo, and Minister of Mines, Obert Mpofu.

Shock Therapy and Pre-emptive Strikes

Through the control of power ZANU has also been able to administer significant amounts of shock therapy to its co-signatories to the GPA both as a public display of its power and as a series of pre-emptive strikes in the face of any perceived threat to the status quo. The instrument of this therapy is arrest or imprisonment or allegations of misconduct followed by arduous legal cases containing the threat of imprisonment. Treason charges are reserved on the menu for presidential aspirants. This tried and tested strategy has been used against political opponents since independence with impressive results. It is simply meant to wear them out and divert their attention from the actual political struggle. Nearly all contenders for the post of president in Zimbabwe have been charged with treason: Abel Muzorewa, Ndabaningi Sithole, Morgan Tsvangirai, Paul Siwela and, more recently, Job Sikhala. Invariably, all the cases of treason have been lost in court and, perhaps predictably, many have been quick to celebrate this victory as if ZANU-PF or Mugabe wanted to win the cases in the first place. The strategy, however, is intended simply to fatigue the opponent while ZANU-PF uses the time to restrategise and strengthen itself.

Under the GPA, ZANU-PF has continued to arrest a significant number of MDC MPs. Not that it was not doing so previously, but it simply has raised the tempo. On 25 August 2008, five months after the election, Parliament was scheduled to resume but during the swearing-in ceremony, two MDC legislators, Shuwa Mudiwa and Eliah Jembere, were arrested with the police forcibly taking Mudiwa out of the Parliament building. They were also said to be looking for five other MDC MPs in connection with various alleged crimes. This move happened against the backdrop of the GPA negotiations and was meant to cajole Tsvangirai into signing the agreement. Earlier on, Tsvangirai had criticised the opening of Parliament in the context of the negotiations deadlock.[46] Between May and July 2008 over eleven MDC MPs and senators-elect were arrested on various charges; five were held without charge, ten were on the police wanted list and were in hiding, while four had been exposed to one or another form of violent harassment.[47] Notable amongst the arrests was Naison Nemadziwa, MP-elect for Buhera South, who was arrested outside the Mutare High Court soon after winning a court case against his electoral opponent, ZANU-PF member and war veterans' leader Joseph Chinotimba. Tendai Biti, MDC's Secretary General and MP-elect for Harare East was arrested and charged with treason for, amongst other things, announcing MDC victory in the parliamentary elections ahead of the official announcement. He was held for 21 days and subjected to various forms of torture. Eric Matinenga, who was arrested on charges of inciting public violence on 31 May 2008, was released on 5 June after the state failed to prove its case; he was rearrested on 7 June and detained until 26 June, despite a court order to release him issued on 9 June. This onslaught was designed in the initial stages to diminish an MDC majority before the election of the Speaker of Parliament when the MPs were sworn in and in the long term to replace the MPs and senators if their seats fell vacant by conviction or prolonged absence from parliamentary sessions.

The arrests of MPs subsided after the signing of the GPA as the attention turned to some civic leaders. The case of Jestina Mukoko, the director of Zimbabwe Peace Project gripped the Zimbabwean public when she was abducted on 3 December 2008 and detained for 21 days with her co-accused, who included a 72-year-old man and a two-year-old baby. She was charged with recruiting an ex-policeman in a plot for a military coup.[48] In February 2009 MDC's Treasurer General, Roy Bennett, was arrested on charges of treason on the day he was supposed to be sworn in as Deputy Minister of Agriculture. These charges arose from a state witness Peter Michael Hitschman who 'confessed' after his arrest in 2006 that Bennett possessed guns which he intended to use in acts of sabotage against the state. Hitschman's evidence was found to be inadmissible in 2010 by the Attorney General.[49] Bennett was later released and went into exile, so being effectively barred from occupying the post of Deputy Minister of Agriculture.

The arrests of MDC officials continued throughout the tenure of the GNU but ZANU has also been able to apply its 'catch and release' tactics as a tool to pre-empt any perceived threat to its hegemony. In June 2011, an investigation by the national broadcaster ZBC alleged that the MDC had obtained funding in excess of three million pounds from Britain to bankroll journalists on a project to denigrate the person of President Mugabe. These funds were allegedly administered by Minister of State in the Prime Minister's Office, Jameson Timba, who was immediately arrested, detained and tortured.[50] At this time, ZANU-PF propaganda was feverish about the 'regime change' agenda and its 'agents' following the release in November 2010 of leaked US State Department cables. In August 2011, however, several of these 'WikiLeaks' on Zimbabwe were released, which implicated a number of senior members of ZANU-PF and the Zimbabwean military in the so-called 'regime change' discourse.

In December 2010, an event in Tunisia sparked a wave of protests that eventually toppled the government on 14 January 2011; protests rapidly swept across the Arab countries of Lebanon, Oman, Syria and Morocco; in Egypt, the president, Hosni Mubarak, was forced to resign. Slowly this 'Arab Spring' engulfed all the Arab countries in North Africa and the Middle East, overthrowing long-term dictatorships. Protesters were reportedly using internet and mobile phone-based social networks such as Facebook and Twitter to coordinate their activities. In February protests began in Libya against the regime of Mugabe's close ally Colonel Muammar Gaddafi beginning a civil war that ultimately led to the intervention of NATO forces and Gaddafi's defeat and capture in October. As the events were beamed on satellite channels, which have become commonplace in many Zimbabwean households due to the poor and partisan showing of the national television broadcaster, Zimbabweans easily compared the unfolding North African situation with their own. On 22 February 2011, 46 people including former MDC Highfield MP and International Socialist Organisation co-ordinator, Munyaradzi Gwisai, were arrested on charges of plotting an 'Egyptian style' revolution to topple the Mugabe regime.[51] The basis of the accusations were a videotape they had watched in Harare and speakers who had allegedly addressed the gathering calling for the need to overthrow the Zimbabwean government in the Egyptian way. While 39 of the group were later released, Gwisai and five others were held for a statutory 21 days and only released on bail on 15 March.[52] In the same month, three leaders of a separatist movement, the Mthwakazi Liberation Front, calling for the secession of Matabeleland from Zimbabwe, were arrested for distributing flyers under their movement's logo allegedly advocating an 'Egyptian style' overthrow of Mugabe. The trio, Paul Siwela (who had once run as a presidential candidate), Charles Thomas and John Gazi were charged with treason and held for 86 days.[53] As these events were unfolding, it came to light that Zimbabweans had also turned to using cyber-social networks to organise a 'Million Citizens March' on 1 March 2011. On 25 February security operatives picked up MDC-99 leader, Job Sikhala, who was then tortured in police custody using electric cables; he was also beaten with an iron bar causing a hip dislocation. After spending a whole weekend in their custody, police issued a warrant to detain Sikhala for a further 48 hours, a move his party argued was meant to ensure that he would be in their hands on the day of the so-called March. He was later charged with kidnapping someone in Mutare and released.[54] This was not the first time Sikhala, who is known for pulling stunts within the system, had been tortured. In 2007, he was detained and exposed to serious torture after being linked to a coup plot where he was alleged to have been bankrolled to win over Zimbabwe's service chiefs in a plan to overthrow Mugabe and replace him with Tsvangirai. It was supposed to add value to the on-going Tsvangirai treason trial in which one of the service chiefs testified. Tsvangirai was later acquitted; his biography offers intricate details of this arrest and trial. Thus, suffice it to say, for all the political arrests during the tenure of the GPA, none have contained enough valid evidence to warrant convictions. As previously stated, ZANU-PF has simply used them to either divert the attention of its political opponents, or to wear them down, while at the same time gaining much needed political ground. In most cases these actions were psychological in purpose and effect, directed at the wider Zimbabwean public to warn them of the consequences of any confrontation with the state.

ZANU-PF and the People's Mandate: Internal Democracy and the Politics of 'Restructuring' in the Era of the GNU

ZANU-PF has consistently stuck to the position that it acquires its mandate to rule from the people through the direct participation of the grassroots in its internal democratic structures. The spectacular exercise of routine party elections saturates the national media to drive home this point. In July 2012, ZANU-PF decided to abolish the lowest structures of this so-called ladder of democratic expression – the District Co-ordinating Committee (DCC) elections – for the simple reason that they were sowing seeds of division in the party by the imposition of candidates not elected by the people. This came in the wake of intra-party violence during the 2012 DCC elections in Manicaland and Masvingo provinces. A special Politburo meeting passed the resolution to abolish this structure, recognising, according to the party's spokesperson, that they were never part of its historic practice.[55] This painful decision was nonetheless self-inflicted, coming as it did from ZANU-PF's undue pressure for elections in 2012 to end the GPA. ZANU has always wanted elections for itself as a party and within the country. It has scrupulously observed this axiom. Masunungure has argued that Zimbabwe falls squarely within the definition of a minimalist 'pseudodemocracy': legal opposition parties exist as do other constitutional features of an electoral democracy but they fail to engender an appropriate environment for a fair contestation where a ruling party can be turned out of power.[56] It may be useful to apply this analysis to ZANU-PF as a party – one which has a fervent adherence to its own internal democratic process – to explore whether they function for their intended purpose. This task is complicated by the twin factors that ZANU was founded on the Marxist-Leninist ideology of 'democratic centralism' and that during the three-decade long post-independence period, ZANU-PF has continued to function as a liberation movement rather than a political party in a modern democracy.

I have elsewhere documented how ZANU arrived at Marxism-Leninism as the official party ideology in the 1970s and how 'democratic centralism' was used to maintain party discipline during the liberation war.[57] My argument will not be repeated here and ZANU itself has sufficient sources describing this process.[58] Senior ZANU politicians were however skeptical about the ability of this principle to deliver internal democracy within the party and the liberation movement. They even feared that it would turn the party's leader into a dictator. Edgar Tekere, the party's secretary-general during the war, revealed to Heidi Holland that Rugare Gumbo, the chief exponent of 'democratic centralism' and ZANU's Secretary for Information and Publicity from 1973 to 1978 (when he was arrested by ZANU for (ironically) plotting a coup against Mugabe), was responsible for turning Mugabe into a dictator through this ideology:

> *[Gumbo] was a very effective propagandist, an ideologue. He began preaching Marxism, Mugabe liked the sound of this ideology and before long, he had completely fallen for it and began to sing the Marxism/Leninism song. But that was all rhetoric. There was no genuine vision or belief behind it.'...Rugare was very fond of Democratic Centralism. He preached it a lot and it got into the*

head of Mugabe. *Put simply, it was the idea that numerous as the people are and as welcome as they are to express their views, what matters finally is only the view of the leader. It's a recipe for dictatorship...the problem was that Gumbo – and later many others – kept telling Mugabe, 'you are the leader: what you say is final.' It was seductive and Mugabe got used to it. He became corrupted by it. At the same time, Mozambique's president Samora Machel was continually preaching central control. And the whole of Africa under its earlier chieftain system of governance was used to the idea of central control anyway. I remember Mugabe telling me just before we went back home after Lancaster House that Machel had urged him to keep tight centralised control over the whole country once he was in power. These were bad influences on Mugabe at that crucial time. Men like Simon Muzenda... would stand up quite unashamedly and state during a debate 'why are we still talking about this? The president has stated his opinion; the president has spoken. What is there to discuss anymore? Or they would turn to Mugabe and say, 'What does the President believe?'...they pandered to his vanity....it was the start of the Mugabe personality cult.*[59]

There is no reason to think that the re-emergence of Rugare Gumbo to his historic post as Publicity Secretary of ZANU-PF has re-kindled sentiments of democratic centralism, which have necessarily led to disbanding the DCCs. But the decision to dispense with a unit so instrumental in defining the party's grassroots structures during the preparation for elections is unfathomable, more particularly as ZANU-PF has been calling for elections sooner, rather than later. It is possible, as the party has argued, that DCC elections were sowing seeds of division as evident in the rifts and factionalism displayed in these elections, and that the ZANU-PF leadership has genuinely felt the need to intervene to stem a possible implosion. But ZANU history has also demonstrated that the decision-making powers that purportedly reside in the party's grassroots structures stand good if they are acceptable to the leadership; where and when they are not, they stand 'guided' or are simply whipped into line by the same leadership.[60]

Several Central Committee meetings on the state of the party and a report of the commissariat department culminated in this decision. There are, however, also external factors directly related to the developments in the GPA, in particular, the firm decision taken by SADC leaders at their June 2012 extra-ordinary summit in Luanda to ensure that all parties to the GPA abide by the Election Road Map and prepare for a free and fair election within twelve months from July 2012. Prior to the Luanda meeting, ZANU had piled on pressure for an early election arguing that the lifespan of the GPA had expired. They also reasoned that it was in Zimbabwe's interest to hold elections in 2012 because it was due to host the General Assembly of the United Nations World Tourism Organisation in August 2013. It proceeded to issue ultimatums to COPAC to submit the draft constitution and cajoled its members to duly prepare for such an election.[61] After Luanda, ZANU seems to have abandoned their election push even as COPAC is wrapping up its work. In addition, of all things, ZANU has disbanded its DCCs. Analysts have reasoned that the SADC decision, dubbed a 'game changer' by one MDC negotiator, have made it difficult for elections to be held in 2012 under any constitution whether new or old. One argument has been that ZANU-PF's push for an early poll was to secure an early victory under Mugabe (and perhaps the old constitution) and then deal with its succession issues afterwards.[62] This argument has seen the increased militarisation of ZANU-PF structures as a calculated move to prepare for the takeover of the party by securocrats involved in the succession plan. A list of serving and retired military, police and intelligence personnel eyeing ZANU-PF parliamentary and senatorial constituencies currently under civilians has been circulated in the press and the general chaos that characterised the 2012 DCC elections has been attributed to this operation.[63]

There is no doubt that the SADC Luanda declaration has forced a strategic rethink within different ZANU-PF structures, and that this began to manifest itself in the factionalism and violence that rocked the DCC elections, thus calling for the rapid intervention by the party's top brass. What is curious to note is that the leadership did not only veto the disbanding of the DCCs but transferred their responsibilities and management to its provincial leadership. Party spokesperson Rugare Gumbo was quoted saying members of the disbanded DCCs would either be co-opted into provincial structures or simply 'go home and rest and wait for new opportunities in the party'.[64] Some of the party leaders went so far as to argue that DCCs were never a part of the party's history at its inception in 1963. A more robust analysis of ZANU's political history will render such assertions quite mischievous and may record more revealing cases of intra-party violence in ZANU-PF's DCC and primary elections especially during the period after 1995. Vote-buying, intimidation, rigging and imposition of candidates were as rampant as they are now, but none of them resulted in the need to terminate the exercise. In fact, two of ZANU-PF's National Commissars, Border Gezi and Elliot Manyika, lost their lives on duty and in succession, each at the peak of highly controversial party 'restructuring' exercises.

Restructuring reflects the broader power politics in ZANU-PF. After his election as party president in 1977, Robert Mugabe embarked on a restructuring exercise designed to engender a disciplined party. The result was a centralised administration which struck a permanent alliance between the functional organs of the party, the office of the president, and the departments of defence, security and the commissariat. In 1978, a Central Committee resolution elevated the office of special assistant to the president to the party's secretary for security and intelligence while the commissariat was given more responsibility to regulate, oversee and politicise the masses. The ideological drive of the work of Mayor Urimbo is a significant feature of the party after this period, as were several reports of harassment by the party's security agents.[65]

At independence ZANU-PF imposed the party's *de facto* supreme decision-making body, the Politburo, which is appointed by the party president from members of the Central Committee, to act on behalf of the *de jure* supreme organ, the Congress, when it is not in session. Elections to all the other structures of the party naturally facilitate changes but are overseen by the commissariat department. It, in effect, endorses the exercise, which the party prefers to refer to as 'restructuring'. The Politburo may be likened to the Cabinet, because it is hand-picked by the president, who can 'reshuffle' it. Normally, the politics affecting the 'restructuring' exercise arise from ZANU-PF's primary elections and Mugabe's relations with individual members inform the reshuffling of these organs. Thus, on the one hand, the disbandment of the DCCs was an acknowledgement of their irrelevance to the decision-making process within ZANU-PF; on the other hand it also revealed how the 'democratic' process remains a preserve of the higher organs of party authority. This anomaly explains ZANU's leadership succession crisis. If one accepts the argument that ZANU-PF entered the GPA carrying the burden of two main factions led by Emmerson Mnangagwa and Joyce Mujuru, it will emerge that candidates loyal to the Mujuru faction had effectively lost the DCC elections throughout the country.[66] Under this argument, it has, therefore, been suggested that the DCCs were stopped to prevent a possible Mnangagwa triumph.

With regard to the question of leadership succession, ZANU-PF seems to have two potentially contradictory systems, both of which are based on the people's vote: the first, a hierarchy based on seniority in the party (i.e. based on first come first serve order), the second, based on a popular vote by Congress. In each case the Presidium (the president, two vice presidents, and chairman) constitutes the highest offices, and members of the Central Committee (secretaries and their deputies) occupy portfolios in accordance with their sequence in the pecking order. All these posts are, however, supposedly elected and a candidate may lose this post by either demotion or incapacitation. So, in an ideal scenario, the popular vote at a congress should determine positions within the hierarchy. Practically, however, congress is also 'guided' in its voting, and seniority may be defined differently within different historical contexts or according to amendments to the ZANU-PF constitution. In addition, both the Politburo and Central Committee can make decisions on behalf of congress and can be manipulated to serve the interests of the leadership. This is the central source of ZANU-PF's succession crisis, which it has failed to solve throughout the tenure of the GNU.

Ibbo Mandaza has argued that every other ZANU-PF Congress since 1994 has held out the possibility of discussion or even decision over succession, although party members have never considered a life-presidency.[67] Since 2004, Mugabe, for his part, has offered conflicting positions on his intention to retire. It was in 2004 that succession struggles were concerned with the party's vice-presidency, which fell vacant after the death of Simon Muzenda. Mnangagwa, then the party's secretary for administration, the fifth senior position in the party, had secured the support of seven of the country's ten provinces ahead of the 2004 congress. He was, however, 'beaten' by Joyce Mujuru through a technicality when the party's constitution was amended to make one of the vice-presidents a woman. His defeat was preceded by a suspension from the party of six chairpersons of the seven provinces who had supported his bid and had attended an *indaba* in Tsholotsho. Amongst them were Jabulani Sibanda, who doubled as the leader of the war veterans, and Jonathan Moyo, then Minister of Information and a Politburo member who was allegedly the key conspirator of the Mnangagwa bid. During the congress, Mnangagwa lost his post as Secretary for Administration while the seat Jonathan Moyo was eyeing in Tsholotsho was reserved for a female candidate. Mnangagwa was further humiliated by being appointed Minister of Rural Housing and losing the powerful post he occupied as Speaker of Parliament.

In 2006, Mugabe indicated that he had no intention of resigning, when he tabled a motion at ZANU-PF's annual people's conference in Goromonzi, that his term be extended by Parliament to 2010 after it expired in 2008. Jabulani Sibanda, the war veterans' leader, who remained suspended in the party, had led controversial marches in support of Mugabe prior to the conference. Despite this, Mugabe's motion was rejected by ZANU-PF. Indeed, by the beginning of 2007, it seemed likely that Mugabe would not receive popular endorsement as the party's candidate in 2008. He therefore resorted to finding confirmation of his candidature from higher organs in the party, something democratic centralism facilitates with ease, and in March the ZANU-PF Central Committee did as he wanted. Meanwhile, Jabulani Sibanda, acting as agent provocateur – he had remained suspended and had fallen out with the Matabeleland leadership of the party – went on a countrywide campaign for a Mugabe re-election bid. His drive was sufficient to beat party members into line to accept an extraordinary congress in December 2007, whose main agenda was to confirm Mugabe as the ZANU-PF candidate for the 2008 presidential election. Jonathan Moyo has argued that this drama unfolded under the watchful eye of the Zimbabwean military.[68] Similar contestations between democratic processes and the leadership's preferred choice emerged over the vacancy of the late ZANU-PF vice-president Joseph Msika, where the preferred appointment, John Nkomo, beat his contenders by neither a popular vote (which Obert Mpofu has always enjoyed in Umguza constituency) nor seniority (which Naison Kutshwekaya Ndlovu claims from ZAPU).

In the light of the above, it is clear that ZANU-PF's democratic processes were not engaged in the choice of a presidential candidate in 2008 and that this remains a source of divisions in the party. After failing to obtain popular endorsement in 2006, Mugabe avoided this process in 2007 in favour of using senior organs of the party's structure, which facilitated decisions in his favour. Factions within ZANU-PF have grown along these fissures throughout the tenure of the GPA. Mugabe failed to contain them in Goromonzi; they were merely postponed, and we can now see that they have mutated throughout the tenure of the GNU. They now rear their ugly head in the controversy over the DCC elections in 2012, which comes at a time when the option of an early election under ZANU-PF terms no longer exists and the prospect of a highly regulated one is less than a year away. While disbanding the DCCs is a way of containing internal dissent, it also amounts to throwing the baby out with the bath water.

ZANU-PF and the Battle for Hearts and Minds in the Tenure of the GNU
PROPAGANDA AND THE HISTORIC ROLE OF ZANU's PUBLICITY OFFICE

Rugare Gumbo, the current ZANU-PF Secretary for Information and Publicity, can be credited for elevating the ZANU information and publicity department to an effective and useful propaganda tool during its time of crisis in the mid-1970s. While studying in the United States, he co-ordinated the publication of ZANU's official organ, the *Zimbabwe News,* which significantly improved in its intellectual depth and coverage and even the quality of paper on which it was printed.[69] When Gumbo was imprisoned in Zambia after the Chitepo assassination in 1975, Eddison Zvobgo, who was also in the USA at the time, oversaw the publication of the *Zimbabwe News* and spent the better part of 1975-76 priming the readership to anticipate a Mugabe takeover of ZANU. Zvobgo fell short of running an international campaign for Mugabe, dedicating pages on end of the magazine extolling his virtues as a morally upright leader fit take over the reins of the beleaguered liberation movement.[70] Zvobgo, who was elected Deputy Secretary General at the ZANU Congress in 1963, went to prison with other nationalists but was released in 1971 ahead of the Pearce Commission when he became a part of Bishop Abel Muzorewa's African National Council (ANC) before going on to study in the USA. In 1975, armed with a doctorate in law, he was making his bid to return to ZANU when the ANC was torn asunder by a bitter leadership struggle between Muzorewa and Joshua Nkomo. Zvobgo then teamed up with Gumbo in a campaign for Mugabe to take over the leadership of ZANU, while the latter was in the political wilderness of Quelimane. Their support won Mugabe recognition from the Frontline States leadership in general and Mozambique's Samora Machel in particular. For his labours, Mugabe rewarded Zvobgo by drafting him into the ZANU legal team at the 1976 Geneva negotiations, joining a troupe of other educated technocrats brought into ZANU at this time with little or no political and military experience. Rugare Gumbo retained his post as Secretary for Information and Publicity in the ZANU Chimoio Congress of 1977, but less than a year later he was caught up in a coup plot that landed him in a ZANU prison. Zvobgo took over the publicity division filling up this void but found himself pitted against Nathan Shamuyarira who also wanted access to this unit to wash himself clean of a previous association with a splinter movement of ZANU, the Front for the Liberation of Zimbabwe (FROLIZI). Both Zvobgo and Shamuyarira fought hard to ward off suspicions that they were CIA agents given their prolonged backgrounds in the USA. Their turf war is recorded by Edgar Tekere, who quotes an incident when Shamuyarira allegedly hatched a smear campaign against Zvobgo by circulating an anonymous letter in Maputo alleging that he was a CIA agent. He writes:

> ...I then called in Zvobgo and gave him a copy of the letter. I told him the problem was not he, but Shamuyarira, who had written the letter. At this Zvobgo became very disturbed and began to cry... at about four o'clock that same day, there was a sudden commotion and some of our people rushed in to tell me that Zvobgo had gone wild, had picked up an axe, and was on his way to Shamuyarira's house to kill him.[71]

Zvobgo eventually took control of the publications and propaganda unit. One notable emphasis in his discourse is the celebration of ZANU's history of violence packaged under a concept he christened the 'ZANU Idea'. A key publication of this time was the ZANU 'hit list' entitled 'Zimbabwe Traitors: This is a time of Decision'; it was targeted at those Africans who had joined the 1978 Internal Settlement and it warned:

> ...the PF wants to give these Zimbabweans the first and last opportunity to withdraw from their criminal collaboration with the Ian Smith racist regime. If they comply with this warning, all will be forgiven, if they persist, they will be doomed as their principals...[72]

Some of the principal targets appearing on its 'A' List were Enoch Dumbutshena (Zimbabwe's First Chief Justice), Olivia Muchena (current Minister of Women's Affairs), James Dzvova (who became a ZBC hagiographer) and Micah Bhebe (who was ZANU-PF MP for Bubi-Umguza until 1995). This list ironically reveals ZANU's exceptional ability to recycle people, and the emptiness of its 'sell-out' rhetoric in that the same so-called sell-outs turned into patriots overnight.

Rugare Gumbo was in the political wilderness after 1980 when he joined Ndabaningi Sithole's ZANU in bitterness due to his imprisonment by Mugabe. He bounced back in the 2000 parliamentary election after beating the MDC's Sekai Holland; in 2005, he retained the seat after losing the ZANU-PF primaries and was appointed Minister of Economic Development (2005-07) and

Minister of Agriculture (2007-09). At ZANU's Congress in 2007, Gumbo regained his historical position as ZANU-PF's Secretary for Information and Publicity. With the advent of the GPA, Gumbo became a full-time party functionary with no other responsibility in government; it is through his office that the ZANU-PF's official position on all matters to do with the GPA has been communicated. In his customary relaxed tones, Gumbo has often reinforced entrenched and uncompromising ZANU positions. For instance, when one of the negotiators Patrick Chinamasa suggested that as the matter stood, it was not likely that Zimbabwe would be ready for elections in 2011 or 2012, Rugare Gumbo responded that 'Chinamasa was expressing his own opinion. The party position, as the president has always said, is that elections would be held this year 2011.' When the ZANU-PF COPAC representative, Munyaradzi Paul Mangwana, intimated that the earliest a referendum could be held on the draft constitution was December, Gumbo responded that the ZANU-PF's position was that elections would be held in 2012.

The ZANU Publicity department has always been a hotbed where incumbents have often sought to outdo each other in praising the president; turf wars have been the order of the day. Post-independence, such cases have involved Jonathan Moyo and Nathan Shamuyarira, and later Jonathan Moyo and the presidential spokesperson George Charamba, who is generally perceived to be the author of the *Saturday Herald* column using the pseudonym, Nathaniel Manheru. When Jonathan Moyo was fired from ZANU-PF and became independent MP for Tsholotsho in 2005, he became a columnist for a website <www.newzimbabwe.com> which he used to expose the ZANU-PF propaganda tactics, particularly the strategy behind the Manheru column. Not only did he unmask Charamba as its author, but went on to call him a 'useful idiot' because:

> *Charamba's... Manheru column in* The Herald *on Saturdays is not altogether useless. In fact it has been a gold mine as a media and diplomatic source of juicy state secrets and other information about goings on in government. This is because there have been numerous occasions when Charamba has thoughtlessly used his column to leak juicy tit bits he overhears at the Monday briefing meetings and other encounters with Mugabe which he attends with state securocrats and other key bureaucrats.*[73]

Moyo was readmitted back into ZANU-PF in 2009 after the GNU had been established but his hostility towards Manheru has not altogether dissipated. He has secured his own column in the *Sunday Mail* where he ladles out his own version of ZANU-PF propaganda on the GNU. Both columnists wax verbose: Manheru sporting a Victorian style steeped in anectode and metaphor while Moyo's sermons swing between propaganda and pure vitriol against people or organisations holding perspectives that differ from his own. To this can be added the tired 'redemptionist' Black Atlantic perspectives of Tafataona Mahoso in the *Sunday Mail*, the several other amateur or fly-by-night columnists in the national papers, and the partisan daily broadcasts of the national radio and television stations. Despite a lack of co-ordination, and evidence of internal contradiction, ZANU-PF has been successful in using these various propaganda tools throughout the GNU to invent and echo terminology that has gradually formed part of the discourse of negotiations with the MDCs.

ZANU's 'Comprador Bourgeoisie', Indigenisation and the GPA

Just before presenting his 2012 mid-term budget review at the end of June, Minister of Finance, Tendai Biti called for an emergency Cabinet meeting to announce that the government was broke. His budget estimates, based on projected remittances from the sale of diamonds, had not been realised because most diamond companies operating in Chiadzwa had not surrendered their earnings to treasury. Addressing Parliament in the last week of June, Biti announced that he would have to review downwards by half his budget estimates of the previous year and expressed fears that ZANU-PF was using the earnings from diamond sales to fund a parallel government from the GNU.[74] ZANU-PF has always maintained that the full potential of diamond sales cannot be realised because of the sanctions imposed on Zimbabwe and its mining sector, a position often forcefully emphasised by the Minister of Mines, Obert Mpofu, and the Chairman of the Zimbabwe Mining Development Corporation, (ZMDC) Goodwills Masimirembwa. Mpofu was quoted as saying that the public announcement by Biti that Zimbabwe was expecting US$600 million from diamond sales was enough to encourage other countries sympathetic to the West to impose sanctions on the sale of Zimbabwean diamonds.[75]

It was ironic however that the biggest spenders in government were the ministries of Defence and Home Affairs, both of which had over-recruited without permission from treasury.[76] A report published by the international human rights organisation Global Witness confirmed in June that most of the diamond companies were wholly or partly owned by the Zimbabwean military in joint ventures with international companies. One company implicated in the failure to remit diamond revenue to treasury is a Chinese company half of whose shares were owned by a serving lawyer of the ZNA; its board of directors were drawn from senior members of the Ministry of Defence, two police commissioners, a ZANU-PF party officer and two retired army colonels.[77] Biti, in his address, castigated ZANU-PF ministers on a 'property-buying spree' and singled out the Minister of Mines who had allegedly acquired the majority shares in a local bank in the recent past.[78]

But where did ZANU's 'rich and famous' emerge from in a party that has socialist roots, which had at one point even adhered to a leadership code and still identifies with the rural poor? Alex Magaisa, a political commentator, has equated ZANU-PF to a 'mafia' with Mugabe as its 'Godfather'. ZANU-PF, he maintains, '…is more than an organisation – it incorporates a way of life, with its own set of values and codes of practice and it is within this context that the behaviour of its members can best be understood.'[79] Invoking the parlance of the Italian mafia, Magaisa equates ZANU-PF to a 'family' with its own 'made men' (and women) and a criteria of making them; and for ZANU-PF it is credentials of the liberation struggle or connections with it. The main advantage of being 'made' in the mafia is having certain territorial control and the protection of the family and for Magaisa:

> …in the Zanu PF Family, the made men and women have their own territories in which they operate. Some are in tourism, energy, mining, manufacturing, finance, etc – the made men in Zanu PF guard these territories jealously and exploit them with ruthless efficiency (ibid.).

Magaisa concludes his analogy by arguing that power in the mafia revolves around the Godfather who has a wealth of information on everybody in the family and the enforcers of its code; and 'whomsoever attempts to break the code is immediately brought to book and dispatched with brutal efficiency'. He cites cases in ZANU-PF of the fate of the plotters of the Tsholotsho succession bid as well individuals like Chris Kuruneri, James Makamba, and Charles Nherera, amongst others, as examples. Magaisa suggests that ZANU-PF is also, by and large, a business consortium.

ZANU-PF: FROM SOCIALISM TO CAPITALISM

Useful as it may be, Magaisa's analogy suffers from a lack of a chronological context. In other words Magaisa fails to explain for when this mafia ideology began in ZANU-PF and why. This is critical for a party that assumed state power with a socialist ideology and required its senior membership to adhere to a strict leadership code that was anti-accumulation. As has been shown already it also sought to project the image of its leader, Robert Mugabe, as incorruptible. In 1978, ZANU published a comprehensive list of British and American companies and subsidiaries understood to be 'looting and exploiting Zimbabweans' and issued a stern warning:

> ...we know who you are, what you are the for (sic). Should you elect to be our adversary, you will be welcome. On the other hand, if you will be our partners in building a new socialist Zimbabwe, time for proof has arrived.

And an unequivocal commitment:

> ZANU is sworn to amputate the capitalist tentacles that stretch into Zimbabwe and introduce a radical socialist development model based on scientific socialism – thereby placing the people of Zimbabwe in control over their economy and natural resources to their immense benefit.[80]

So the question is really: what happened to turn ZANU into a rapacious capitalist enterprise fitting modern descriptions of a mafia? Before this may be answered it is necessary to point out that prior to assuming state power both ZANU and ZAPU had business interests managed through holding companies. At independence ZAPU owned two farms and five business enterprises; it later established a holding company, Nitram, ostensibly for the purpose of looking after ZIPRA ex-combatants.[81] Within a year Nitram had also acquired hotels, farms and other businesses using money contributed by ZIPRA ex-combatants.[82] In 1989, Joshua Nkomo formed the Development Trust of Zimbabwe (DTZ), which purchased the Nuanetsi Ranch, of which more below. ZANU's business interests dated back to the pre-independence period when it operated a business enterprise known as M&S Syndicate. Ironically, its first holding company, Zidco, was established in 1979, a year after it had threatened British and American companies. Geoff Nyarota's autobiography reveals that Zidco was formed as a joint venture between M&S Syndicate and a British company Unicorn Import and Export.[83] Nyarota's account exposes the direct involvement of Zidco in the 1989 Willowgate vehicle scandal which sucked in most ZANU-PF senior leaders. He shows that by the 1990s Zidco owned twelve Zimbabwean companies and more than 50 properties. All these companies thrived on government contracts and Nyarota names and shames individual ZANU-PF leaders who won tenders, used proxies or awarded lucrative deals to family and friends.[84] Unlike Magaisa's analogy of the infallibility of the mafia leader, Nyarota attributes Mugabe's failure to discipline his colleagues as an essential weakness of his leadership, traceable to the Willowgate scandal which inelectably sucked him in to the world of corruption.

What is implicit but not vigorously pursued in Nyarota's account is ZANU-PF's alliances with capitalist individuals who have in the past underwritten ZANU's political projects. This has become even more evident in recent years and ZANU leaders openly and publicly confess these alliances, although he makes reference to Manilal Naran and Sam Levy's links with ZANU-PF and their involvement in the 1989 Willowgate Scandal. It is interesting to note how these alliances are well established in ZANU-PF history. In 1974 ZANU leaders of the Nhari Rebellion were accused of working with the capitalist Lonhro chairman, Tiny Rowland, to prevent a communist takeover of Zimbabwe. Rowland continued to be an important force in independent Zimbabwe, building alliances with successful local ZANU-PF aligned business people such as James Makamba.

The Different Hues of ZANU-PF Indigenisation

At Independence ZANU-PF was confronted with a policy conflict in its desire to preserve white capital while at the same time seeking to deliver on the liberation promise to the predominantly poor and previously disadvantaged African population. This is how it adopted the policy of 'Growth with Equity' which has been summarised by Brian Raftopolous as a welfare strategy dilemma seeking to reconcile growth with more equitable distribution and initiate change without serious destabilisation.[85] By 1990, when the ZANU-PF government decided to adopt the Economic Structural Adjustment Programme (ESAP), white private capital, which had successfully alienated the African petty bourgeoisie and monopolised lines of credit, played a central role. It came together under the collective banner of the Confederation of Zimbabwe Industries (CZI). Around this time, however, African business-people had become aggressive in lobbying government for increased participation in the national economy and formed the Indigenous Business Development Corporation (IBDC). Although the state offered concessions to the IBDC and sub-contracted 'non-core business' of government departments to some of its members, it was no more than adhering to the ESAP requirements of downsizing and reducing fiscal expenditure. The result was mass retrenchments and the collapse of most indigenous business ventures in the absence of adequate credit support. ZANU-PF preferred instead to work with patronage, issuing tenders to cronies and client briefcase organisations such as the Affirmative Action Group (AAG) which literally turned vegetable vendors into millionaires overnight. Independent black businessmen working outside the orbit of the state were either thwarted, as in the case of Strive Masiyiwa, or hounded into exile, as were James Makamba and Mutumwa Mawere amongst others. This is the version of indigenisation pursued by ZANU-PF until the enactment of the Indigenisation and Economic Empowerment Act in 2007. By then it was borrowing from the South African version of the policy of Black Economic Empowerment (BEE).

ZANU-PF patronage slowly stretched its tentacles to incorporate former Rhodesian whites who forged alliances with the party to protect their interests from the growing wave of confiscation of property begun by the land occupations in 2000. In a public lecture delivered at Rhodes House in Oxford in May 2012, exiled MDC-T Treasurer General Roy Bennett alleged that there is a 'relatively small but significant' section of whites who work closely with ZANU-PF, including people who used to bust sanctions for Ian Smith, Selous Scouts and others closely connected to the South African intelligence service during apartheid.[86] Bennett, who was careful to sanitise his role despite being one such ZANU-PF sponsor in the past, made these remarks barely a week before the death of a Zimbabwe business tycoon, Sam Levy, in June. Several ZANU-PF bigwigs fell over each other pouring condolences to the Levy family, notably Vice-President Joyce Mujuru who revealed that Levy was an important business partner of her late husband, Retired General Mujuru. He had even paid the general's hospital bills following an operation in South Africa after a helicopter accident.[87] Van Hoogstraten, a British business mogul, once rated Britain's youngest millionaire in the 1960s with over 200 million pounds worth of investments in Zimbabwe, claims a personal friendship with Mugabe and controls vast stakes in a number of companies listed on the Zimbabwe Stock Exchange.[88] John Bredenkamp, who was once in charge of the finances of the Rhodesian army, was involved in sanctions-busting deals for the Ian Smith regime in return for concession in tobacco sales, is alleged to have brokered arms procurement deals for the Zimbabwean army. Bredenkamp is known to have bankrolled Emmerson Mnangagwa's failed bid for the ZANU-PF vice-presidency in 2004 which resulted in the infamous Tsholotsho *indaba*.[89] Lastly, Muller Conrad 'Billy' Rautenbach is the former head of a South

African automobile corporation which controlled the Hyundai franchise until November 1999. He is said to have strong connections with ZANU-PF's Emmerson Mnangagwa who appointed him chairperson and managing director of Gecamines, a Zimbabwe state-owned mining company in the DRC. Rautenbach maintained his mining interests in the DRC and his company Camec managed to establish a stake in Zimbabwe's platinum mines. He was also able to obtain huge amounts of land in Chisumbanje in the Nuanetsi Ranch where his company BioEnergy Zimbabwe has set up ethanol production plant.[90] This project has sparked controversy with its evictions of local people who are supported by the Masvingo ZANU-PF provincial executive which ironically sees the Rautenbach venture as disempowering the African families it displaced. It has also sown division between mostly former ZAPU board members of the Development Trust of Zimbabwe who own Nuanetsi Ranch; they see this venture as an invasion by ZANU-PF stalwarts on the interests and legacies of ZAPU and Joshua Nkomo.[91] Recently ZANU-PF has blamed the MDC Energy Minister, Elton Mangoma, for failing to come up with legislation compelling the blending of Zimbabwean petrol with ethanol from Chisumbanje. Rautenbach's company Green Fuel was forced to halt operations in March 2012 when it ran out of storage space after reaching its maximum production capacity of 10 million litres.[92] Mangoma and the MDC have blamed Green Fuel for poor planning and inefficiency despite government backing in what appears to be an attack on the patronage politics ZANU-PF has enjoyed with the rich whites.

The new empowerment act passed through Parliament in 2007 when ZANU-PF enjoyed two-thirds majority and when most of its leadership were slapped with targeted sanctions by the USA and Canada, the EU, New Zealand and Australia. It was signed into law by Mugabe on 9 March 2008, a few weeks before the harmonised election, and its related regulations were gazetted in 2010 when the GNU was in full swing.[93] A clause compelling all foreign investors to cede 51% of their shares to Zimbabweans has been vigorously pursued by the imposing figure of the Minister of Indigenisation, Saviour Kasukuwere, himself a former member of the AAG, since the formation of the GNU. His crusade has forced several companies to comply or face confiscation by the state, and since the formation of the GNU, ZANU-PF's spectacular success is in the nationalisation of all mines, particularly diamond and platinum mines. This happened against the background of a spirited attempt by Western countries to classify Zimbabwean diamonds 'blood diamonds' and exclude them from the international market controlled by the Kimberley Process (KP) system. The indigenisation campaign has drawn criticism for its selective application of the law in the face of allegations that Chinese businesses have been spared the 51% share requirement because of ZANU-PF's strong relations with China. Wide speculation about the real beneficiaries of the 51% shareholding abounds and ZANU-PF has responded to this by launching Community Share Ownership Trusts in the rural areas where mining activities take place and the mining companies are required to contribute to the trusts, placed under the chiefs. To date, five such trusts have been launched since 2011 with cash injections ranging from $10 to 50 million. This move has been seen by some as ZANU-PF's attempt at vote-buying by using the chiefs.

More recently, Kasukuwere has taken the 51% campaign to foreign-owned banks where he has clashed with several ZANU officials including the Governor of the Reserve Bank, Gideon Gono. Kasukuwere, who himself owned Genesis Investment Bank before it collapsed, was dismissed by Gono as 'not a fit and proper person to deal with banks having been involved with the failed indigenous bank', to which Kasukuwere is said to have responded by accusing Gono of being 'immature'.[94] Gono has been supported by the Minister of Finance, Tendai Biti, and Prime Minister Morgan Tsvangirayi in castigating Kasukuwere's moves as unlawful. Despite this, the Attorney General, Johannes Tomana, has taken sides with Kasukuwere arguing that the Act is law and therefore not debatable: '…debating takes place in Parliament. Gazetted laws should simply be obeyed. It is the abiding of our laws that gives guarantee to foreign investors…' he said.[95] And so the drama continues.

Conclusion

Taking Stock: ZANU-PF in the GPA Scorecard

Attempting to account for a party's action in a Government of National Unity may be equated to shooting a moving target and one could write such a chapter until the next election. The only conclusions to be drawn should be based on its performance and actions so far; such conclusions may change as the country still has nearly a year to run until the expiry of the GNU and it is not the business of historians to prophesy what will transpire. In the foregoing an attempt was made to account for ZANU-PF's actions in the GPA in the context of its own history. At the time of writing, most the preconditions set by SADC with respect to the GPA have been met – the Media, Human Rights, and Electoral Commission Bills have passed through Parliament and the commissioners appointed, while the draft constitution has been submitted clearing the path to a referendum and an election under a new constitution. In this bumpy road, it is critical to determine whether ZANU-PF's interests, as outlined above, have been served and whether the strategies it employed to achieve them were entirely successful. This assessment will be based on what the parties have agreed on and what obtains in the draft constitution, if indeed it is approved. First of all it is almost clear that ZANU-PF successfully resisted security sector reform in the interparty negotiations, thereby leaving the military-civilian alliance, which has always been its pillar of strength, intact. Unless the new constitution empowers Parliament to oversee the appointment of service chiefs or empowers it to prosecute treasonous statements amongst their ranks, security sector reform will remain a pipe dream. Similarly, ZANU-PF retained the power to appoint the Attorney General, who has done so well in effecting the prosecutions and supporting specific laws; the governors, who remain in control of all the provinces and metropolitan towns; and, lastly, the ambassadors where ZANU-PF has only conceded three foreign missions i.e. Senegal, Australia and Germany, to the other signatories of the GNU.

Commissions have been constituted with representatives nominated by all parties to the GNU. Nonetheless, ZANU-PF has been successful in stalling reforms to free the airwaves and democratise the print media. The ZANU-PF Minister of Information has simply ignored or rebuffed directives. It had also successfully secured the agreement that the work of the Human Rights Commission should begin in February 2009, thereby sparing its membership from prosecution from crimes related to electoral violence and other human rights abuses over the previous decade. Through the media it controls, ZANU-PF scored another success in persuading the MDCs to sing from the same hymn-book on the issue of sanctions. MDC Prime Minister Morgan Tsvangirai and his Finance Minister Tendai Biti have all publicly acknowledged and supported an international campaign for the removal of sanctions, which has left western countries with very little justification for them. Lastly, the indigenisation campaign on its own has achieved much in transferring ownership of business and property from particularly Western foreigners, in fact it has achieved as much success in this regard as the controversial Fast Track Land Reform in taking away land from whites. The most spectacular success was scored in the mining sector, where global mining concerns were forced to concede and others, such as Canadile Diamonds, were expelled. In the diamond sector, this war was fought and won almost single-handedly by the fiery ZANU-PF Minister of Mines, Obert Mpofu. Zimbabwe successfully licensed to sell its diamonds on the KP market despite all the odds stacked against it.

However, most of the ZANU-PF successes would seem short-term if considered against the possibility of an election under the new Electoral Act and with a new constitution. This, of course, is dependent upon whether ZANU-PF will find itself able to use the inherent structures of state power, which it successfully defended in the negotiations, to subvert such an election. In the new Electoral Bill that has gone before Parliament, the Zimbabwe Electoral Commission is no longer appointed by the incumbent president, as was the case in the past, but by Parliament. The Commission also oversees the voters' roll which was the responsibility of the Registrar General, another presidential appointee. The voters' roll will remain ward-based as opposed to polling station-based, which ZANU-PF wanted. The MDC pushed for the former to preserve the privacy of voters.[96] In the 2008 elections, ZANU-PF was accused of meting out violence to communities that did not vote for it.

Finally, if – and only if – the draft constitution is approved by Zimbabweans in a plebiscite, the various factors guaranteeing ZANU-PF hegemony stand challenged. One was the strengthening of Parliament, including the subjection of the security sector appointments and deployments to the approval of Parliament. The other was the devolution of power to the provinces and appointment of provincial governors by winning parties in each province. This takes away the presidential privilege of appointing all the governors. The proposed laws allowing dual citizenship empower a number of Zimbabweans who had been disenfranchised by ZANU-PF to exercise the right to vote even in the diaspora. In its first reactions to the draft constitution ZANU-PF was concerned to make the struggle for liberation from colonialism and imperialism the cornerstone of the constitution in the manner that the American Civil War provided the cornerstone for the constitution of the United States of America. They also wanted, amongst other things, chiefs to be given due recognition in the Judicial Service Commission, but all this notwithstanding the party's supreme body approved 'nearly 97%' of the draft document.[97] However, the clause that reportedly consumed most time in the ZANU-PF Politburo deliberations is the section requiring a presidential candidate to have a running mate who would become the vice-president of the winning candidate. This clause challenges the sacrosanct question of succession in ZANU-PF. It would force Mugabe to declare a successor in the event that he wishes to run again, and this person would assume the office of president in the event of death or incapacitation of the incumbent. This single issue has thrown the cat amongst the pigeons and it remains to be seen how ZANU-PF will emerge out of the situation. Readers are starkly reminded that with ZANU-PF, literally anything is possible.

ENDNOTES

1 This paper benefitted much from discussions with contributors to this volume and various engagements with Dr Ibbo Mandaza in Harare and Godfrey Hove in Stellenbosch.
2 M. Tsvangirai (with T.W. Bango), *Morgan Tsvangirai: At the Deep End* (Johannesburg: Penguin, 2011), p. 388.
3 Ibid., p. 418.
4 Tsvangirai does not, however, adequately explain why Welshman Ncube's faction did not want to assume leadership of the breakaway movement.
5 Ibid., p. 509.
6 T. Hoekman, 'The Politics of Negotiation: Opposition and Power Sharing in Zimbabwe', unpublished M.Phil. thesis, Oxford University, 2012, p. 42.
7 Ibid., p. 44.
8 Ibid., p. 48.
9 Tsvangirai and several Zimbabwean activists were screened on international media with broken limbs and swollen faces after detention and assault by the Zimbabwean police.
10 J. Moyo, 'The Wikileaks Saga: National, Regional and International Implications', lecture delivered to the SAPES Seminar Series, 29 September 2011.
11 *The Daily News*, 28 January 2012
12 F. Zaba, 'Soldiers Take Over ZANU-PF Commissariat', *Zimbabwe Independent*, 6 May 2012. For a full list of military and security personal willing to contest elections see O. Gagare and W. Zhangazha, 'CIO, Army Battle ZANU-PF Bigwigs', *Zimbabwe Independent*, 27 April 2012.
13 G.C. Mazarire, 'Discipline and Punishment in ZANLA: 1964-1979', *Journal of Southern African Studies*, 37 (3), 2011.
14 N. Kriger, *Guerilla Veterans in Post-War Zimbabwe: Symbolic and Violent Politics, 1980-1987* (Cambridge: Cambridge University Press, 2003), p. 111.

15 A. Alao, 'The Metamorphosis of the "Unorthodox": The Integration and Early Development of the Zimbabwe National Army', in N .Bhebe & T. Ranger (eds), *Soldiers in Zimbabwe's Liberation War* (Harare: University of Zimbabwe Publications, 1995), p. 117.

16 E. Sibanda, *The Zimbabwe African People's Union: A Political History of Insurgency in Southern Rhodesia* (Trenton NJ: Africa World Press, 2005), pp. 244, 282.

17 Ibid., p. 250.

18 S.J. Ndlovu-Gatsheni, 'The Post-Colonial State and Matabeleland: Regional Perceptions of Civil-Military Relations, 1980-2002', in R. Williams et.al., *Ourselves to Know: Civil Military Relations and Defence Transformation in Southern Africa* (Pretoria: Institute for Security Studies, 2003), pp. 24, 31-33.

19 M. Rupiya, 'Civil-Military Relations in Zimbabwe: Is There a Threat?' in R. Williams et.al., *Ourselves To Know*, pp. 260-61.

20 'The Security-Military Business Complex in the Transition in Zimbabwe', Zimbabwe Institute Discussion Paper, 2008.

21 N. Bhebe and G.C. Mazarire, 'Zimbabwe's Liberation Struggle', Report Prepared for the SADC Secretariat Hashim Mbita Project on the Liberation Struggle of Southern Africa, Dar es Salaam, 2010, p. 99.

22 See Zimbabwe Institute Discussion Paper.

23 E. McCandless, *Polarisation and Transformation in Zimbabwe: Social Movements, Strategy Dilemmas and Change* (Scottsville: University of KwaZulu Natal Press, 2011), pp. 97-98.

24 Ibid.

25 J. McGregor, 'The Politics of Disruption: War Veterans and the Local State in Zimbabwe', *African Affairs*, 101, 2002, pp. 23-36.

26 VOA News, 'Constitution Talks Resume after Chaos', *ZimEye*, 15 July 2009.

27 J. Chimunhu, 'ZANU Creating Bogus NGOs to disrupt Constitution', *ZimEye*, 19 July 2009.

28 B. Chapwati, 'ZANU-PF Rowdy Gangs Disrupt COPAC Meetings in Mashonaland West', *ZimEye*, 25 June 2009.

29 T. Sibanda, 'COPAC to Tighten Security following disruptions by War Vets', *SW Radio Africa*, 16 January 2012.

30 T. Sibanda, 'Jabulani Sibanda rips ZANU-PF apart in Masvingo province', *SW Radio Africa*, 28 June 2011.

31 L. Sachikonye, *When a State Turns on its Citizens: Institutionalised Violence and Political Culture* (Johannesburg: Jacana Media, 2011), p. 106.

32 P. Nyangove, 'Jabulani Sibanda Threatens to Roast Livers of Opponents', *The Standard*, 14 August 2011.

33 'War Vets Leader Told to Leave Masvingo', *The Herald*, 23 June 2011.

34 Ibid.
35 G. Maponga, 'Sibanda to Stay in Masvingo', *The Herald*, 27 June 2011.
36 Zimbabwe Peace Project, *Summary on Politically-Motivated Human Rights and Food Related Violations July 2011*, (28/08/2012).
37 Radio VOP Zim Channel, 'Zim Journos, MDC MP beaten up by ZANU(PF)', 23 July 2011.
38 M. Tsvangirai, *Morgan Tsvangirai: At the Deep End*, p. 207.
39 W. Chiwewe, 'Unity Negotiations', in C.S. Banana (ed.) *Turmoil and Tenacity: Zimbabwe 1890-1990* (Harare: College Press, 1989), pp. 245-246.
40 S. Eppel, 'An overview of the circumstances of the Unity Accord of 1987 in comparison to those of the Global Political Agreement of 2008', unpublished paper, Solidarity Peace Trust, 2009.
41 J. Muzondidya, 'Zimbabwe's Failed Transition? An Analysis of the Challenges and Complexities in Zimbabwe's Transition to Democracy in the post-2000 Period', in T. Murithi and A. Mawadza (eds) *Zimbabwe in Transition: A View from Within* (Johannesburg: Jacana Media, 2011), pp. 23-4.
42 M. Huni, 'Service Chiefs Thwart Threat', *The Sunday Mail*, 7 July 2012.
43 D. Matyszak, *Law, Politics and Zimbabwe's 'Unity' Agreement* (Harare: Konrad Adenauer Stiftung, 2010), p. 96.
44 Ibid. p. 98.
45 M. Tsvangirai, *Morgan Tsvangirai: At the Deep End*, p. 510.
46 A. Shaw, 'MDC Says 2 MPs arrested before Swear In', NewZimbabwe, 12 November 2009.
47 US Embassy Zimbabwe, Cable 08HARARE622, 'ZANU-PF Targets MDC Officials'. Accessed on 14/6/12.
48 D. Howden, 'Jestina Mukoko: Mugabe's Henchmen came for me before Dawn', *The Independent* (UK), 17 January 2009.
49 'AG Attacks on Witness, Fails to Build A Case Against Bennett', *Prime Minister*, 13 January 2010.
50 'What was the real Reason of Jameson Timba's arrest?' *The Zimbabwe Review*, 29 June 2011.
51 'Gwisai, 45 Others Charged with Treason', *Daily News*, 23 February 2011.
52 The MDC Minister of Energy and one of the negotiators of the GPA were also arrested in the same week on allegations of criminal abuse of office for authorising the procurement of fuel from a South African company. Other MDC MPs Douglas Mwonzora, Roger Tazviona and Shepherd Mushonga had been arrested and released in the previous weeks.
53 'Siwela Set Free', *NewsDay*, 3 June 2011.
54 I. Madongo, 'Sikhala arrested and Tortured', *SW Radio Africa*, 28 February 2011.

55 T. Maodza, 'ZANU-PF DCCs Disbanded', *The Herald*, 2 July 2012.
56 E.V. Masunungure, 'Introduction', in E.V. Masunungure (ed.), *Defying the Winds of Change: Zimbabwe's 2008 Elections* (Harare: Weaver Press, 2009), p. 3.
57 G.C. Mazarire, 'Discipline and Punishment in ZANLA 1964-1979', *Journal of Southern African Studies*, 37 (3), 2011.
58 See for instance ZANU, 'ZANU's Political Programme: *Mwenje no. 2*, Lusaka, 1972', in C. Nyangoni & G. Nyandoro (eds) *Zimbabwe Independence Movements: Select Documents* (London: Rex Collings, 1979), pp. 249-251.
59 H. Holland, *Dinner with Mugabe: The Untold Story of a Freedom Fighter Who Became a Tyrant* (London: Allen Lane, 2008), pp. 49-50.
60 J.M. Makumbe and D. Compagnon, *Behind the Smokescreen* (Harare: University of Zimbabwe Publications, 2000), Chapter 4.
61 'ZANU-PF Central Committee Meets to Discuss Issues affecting the Party', *Zimbabwe Independent*, 1 July 2012.
62 'I am ready to rule: Ngwena', *Zimbabwe Independent,* 11 May 2012.
63 'CIO, Army Battles ZANU-PF Bigwigs', *Zimbabwe Independent,* 27 April 2012.
64 'ZANU-PF off the Rails', *NewsDay*, 2 July 2012.
65 G.C. Mazarire, 'Discipline and Punishment in ZANLA', *Journal of Southern African Studies*, 37 (3), 2011, pp. 589-591.
66 'ZANU-PF In-fighting Intensifies Following DCC Elections' *Short Wave Radio* 17 April 2010.
67 I. Mandaza, 'Will ZANU-PF Survive after Mugabe?' Unpublished paper, n.d., pp. 40-43.
68 See J. Moyo, 'Unravelling ZANU-PF's Extra-Ordinary Congress' www.newzimbabwe.com (Dec. 2007).
69 Beginning 1974, the number of issues of the *Zimbabwe News* increased and it began to appear in a glossy and coloured paper.
70 G.C. Mazarire, 'Discipline and Punishment in ZANLA 1964-1979', pp. 583.
71 E.Z. Tekere, *A Lifetime of Struggle* (Harare: SAPES Books, 2007), p. 98.
72 'Zimbabwe Traitors: This is a time of Decision', *Zimbabwe News*, 10 (5) 1978, pp. 57-58.
73 J. Moyo, 'The Useful Idiot has Gone too Far this Time', www.newzimbabwe.com 2006.
74 'MDC Accuses Diamond Miner of Funding Shadow ZANU-PF', *Mail and Guardian*, 29 June 2012.
75 O. Kazunga, 'Illegal Sanctions a threat to Diamond Sales', *Chronicle*, 11 May 2012; see also 'Mbada Diamonds injects $300 million into national coffers', *The Herald*, 22 May 2012.
76 'Biti, Mnangagwa Clash over Army', *The Daily News on Sunday*, 10 June 2012.
77 Global Witness, *Financing a Parallel Government: The Involvement of the Secret*

Police and Military in Zimbabwe's Diamond, Cotton and Property Sectors, June 2012.
78 'Zimbabwe: Envoys Misled During Tour of Marange Diamond Fields', *New Zimbabwe Forum*, 29 June 2012.
79 A. Magaisa, 'The Godfather of the ZANU-PF Mafia', newzimbabwe.com, 11 December 2009.
80 'British Companies Looting in Zimbabwe', *Zimbabwe News*, 10 (1) 1978, pp.47-48.
81 J. Nkomo, *The Story of My Life* (London: Methuen, 1984), pp. 226-227.
82 J. Todd, *Through the Darkness: A Life in Zimbabwe* (Cape Town: Zebra Press, 2007), pp. 28-34.
83 G. Nyarota, *Against the Grain: Memoirs of a Zimbabwean Newsman* (Cape Town: Zebra Press, 2006), p. 204.
84 Ibid., pp. 202-204. Apart from showing that Zidco was chaired by ZANU-PF's most powerful men in succession, i.e. Enos Nkala and Emmerson Mnangagwa, Nyarota exposes the alliance between Maurice Nyagumbo and his cousin Jonathan Kadzurai in the Willowgate Scandal, Mnangagwa and the Joshi brothers in ZANU Properties, Mugabe and his nephew Leo Mugabe in the Harare International Airport tender, and Mugabe and Nkomo's involvement in the establishment of the Commercial Bank of Zimbabwe (CBZ) after the collapse of the American Bank BCCI amongst other things.
85 B. Raftopolous, 'Beyond the House of Hunger: Democratic Struggle in Zimbabwe' *Review of African Political Economy*, 54, 1992, p. 64.
86 V. Langa, 'White Farmers Sponsoring ZANU-PF', *NewsDay*, 31 May 2012.
87 'Vice President Mujuru consoles Levy Family', *The Herald*, 8 June 2012.
88 *The Times* (London), 3 July 2009.
89 T. Nyasha, 'Bredenkamp flees Zimbabwe' *newzimbabwe.com, n.d.*
90 *Mail and Guardian*, 20 November 2009.
91 J. Mujere and S. Dombo, 'Large Scale Investment Projects and Land Grabs in Zimbabwe: The Case of Nuanetsi Ranch Bio-Diesel Project', paper presented to the International Conference on Global Land Grabbing, IDS, University of Sussex, 6-8 April 2011.
92 'ZANU-PF Blames Mangoma for Green Fuel Failure', *ZimEye*, 11 April 2012.
93 'Chiyangwa's AAG Blasts Kasukuwere', *The Zimbabwe Mail,* 6 July 2012.
94 'Zimbabwe Minister, Central Bank Chief Spar over Indigenisation of Banks', *VOA News*, 6 July 2012.
95 'Chiyangwa's AAG blasts Kasukuwere'.
96 'Parties Quarrel over Electoral Act', *The Herald*, 3 July 2012.
97 M. Mkwate and K. Bwititi, 'Draft Constitution: The Drama Begins', *The Sunday Mail*, 29 July 2012.

CHAPTER 4

Turning Confrontation into Critical Engagement:
The Challenge of the Inclusive
Government to Zimbabwean Civil Society

BERTHA CHIRORO

Introduction

The signing of the Global Political Agreement (GPA) on 15 September 2008 brought numerous challenges, dilemmas and opportunities for Zimbabwe's civil society. The establishment of the Inclusive Government (IG) came in the context of civil society already having been much eroded, most noticeably from 1998 onwards, by authoritarianism, political violence, and economic hardship. Nonetheless, the establishment of a new political order drew considerable hope, resources and renewed energy from civil society organisations (CSOs), which began to open the space for critical engagement with the IG. This chapter will analyse the dilemmas faced by CSOs seeking to come to terms with the uncertain transition, as well as the processes and initiatives taken by them in adapting themselves to the changed context. The role of donors in supporting civil society developments and networks will also be examined.

We will begin by outlining the history and challenges of Zimbabwe's civil society's relationship with the state as well as the various developments that ensued in the sector as a response to the GPA and IG. The chapter mainly argues that while civil society has given priority to advocating for a free and fair electoral environment, documenting human rights violations, and monitoring the GPA and the constitutional reform process, its engagement with socio-economic issues has been limited, leaving the voices of the poor, vulnerable and marginalised, their needs and insights, excluded from major political developments.

Cleavage and Contestation: Civil Society as a Reflection of Politics in Zimbabwe

While the decline of civil society's influence on political developments between 1998 and 2008 has been widely noted, a vocal and heterogeneous sector is still evident. The National Association of Non-Governmental Organisations (NANGO) estimated that by January 2012 about 4,000 NGOs were operating in Zimbabwe.[1] Among them are trade unions, faith-based organisations, residents' associations, media advocacy groups, women's and youth organisations and various community-based groups that are organising outside the control of the state. Since 2008, approximately 1,990 organisations have registered as trusts, though it is not clear how many of these are family trusts and how many are CSOs. Moreover, 1,038 organisations have registered under the Private Voluntary Organisations (PVO)[2] Act (which provides for the registration of local and international NGOs, under the Ministry of Labour and Social Services) in the three years since the formation of the Inclusive Government.

Since 1997, Zimbabwe's civil society has been divided between those groupings which uphold the international human rights agenda and are, in general, aligned to the opposition, and those that are aligned to ZANU-PF.[3] The list of civil society organisations that has operated in an organic alliance with ZANU-PF in its advocacy for radical social and economic change, especially in relation to the ownership of land, include the Zimbabwe National Liberation War Veterans' Association, Zimbabwe Liberation War Collaborators and the Zimbabwe Political Detainees and Restrictees Association. These organisations, as well as the youth militia, were involved in violent campaigns against MDC supporters, white farmers and black farm workers shortly after the constitutional referendum of 12-13 February 2000, as well as during the 2000 parliamentary and the 2002 presidential elections.[4]

Confronting these ZANU-PF-aligned CSOs has been a host of others aligned to the MDC whose chief concerns have been constitutionalism, human rights and finding ways to resist state power. Examples of such organisations are the National Constitutional Assembly (NCA), the Crisis Coalition of Zimbabwe, Zimbabwe National Students Union (ZINASU), Women of Zimbabwe Arise (WOZA) and the Zimbabwe Congress of Trade Unions. These organisations have generally been confrontational to the ZANU-PF regime and opposed to its violence and repression. A clear divide thus exists within Zimbabwean civil society between civics which, in their confrontation with ZANU-PF, have depicted themselves as the 'real civil society' and those that work hand-in-glove with ZANU-PF and depict those opposed to the party as 'sell-outs' and 'puppets' of international interests.[5] The tendency in general has been to view the CSOs aligned to the MDC as more progressive, while excluding those organisations that are aligned to ZANU-PF, which are generally regarded as 'uncivil'.[6]

This duality has continued into the present era of the IG with civil society organisations aligned to the MDC projected as democratic whilst those aligned to ZANU-PF have been depicted as 'violent thugs' trying to defend an unpopular regime. This polarisation has generated different perceptions among civics about what democratic social change should entail and how it should be achieved in both political and socio-economic terms.

The international donor community and the Zimbabwean state have both played significant roles in influencing current divisions within civil society. Donors have supported civil society that agitates for civil and political rights, and the ZANU-PF government has sponsored the component of civil society supportive of its political agenda. Zimbabwe thus illustrates the Gramcian notion that civil society can become a battleground for powerful national and international actors to intervene with hegemonic interests, or projects.[7] The civil society sector in Zimbabwe is, thus, a highly contested terrain, with competing claims as to which elements represent legitimate civil society. The divisions and polarisation within civil society have had a debilitating effect on its ability to critically engage with developments under the Inclusive Government. A major strategic dilemma underlying civil society in Zimbabwe is that it has not been able to bridge the divide that has emerged between constitutionalism and human rights on one hand, and socio-economic rights on the other – the rights/redistribution dilemma.[8]

In order to understand fully the dynamics shaping civil society activism within the context of the GPA, it is necessary to examine briefly the history of civil society activism since independence.

Phases in the Development of Zimbabwean Civil Society Since Independence

Zimbabwe's civil society has gone through several very different phases since 1980. In the immediate aftermath of independence, government was chiefly concerned with issues of state-building and economic development and, as a result, civil society, inspired by the ideals and values of the liberation struggle and socialist ideology, assumed a largely supportive developmental role.[9] In their assessment of civil society in the early independence period, Sam Moyo, John Makumbe and Brian Raftopoulos identified four phases: the 'welfare phase' (1979-81); the 'development phase' (1982-86); the service NGO phase (1987-1990); and the Economic Structural Adjustment Programme (ESAP) phase (1991-94). During the early phase, civil society was concerned with education and welfare, involving organisations such as the Association of Women's Clubs (AWC), which was linked to the Ministry of Community Development and Women's Affairs.[10] Later, in 1996, the AWC disputed a government action that had suspended twelve members of its executive committee. The women filed a suit with the Supreme Court and challenged the constitutionality of the applicable section of the PVO Act. They alleged that the powers given to the Minister of Labour, Social Welfare and Public Service were in conflict with the constitution which guaranteed freedom of association, freedom of expression, and the right to a fair hearing. The women won their case, and resumed their roles and duties within the AWC executive, having had their legal costs paid by the Ministry.[11]

Labour also formed a core element of civil society, and a relationship of common interests developed with the state. Government was instrumental in the formation, in 1981, of the Zimbabwe Congress of Trade Unions (ZCTU),[12] and ensured the enactment of laws that protected the labour force and established a minimum wage.[13] The respective interests of the ruling ZANU-PF party and of labour were thus inextricable, and government frequently presented itself as representing the needs of labour. This symbiotic relationship changed dramatically in the late nineties when, amid growing economic hardship, the labour movement became more militant in its demands. Repressive laws, such as the Law and Order Maintenance

Act, were used to stifle opposition in the name of development, security and maintaining state sovereignty.[14]

The second phase, 1982-86, witnessed the growth of income-generating organisations, which focused on training members of communities in, for example, market gardening, poultry breeding and soap-making. Organisations such as the Organisation of Rural Associations for Progress, the Organisation of Collective Co-operatives in Zimbabwe, and the Zimbabwe Foundation for Education with Production provided training and others such as the Environmental and Development Agency provided technological know-how.[15] One NGO which is important to mention is the Zimbabwe Project Trust (ZimPro) which has recently celebrated three decades of work in Zimbabwe since 1980. ZimPro was registered in Zimbabwe as a PVO in 1982; its vision was to ensure a poverty free society by empowering poor, disadvantaged and marginalised communities by working on issues of food security and public health – though it began by working with ex-combatants, assisting with education skills training, and co-operative development. As an NGO, its history[16] charts the changing political and socio-economic development and political climate in Zimbabwe and reflects the way in which it has adapted to change. In the process, it has worked with other organisations, communities and individuals on issues spanning emergency responses, social protection, food security and livelihoods, mainstreaming HIV and AIDS and advocacy.[17]

The third phase, 1987-91, saw the growth of a new generation of service NGOs and human rights groups addressing issues of HIV and AIDS, women and the environment. The fourth phase, the ESAP phase, led to a shift in focus towards policy and advocacy. Many NGOs focused on relief work during the 1992 drought, and the negative impacts of retrenchment and high inflation.

From 1995 onwards, most CSOs – notably the ZCTU and church organisations such as the Catholic Commission for Justice and Peace, in alliance with the international donor community – began focusing on governance, human rights and democracy processes, campaigning specifically for a level playing field during elections. There was also significant growth in advocacy groups, and this changed the tempo of civil society's engagement with the state. By 1997, the ZCTU made this change evident when it began to link the general problems of workers to broader governance issues, aligning itself with the newly formed National Constitutional Assembly (NCA) and other NGOs. This alliance reflected a shift in the relationship between labour and the ZANU-PF government, which until 1991, had been based on the values of liberation struggle. The student movement (ZINASU), along with the ZCTU, increasingly clashed with the government over social and economic issues and, subsequently, over legislative instruments used to curb their activism and organisational activities.[18] Political debate went beyond the merits and demerits of one-party and multiparty systems and embraced other questions such as the accountability of government and party institutions, the forms and level of popular democratic participation, and relations between civil society and the state.[19]

Dissatisfaction with government policies and behaviour ensued, along with agitation against the outcome of the ESAP process, resulting in a mushrooming of organisations and new tactics. A vibrant civil society emerged, styling itself as a deliberate countervailing force to the totalitarian tendencies of the ZANU-PF regime. Instruments included networking, mass protests and stayaways and a significant flow of information from media advocacy groups, the few independent newspapers, and research think tanks. Zimbabwe witnessed an extraordinary departure from earlier civic activism when civil society had represented praise-singers who would go onto the streets in support of government policy. A more radicalised and politicised sector emerged, one which demanded inclusion on all issues of governance.

Most notable within this change was the press, which continually asserted its critical independence; a more militant and radicalised ZCTU, with more than 37 affiliates; and the NCA, which emerged in 1997 as the umbrella body for the NGOs representing good governance and human rights. With a membership of more than 150 organisations, and more than 10,000 individual members, it quickly assumed a status not unlike that of an opposition party, certainly filling this gap until the emergence of the Movement for Democratic Change (MDC) in 1999. A vibrant and confrontational civil society thus quickly developed between 1997 and 1999, emerging within an environment of weakening law and order, a decaying state, the fragmentation of society, and the absence of any viable political party through which to oppose government.

The formation of the MDC affected the efficacy of the civil society movement, as many leaders of the CSOs migrated toward the MDC, thereby creating a leadership vacuum within the movement. The ZANU-PF government made maximum use of the legal means at hand, including the Public Order and Security Act, (POSA) and the Access to Information and Protection of Privacy Act (AIPPA) (see below), to curb civil society activism and to shrink civil and political freedoms.

Civil Society and the Zimbabwe Crisis 2000-07

There have been different interpretations of the Zimbabwe crisis.[20] On the one hand, scholars such as Sam Moyo and Paris Yeros have emphasised issues of national sovereignty and re-distributive justice as being at the heart of the crisis. On the other hand, scholars such as Brian Raftopoulos, David Moore and Ian Phimister have stressed the centrality of political and economic governance, transparency and accountability.[21] Zimbabwean civil society, in general, has viewed the crisis as a result of the repressive and violent nature of the ruling ZANU-PF regime and its violation of human rights. Civil society responded to the crisis of governance by forming coalitions to articulate a national, regional and international response to the debilitating situation in the country.

The most significant result of civil society mobilisation against the ZANU-PF government was the rejection of the government-sponsored constitution of 2000 when civil society organisations, led by the NCA, successfully campaigned for a 'No' vote. The ZANU-PF reaction was immediate. They turned to a violent campaign against the civics and the opposition MDC, and enacted new repressive legislation, such as AIPPA (2002), meant to control freedom of expression and the media, POSA (2002) and the NGO Act (2004).[22] The run-up to the subsequent 2000 and 2002 parliamentary elections was marked by an intensification of the intimidation, violence, torture and death that is outlined in numerous human rights reports.[23] The economic repression and brutalisation of civil society activists in the post-2000 period severely weakened the opposition and the social forces. So did the mass emigration of Zimbabweans, including some of the experienced civil society leaders and activists. It is estimated that about 3.5 million Zimbabweans have left the country because of the deepening economic and political crisis, many of whom are working in South Africa.[24]

However, during the Save the Zimbabwe Campaign of 2007, led by the Zimbabwe Christian Alliance, civil society was able to make another unified onslaught on the authoritarian state. The Campaign was an alliance of faith-based groups, labour, opposition and NGOs, launched in February 2006 to mobilise regional and international solidarity to increase pressure on ZANU-PF when all avenues to resolving the Zimbabwe crisis appeared closed. A crackdown on a protest prayer rally organised by the Alliance on the 11 March 2007 not only displayed the brutal force by the police against the opposition figures and civil society but also sent shock waves across the world, putting the Zimbabwean governance crisis squarely on the agenda and leading to international condemnation and a call by SADC for an emergency meeting on the crisis.

From 2007 through to the bloody presidential election run-off of June 2008, civil society, although suffering from fatigue generated by the sustained repression, maintained domestic pressure to end a violent and authoritarian rule in Zimbabwe.[25] Zimbabwean civil society continued to participate in regional and international advocacy to highlight the crisis and to ensure that the national, regional and international community had objective information regarding the root causes of the crisis, the continuing human rights violations, and their far-reaching consequences for the peoples of Zimbabwe.

Civil Society Dilemmas in Coming to Terms with the GPA

The signing of the GPA precipitated much dissension and even chaos among Zimbabwean CSOs. There was disbelief at the MDC's willingness to enter into a deal with ZANU-PF, brokered by a mediator, South African President Thabo Mbeki, whose policies had been widely seen as an obstacle to transition in Zimbabwe. The sense of betrayal was widespread, not least because, historically, power-sharing arrangements with ZANU-PF, such as the 1987 unity accord between ZANU and ZAPU, had generally led to the annihilation of those who had entered into the arrangement, rather than real co-operation in the responsibilities of government. CSOs were also concerned that the MDC had gone into the compromise weak, having been worn out by Mugabe: 'In situations of such prolonged struggle and attrition, the assets of energy and idealism and commitment can be sapped by fatigue, burn-out, reactive-ness and diminution of resources.'[26]

In addition to the above, civil society also had numerous concerns about the GPA itself. These included the delays in the release of the 2008 election results, disputes over the results, and concerns that justice and reconciliation demands would never be fulfilled. (The presidential election results were announced five weeks after the polls, thereby fuelling anxiety, tension and suspicions of vote manipulation leading to the violence that besieged the country up until the time of the presidential election run-off on 27 June 2008.)[27] Different groups reacted differently to these questions, with a groundswell of demand for justice for past atrocities. While some CSOs, such as NANGO, focused on the possibility of peace, and on supporting the Inclusive Government, the more radical groups, such as the NCA, ZCTU, and Zimbabwe Human Rights NGO Forum, argued that there could be no real and lasting peace without a truthful confrontation with past violations and the establishment of a process of accountability. They demanded that responsibility be assumed for the 'stolen' vote, the related violence in the lead-up to the 2008 presidential election, and the ZANU-PF state's role in both. Some CSOs went even further, demanding both acknowledgement of the violations from the period immediately subsequent to the GPA as well as justice for other grave human rights violations committed since independence – the Gukurahundi massacres in Matabeleland and the Midlands in the early 1980s; and Operation Murambatsvina, in 2005, when over 750,000 people's homes or livelihoods were destroyed.[28]

In order to show the diversity of responses to and the fracturing of CSO opinion that succeeded the GPA, it may be useful to examine the responses of a few prominent CSOs in the country, such as the ZCTU, Women of Zimbabwe Arise (WOZA) and the International Socialist Organisation (ISO). The ISO, for instance, dismissed the deal as one made between 'bourgeois elites that have fundamental interests in common'.[29] It denounced the MDC for having reached a 'sell-out agreement with the ZANU-PF dictatorship that will not benefit the poor and the working people', and highlighted the role within the MDC of petite bourgeois elements 'who long ago prostrated themselves before western neo-liberal political and economic forces and are now eager to get into state power, even as junior partners, and accumulate as a neo-liberal dependent capitalist class'.[30]

The ZCTU, aggrieved by its exclusion from the dialogue process, denounced the GPA and the secretive manner in which the negotiations had been conducted, describing it as a flawed process. It proposed the establishment of a 'Neutral Transitional Authority', as the preferred solution to the current electoral dispute.[31] It further criticised the power-sharing deal as 'not a transitional government but a structure incorporating losers'; and one, moreover, which was silent on the critical issue of corruption. The ZCTU also denounced the use of a Parliamentary Select Committee to lead the drafting of a new constitution, and argued that the GPA was merely 'a temporary stop gap measure', with which it would engage as such, and such only.[32]

To highlight the diversity in civil society opinion and responses, on 29 September, 2008 over 600 members of WOZA took to the streets in Bulawayo demanding that the government should be formed immediately. WOZA wanted the new IG to grasp the urgency of the everyday social and economic problems Zimbabweans were facing, including shortages of food, electricity, and water. They demanded that talks should cease and the new government should start to deliver instead of haggling over ministries and positions.

Another issue that presented CSOs with a dilemma was the drafting of the new constitution. While organisations such as the NCA, ZCTU, and ZINASU vehemently opposed the leading role allocated to parliament by the GPA in this endeavour, some CSOs, such as NANGO, felt that civics would still have a positive role to play in the process.

The labour movement's participation in the broader political and governance issues that have emerged from the GPA has been marked by splits and divisions. Personality squabbles and splits over control in the ZCTU have weakened the labour movement, preventing it from playing a meaningful role in the transition. The ZCTU split into two rival factions in 2011 in the run-up to a congress meant to elect a new leadership. There is still no institutionalised forum within which government, business and labour can meet. The IG has so far failed to convene the National Economic Council. In addition, the severity of the economic crisis and the informalisation of labour, the massive exodus of skills, and high levels of unemployment have weakened the labour movement's position in the political landscape and vis-à-vis the GPA. Contributing to the weakening of labour was the decomposition of the teaching sector between 2006 and 2008 as the economic crisis deepened, and some teachers left the country and others left the profession. Nonetheless, in early 2012, the Zimbabwe Teachers' Association called for a strike, supported by the ZCTU. They were demanding improved working conditions and a living wage. These strikes, however, are no longer commanding the same attention and voice that they did between 2000 and 2008 when such actions were linked to broader calls for democratisation.

Teachers strike for more pay.

The church has responded to Zimbabwe's economic and governance crisis in a subtle manner, but has found itself marginalised and unable to provide leadership among civil society in response to the GPA, with the occasional exception of a few individuals and organisations who have denounced ZANU-PF authoritarianism. A number of churches have taken partisan positions, with senior clerics or their associates directly or indirectly supporting one side over the other. The Anglican church has been torn apart by a feud in which the excommunicated Bishop Nolbert Kunonga, who has openly supported ZANU-PF, continues to assert that he is the leader of the Anglican Church in Zimbabwe, and has co-opted all Anglican church property – schools, hospitals, orphanages and churches. The official Anglican Church of the Province of Central Africa is currently suing him for restitution of their properties.[33]

Perceptions of partisan positions among church leaders have eroded the church's ability to lead in a situation framed around compromise, namely the GPA. Ironically, one result is that churches now find themselves marginalised in their efforts to promote healing and reconciliation – goals purportedly integral to the GPA, which the churches might have been expected to fulfil.[34] Instead, their role is limited to offering opening and closing prayers at important events, while political figures deal with the real affairs of state.[35] That said, one area in which the churches have remained active is in their continuing call for fresh elections, including identifying the electoral and institutional reforms needed for these to take place, and the benchmarks for demonstrable government commitment to adhering to the rule of law, i.e. behaviour required of all state agents if they are to serve in a professional, non-partisan manner.

Women and the GPA

An equally important sector is the female voice: as expressed by the Women's Coalition, (a network of women's rights activists with chapters in Bulawayo, Masvingo, Beitbridge, Gweru, Gwanda, Bindura, Marondera and Mutare) and WOZA during the term of the IG. Although some have expressed their frustration that their participation is no more than 'tokenism and deception',[36] Zimbabwean women have continued to strive for a democratic political environment together with other CSOs. Women's groups have been involved in the demands for a free and fair electoral environment and have been working with other networks, local, regional and international who share similar objectives. However, the harsh economic climate has made it difficult for most women to participate in and mobilise around political developments, overburdened as they are by bread and butter issues. Furthermore, the first-past-the-post electoral system currently in use has not made it easy for women to enter the political arena; nor have political parties made concerted efforts to promote the participation of women in politics, or facilitated their access to leadership positions. Political parties are not compelled by the Electoral Act to ensure gender equality or representation.

However, civic organisations such as the Women's Coalition of Zimbabwe and the Women and Politics Support Unit, have tried to ensure that women's rights are recognised in the democratisation agenda, and in the constitutional reform process. They have also lobbied SADC, the African Union (AU) and the United Nations for a more gender sensitive electoral road map. Since its formation in 2003, WOZA has continued to push the boundaries by staging fearless campaigns and protests despite the restrictive political environment.[37]

Continuities and Contradictions within Civil Society

In a transition established as a result of agreement between political elites, civil society is often both immobilised and atomised.[38] The exclusive process by which the agreement was established, as well as the dilemmas and challenges to civil society that have subsequently ensued, have limited the prospects for a thoroughgoing transformation of Zimbabwean society and may have led into a situation that could be described as a 'frozen democracy'.[39] The transition has not resulted in a complete break with the past, of the sort defined by O'Donnell and Schmitter as 'the interval between one political regime and another ... delimited on the one side by the launching of the process of dissolution of an authoritarian regime and on the other by the installation of some form of democracy, the return to some form of authoritarian rule, or the emergence of a revolutionary alternative'.[40]

Furthermore, the lingering economic crisis has had a debilitating impact on civil society. With unemployment estimated at over 80% and people struggling to survive, CSOs have battled to mobilise an increasingly disillusioned and apathetic population. In addition, the dollarisation of economy, and the growth of the informal sector through vending, barter, cross-border trade, repair and maintenance, etc., have adversely impacted on the formal sector, thereby affecting the labour movement as a force for social and political change.

Zimbabwe's civil society has also continued to suffer from a lack of autonomy as it continues to rely heavily on foreign funding, rather than membership subscriptions, for sustainability.[41]

The issue of funding has had an important impact on civil society activism in the country. The flow of donor money to CSOs in Zimbabwe has largely been influenced by the persistent economic and governance crisis and has led to tension and conflict between ZANU-PF and a number of the CSOs. Worried about the potential abuse of their funds by government officials through corruption, most donor funds have gone to governance and human rights organisations to 'strengthen democratic forces'. As a result, there are strong, though not necessarily correct, perceptions that donor agendas have dictated and defined the work of CSOs.

Critics have also pointed out that the funding of civil society has concentrated on NGOs at the expense of other civil society actors that have a broader membership. Donors have often devoted attention to those organisations they already know, or with whom they have a good working relationship. Furthermore, donor support also tends to favour urban-based NGOs to the exclusion of more community-based organisations (CBOs). Mass-based organisations and CBOs receive little attention from donors in spite of their potential to mobilise people for development. Most of the urban-based CSOs that receive funding have a local rather than a countrywide reach and constituency, are imbalanced in their political, ethnic and gender representation, and some continue to be linked to the political establishments – either ZANU-PF or the MDC. This makes it difficult for some CSOs to play a non-partisan watchdog role vis-à-vis the Inclusive Government.

The legitimacy of NGOs is also questionable as they are largely accountable to their counterparts in the North instead of to local constituencies. Thus, many NGOs appear to operate as consulting companies – a type of organisation new in Zimbabwe, being non-profit, but acting like a commercial consulting firm, financed by the external mandates. This commercialisation of civil society, especially within the advocacy forum, discourages more credible local actors who are not receiving funds from participation or becoming active.[42] Civic engagement is at risk of being dominated by the 'commercial' NGOs, which may well weaken the development of a vibrant civil society in the long term.

Another important issue that has affected the efficacy of civil society engagement with the ongoing political transition in the country is that of programmatic overlaps in the activities of the many CSOs. For instance, overlapping of activities within the field of human rights and governance has led to 'turf wars' among the organisations working in the field and competing for the same funds. This has militated against effective collaboration, complemenatry programming, sustainability, and the formation of real movements for social change. Moreover, the brain drain has not spared the CSOs, and a number of NGOs are now run by young officers who lack sufficient experience. As a result, CSOs have failed to command the same respect and mobilisation capacity as their predecessors.

Moreover, having been caught by surprise by the establishment of the GPA government, which came at a time when most civics least expected it, civil society has struggled not only to adjust to the new IG environment, but also to develop appropriate responses to it. As a result, they have tended to be reactive rather than proactive, and singular rather than co-ordinated in their interaction with the new government.[43]

The real problem for civil society is that the burden of keeping the IG under observation continues to fall on the shoulders of a small number of very committed, hard-working but greatly overstretched activists. Important achievements in this context have included the development of evidenced-based advocacy strategies as well as detailed situation analyses providing an accurate picture of developments in Zimbabwe. Such reports have yielded results, especially in the SADC mediation process, while also providing an alternative perspective to that of the government on the prevailing political and economic environment. Related to this, has been the importance of transmitting coherent and effective messages to regional and international actors and building coalitions in the progress toward free and fair elections. Partnerships among CSOs such as the Zimbabwe Electoral Support Network (ZESN), Crisis Coalition and NANGO have helped to pool together resources and expertise by bringing different groups together to develop strategies for action.

This, however, does not mean that the differences in values and orientations have made it easy for organisations to respond to the IG. Consensus is still difficult to find. Many CSOs, moroever, tend to focus on the negative developments in the country rather than what has been achieved, in order to attract funding.[44] The challenge for most of Zimbabwe's CSOs is to present the real socio-economic problems that the country is facing, rather than identify problems in response to potential project funding.

Civil Society and Monitoring of the GPA

Despite the challenges posed by the GPA, and the fracturing that has ensued, civil society in Zimbabwe has sought to provide some serious monitoring of the GPA Agreement, without having been part of the Joint Monitoring and Implementation Committee (JOMIC) – which comprised only representatives of the two MDCs and ZANU-PF. Civil society was thus gravely aware of the potential consequences of the compromises that had been forged. As a minimum response, a grouping of 40 CSOs[45] established an independent monitoring mechanism, The Civil Society Monitoring Mechanism (CISOMM), on 25 February, 2009, ten days after the formation of the IG. This monitoring structure was one of civil society's most pragmatic responses to the IG.

The CISOMM initiative has been an opportunity for local NGOs to play a watchdog role independent of the guarantors of the GPA, namely, the AU and SADC. CISOMM established clusters according to various thematic issues: economic recovery, constitutional reform, human rights, institutional transformation, humanitarian and food assistance, media reform, freedom of expression, and national healing. Each cluster was established according to the levels of resources, capacity and technical expertise of the organisations and individuals involved. CISSOM has subsequently been able to identify and declare non-compliance in each area as well as to provide recommendations that may assist policy makers. The reports issued by each cluster are shared with parliamentarians, SADC, libraries, researchers, international lobby groups, JOMIC, civil society actors, regional and international groupings, donors and the international community. CISOMM has also established, as a strategic priority, engagement in the rural areas – taking information and evidence of progress or lack of it to the rural populations. The value of CISOMM is that it has viewed the IG as one entity, accountable as such, whereas individual CSOs tend to focus on the parties of which it is comprised. In concrete terms, the monitoring and evaluation mechanisms developed cover all parties within the GPA, demanding accountability from them as government rather than mobilising alongside one party or against another.

Among the problems evident in CISOMM is that very few groups are monitoring economic developments, in particular issues of economic empowerment, indigenisation, and the diamond industry. Another is the constant challenge to achieve consensus among the 40 organisations involved, as when, for example, one or another CSO may wish to issue a press statement regarding a particular action taken by the IG. The constitutional making process, which will be discussed in detail below, posed a particular challenge. A further problem has had to do with groups producing different statistics, especially on issues of violence; still another is their use of different reporting styles. One CISOMM co-ordinator has complained that some civics exaggerate certain issues because of their political orientation or because of the constituencies they represent.[46] CISOMM generally manages this shortcoming by reporting on trends rather than statistics, leaving organisations to give the public their own statistics. Although CISOMM's outreach into the rural areas is not strong, they have tried to reach rural populations in order to engage them in transitional issues, and efforts for inclusion are being made by the various organisations that represent these constituencies.

Civil Society and the Constitutional Reform Process

The constitutional reform process has been mired in controversy reminiscent of the 1999 process in spite of the fact that there is now an Inclusive Government. From the inception of the Constitution Select Committee (COPAC), there has been no consensus among civil society groups. This, however, has not stopped civil society from engaging with the constitutional reform process in a variety of ways: outreach, data capturing, thematic committee discussions, drafting, and an all-stakeholders conference.

As part of their attempt to influence the process, the Zimbabwe Peace Project, ZESN, and the Zimbabwe Lawyers for Human Rights formed an independent monitoring project known as ZZZICOMP.

ZZZICOMP's goal was to observe the work of COPAC and monitor the constitutional outreach work in an endeavour to ensure transparency, inclusiveness, accountability, and confidence in the process; special emphasis was given to incorporating the views of ordinary people. The outreach began in June 2010, a year later than scheduled because of COPAC's funding problems. Although ZZZICOMP monitors were accredited by COPAC, they nonetheless faced harassment, arrest and even abduction – similar intimidatory tactics were widely reported in the COPAC meetings as well as in the media.

This shadowing exercise by ZZZICOMP helped to shed some light on the constitutional reform process, the problems faced, and the levels of violence experienced during meetings. Clearly one of the most critical responses to the Inclusive Government, the ZZZICOMP has nonetheless struggled to ensure its recommendations are taken into consideration.[47]

The attacks on the first unofficial draft constitution published in *The Herald* on 10 February 2012 reflected the ideological differences and the polarised nature of Zimbabwean society. The NCA, which led a similar constitutional review process in 1999, has taken a position to campaign for a 'No Vote' – this, within the framework of their larger 'Take Charge Campaign,'[48] a revolt against the exclusivity of the government-led process. They advocate that the newly elected government would have to focus on a new constitution. They have been supported in this position by the ZCTU, ZINASU, The Zimbabwe Chamber of the Informal Economy Associations and the National Council of the Disabled Persons in Zimbabwe.

The NCA has dismissed the first draft of COPAC's proposed constitution as a replica of the Kariba draft, which was crafted by the representatives of the three main political parties in 2007. The tensions over the constitution have been heightened as the war veterans called for COPAC to be disbanded, claiming that the people's views on homosexuality, property rights, citizenship and the land issue had been distorted.[49] The controversy over the constitution and what the draft contains clearly demonstrates a nation struggling with competing transformative projects, legitimacy and development as well as neo-liberal conceptions of elections, democratisation and what constitutes Zimbabwe as a nation.

Civil Society and Advocacy Around Elections

Elections have been a major advocacy issue for Zimbabwean civil society since the establishment of the Inclusive Government. According to most representatives of human rights and governance organisations, the election issue cannot be avoided as Zimbabwe does not have a legitimate government with sufficient tenure to take the country towards a clearly defined developmental policy.[50] Whilst hunger, poverty, unemployment and disease are real dangers to a new Zimbabwe, the country cannot tackle these ills without credible institutions and structures. Furthermore, the IG is seen as a temporary arrangement that should provide a framework to facilitate an enabling environment for elections.

Following the painful aftermath of the 2008 elections, many CSOs are trying to develop ways to collaborate so as to avoid fragmentation of their efforts. For example, ZESN the largest election-related organisation with a membership of 30 CSOs (including religious entities such as the Zimbabwe Council of Churches and the Ecumenical Peace Initiative), has segmented its work into four broad thematic areas: election monitoring, public outreach, media and information, and research and advocacy. Many other CSOs have concentrated on civic education, while others, such as the Crisis Coalition in Zimbabwe, have focused on advocacy.

Civil society seems to have made progress in forming a united front and calling for major changes in the electoral framework, both within Zimbabwe and at SADC meetings. Their strategies for dissemination have included focused meetings with relevant institutions such as Parliament's Justice and Legal Portfolio Committee, the Women's Caucus, or with select groups such as ambassadors, as well as public meetings. They have also acted as a lobbying force at Regional Economic Communities (RECs) often by holding parallel events at, for example, the SADC and AU Heads of States and Government Summits.

Civil society organisations such as ZESN, the Media Monitoring Project Zimbabwe (MMPZ), MISA-Zimbabwe, and the Zimbabwe Journalists for Human Rights have also been demanding substantial media reforms as part of the road map to democratic elections in the SADC mediation process. Areas identified as in need of reform are:
- the appointment of a new board for the Zimbabwe Broadcasting Corporation;
- the appointment of a new Board for the Broadcasting Authority of Zimbabwe;
- the licensing of new Broadcasters;
- the appointment of new Trustees for the Mass Media Trust.

These constitute some of the areas that will enable Zimbabwe's transition to a stable democratic political environment that can guarantee freedom of association, expression and choice within and beyond the electoral process. One real test of Zimbabwe's democratic transition is the democratisation of the airwaves.[51]

The Operating Environment of Civil Society under the Inclusive Goverment.

One of the key issues which has affected civil society activism is the structural environment in which it operates. Although the IG has provided some form of economic stability, the operating environment for civil society has remained fearful. As has been made evident in numerous human rights and media reports, violence, intimidation and even torture continue.[52] A clear example of the repressive environment in which civil society activists continue to operate is the arrest and detention of Munyaradzi Gwisayi and 40 others while attending a meeting, on 19 February, 2011, organised by the ISO. They were accused of holding an illegal meeting and watching footage of the uprisings in Egypt and Tunisia. Although the case against them was later dismissed in court, Gwisayi and five others were held in Chikurubi Maximum Security Prison in solitary confinement for three weeks and tortured before being released on bail. That they spent the year thereafter in and out of the courts is a clear example of the harassment which can threaten activists. Numerous other CSO members have been arrested and detained, including the NANGO

Chairperson and Chief Executive Officer, ZESN staff and the Director of the Human Rights NGO Forum.[53]

The United Nations General Assembly Human Rights Council Working Group on the Universal Periodic Review in its twelfth session in Geneva, which met from 3 to 14 October 2011, also noted these acts of violation and urged Zimbabwe in its recommendations to make the Zimbabwe Human Rights Commission and other human rights institutions operational, as well as to support the Anti-Corruption and Media Commissions in order to ensure national cohesion and good governance. In the same report, it noted that freedoms of expression and the press are still severely restricted.

Although some CSO reports have noted improved economic stability, an improvement in social services and human security, together with less political violence against opposition activists, at the time of writing[54] arrests of MDC members, including Cabinet Ministers, and human rights defenders seem to be on the rise, making a mockery of the notion of an inclusive government[55] and a non-partisan judiciary, police and security sector.

Conclusion: The Challenges of Forging a Transformative Agenda

Whilst the GPA contains many contradictions as suggested above, it also marks a shift away from a humanitarian to a developmental vision within which civil society is integral. The idea of a single structure representing the developmental and redistributive challenges of civil society would be deceptive: the transition is being built on the old rubble and old identities are being redefined in order to develop a culture of pluralism. NANGO is putting forward a different vision of a future for civic organisations and providing different ways of working with the IG. Some civics are still supporting political parties and supporting political party positions. Some have pointed to the dangers of co-option and their subsequent emasculation as the watchdogs of the GPA. At the same time, the capacity of CSOs to adjust to a new and fragile environment is being threatened by declining financial resources from donors and a general failure to come up with new strategies for mobilisation and engagement.

Zimbabwean civil society's response to the IG has continued to reveal ideological tensions between its human rights obligations and its need to deal with broader developmental requirements. Political advocacy around issues of human rights and violence often takes centre stage at the expense of developmental issues and issues of social and economic rights, rural development, poverty and inequalities. While public service delivery has remained very poor, with massive water and electricity shortages, poor waste management and poor sanitation remaining the order of the day, civil society has not made a clear and concerted effort to ensure that these issues are addressed by the IG.[56] Since the inception of the GPA, civic activity has been more pronounced on issues of the political transition and the SADC road map towards elections. Little attention has been paid to issues of poverty alleviation, workers' and consumers' rights, community empowerment, economic justice, class inequalities, economic reconstruction and social transformation.[57] Furthermore, economic policy-making decisions have remained largely in the hands of the state and political parties. Zimbabwean civics have not taken up issues of corporate social responsibility and holding corporate bodies accountable for protecting the poor and the most vulnerable. For example, poor mining practices by huge corporate companies have led to toxic waste and heavy metal pollution in some areas.[58] The continued exclusionary use of violence and rhetoric together with the militarisation of politics have created barriers to genuine power-sharing resulting in a politics of continuity.[59] This has forced civil society to work pragmatically within the limitations of the known rather than pushing for a transformative agenda. Civil society representatives have described the IG as 'two governments in one,'[60] meaning that civil society has to work within this reality. Thus strengthening national and regional networks and solidarity around the pertinent issues of socio-economic and political justice will require a balancing act between political engagement and opposition.

Endnotes

1 These figures and estimates for NGOs were given by the NANGO chairperson, Mr Cephas Zinumwe, in an interview with the author in February 2012.

2 These unconfirmed figures of registered organisations came from a telephone interview with a government officer from the Ministry of Labour and Social Welfare in February 2012.

3 S. Moyo, J. Makumbe, and B. Raftopoulos, *NGOs, the State and Politics in Zimbabwe* (Harare: SAPES Books, 2000); Jonathan Moyo, 'Civil Society in Zimbabwe', *Zambezia*, 20 (1), 1993; Sara Rich, 'NGOs and the State in Zimbabwe: Implications for civil society theory'. Unpublished Mimeo, 1998; E. McCandless and E. Pajibo,

Between Perception and Reality: Are NGOs Really Making a Difference? A Report for Mwengo, 2003.

4 L. Laakso, 'Opposition Politics in Independent Zimbabwe', *African Studies Quarterly*, 7 (2/3), 2003.

5 Ibid. p. 3; E. McCandless, 'Polarisation and Transformation in Zimbabwe: Social Movements, Strategy Dilemmas and Change'. Unpublished Ph.D. thesis, 2011; S. Moyo, K. Helliker and T. Murisa (eds) *Contested Terrain: Land Reform and Contemporary Civil Society in Zimbabwe* (Pietermaritzburg: S&S Publishers, 2008).

6 C. Ncube, 'Contesting Hegemony: Civil Society and the Struggle for Social Change in Zimbabwe, 2000-2008'. Unpublished Ph.D. thesis, University of Birmingham, 2010.

7 See N. Bobbio 'Gramsci and the Concept of Civil society', in J. Kean (ed.), *Civil Society and the State: New European Perspectives* (London: University of Westminster Press, 1988). See also J. Hearn, 'The Uses and Abuses of Civil Society in Africa,' *Review of African Political Economy,* 28 (87), 2001.

8 E. McCandless, 'Polarisation and Transformation in Zimbabwe'. p. 216.

9 Jonathan Moyo, 'Civil Society in Zimbabwe'.

10 S. Moyo, J. Makumbe, and B. Raftopoulos, *NGOs the State and Politics in Zimbabwe.* p. 3.

11 S. Rich, 'The State of NGOs in Zimbabwe: Honeymoon over?' *Southern Africa Report*, 12 (3), 1997, p. 17. Also 'Zimbabwe' http://www.era.lib.ed.ac.uk/bitstream/1842/794/SAR_12_3pdf (accessed 31.10.12).

12 S. Dansereau, 'Liberation and Opposition in Zimbabwe', in H. Melber (ed.), *Limits to Liberation in Southern Africa* (Cape Town: HSRC Press, 2003), p. 28. 13 See B. Raftopoulos and L. Sachikonye (eds) *Striking Back: The Labour Movement and The Post-Colonial State in Zimbabwe 1980-2000* (Harare: Weaver Press, 2001).

14 S. Dansereau, 'Liberation and Opposition in Zimbabwe'. p. 27.

15 Ibid. p. 5.

16 M. Ndlovu, *Against the Odds: A History of Zimbabwe Project Trust* (Harare: ZimPro and Weaver Press, 2012).

17 For the full history of the Zimbabwe Project Trust and its programmes see http://www.zpt.co.zw (accessed 7/10/12).

18 L. Sachikonye, *Democracy, Civil Society and the State Social Movements in Southern Africa* (Harare: SAPES Books, 1995) p. 147.

19 For the various views on the one-party state debate see I. Mandaza and L. Sachikonye, (eds), *The One-Party State Debate and Democracy: The Zimbabwe Debate.* (Harare: SAPES Books, 1991).

20 See S. Moyo, et al., *Contested Terrain*.

21 See B. Raftopoulos, 'The Zimbabwe Crisis and the Challenges of the Left'. Public Lecture delivered at the University of KwaZulu-Natal, 23 June 2005.
22 Though never passed into law, the bill did have a negative impact on the activities of NGOs since some sections of its provisions were smuggled into other legislation and used to stifle the activities of civil society organisations. See J. Muzondidya and L. Nyathi-Ndlovu, 'The Legislative and Operational Environment for Civil Society in Zimbabwe', in B. Moyo (ed.), *(Dis)Enabling the Public Sphere in Africa: Civil Society Regulation in Africa* (Johannesburg: Southern Africa Trust and Trust Africa, 2010).
23 See Zimbabwe Human Rights NGO Forum Annual Reports. <http:www.hrforum.org/reports> (accessed 18/8/2012).
24 See S.M. Gallo Mosala, 'The Work Experience of Zimbabwean Migrants in South Africa'. ILO Country Office for Zimbabwe, Issues Paper No. 33, 2008.
25 See B. Raftopoulos and T. Savage, *Zimbabwe: Injustice and Political Reconciliation* (Harare: Weaver Press, 2005); B. Raftopoulos and A. Mlambo (eds) *Becoming Zimbabwe: A History from the Pre-Colonial Period to 2008* (Harare: Weaver Press, 2009); L. M. Sachikonye, *Consolidating Democratic Governance in Southern Africa: The Case of Zimbabwe* (Johannesburg: EISA, 2007).
26 Zimbabwe Institute, 'The State of Civics in Zimbabwe'. A report prepared for the Zimbabwe Institute, September 2008.
27 See Zimbabwe Election Support Network Post Election Update No 1, 30 March to 8 May, 2008. http://www.zesn.org.zw/publications_192 (accessed 7/10/12)
28 See S. Eppel and B. Raftopoulos ,'Political Crisis, Mediation and the Prospects for Transitional Justice in Zimbabwe', in S. Eppel, D. Ndlela, B. Raftopoulos and M. Rupiya, *Developing a Transformation Agenda for Zimbabwe* (Pretoria: IDASA, 2009), p.4.
29 See M. Gwisayi, 'Zimbabwe: Elite deal does not resolve underlying crisis – Aluta Continua', in Links, *International Journal of Socialist Renewal*, 23 September 2008. http://links.org.au/node/647 (accessed 18/8/12).
30 M. Gwisayi in a statement, International Socialist Organisation, 23 September, 2008.
31 ZCTU Press Release, 29 September 2008, 'ZCTU meets with Tsvangirai, rejects GNU'.
32 Ibid.
33 See: http://www.financialgazette.co.zw/national-report/14827-veritas-on-the-conflict.html Accessed 2/11/12.
34 E. Chitando, 'Prayers, Politics and Peace: The church's role in Zimbabwe's crisis', *Open Space* Issue 1, June 2011 p. 47.
35 Ibid. p.47.

36 Z. Gambahaya, 'Tokenism and Deception: How women have been sidelined since the GPA', *Open Space* Issue 1, June 2011, p. 151

37 Since the formation of WOZA, its leaders, Jenni Williams and Magodonga Mahlangu have been arrested 47 and 43 times respectively (personal communication, 2/11/12).

38 A. Arato, 'Civil Society, Transition and Consolidation of Democracy'. Paper presented at the International Conference on Democratic Transitions in Latin America and in Eastern Europe: Rupture and Continuity, 4-6 March 1996, Paris.

39 T.L. Karl, 'Dilemmas of Democratization in Latin America', *Comparative Politics*, 23 (1), 1990, pp 1-21.

40 G. O'Donnell and P. Schmitter, *Transitions from Authoritarian Rule: Tentative Conclusions about Uncertain Democracies* (Baltimore: John Hopkins University Press, 1986) p. 6.

41 E. Masunungure, 'Zimbabwe at the Crossroads: Challenges for Civil Society', *Open Space*, Issue 1, June 2011, p. 126

42 T. Paffenholz and C. Spurk, 'Civil Society, Civic Engagement and Peacebuilding', The World Bank Social Development Papers, Conflict Prevention and Reconstruction Paper No. 36, October 2006.

43 Institute for Justice and Reconciliation, 'Zimbabwe's Government of National Unity: A Two-Year Appraisal'. Report of IJR Policy Advisory Workshop, Cape Town, 10 May 2011.

44 This element of competition for funding, and the need to present problems to donors, came out clearly in the interviews undertaken by some representatives of CSOs and NANGO, February 2012.

45 For a list of CISOMM members, see participating organisations on http://www.cisomm.org

46 Remarks about the CISOMM initiative came from an interview with the CISSOM Co-ordinator based at the ZLHR in January 2012.

47 ZZZCOMP, 'Final Report, Shadowing the Constitution Outreach Process', 2011.

48 'NCA Take Charge ... Threatening No'. *The Zimbabwean*, 4 August 2009.

49 'COPAC the New Frontier', *The Herald* online 21 February 2012.

50 This sentiment came out of interviews the author carried out with some of the representatives of civil society organizations, including NANGO, ISO, ZESN and Crisis in Zimbabwe Coalition, in February 2012.

51 For an analysis of the media coverage of the 2008 elections, see *The Propaganda War on Electoral Democracy: A Report on the Media's Coverage of Zimbabwe's 2008 Elections* (Harare: Media Monitoring Project, 2009).

52 Civil Society Statement to the African Commission on Human Rights, November 2011.

53 Report to the African Commission on Human Rights and Peoples' Rights under Agenda Item 5 (e) Statement on the Human Rights Sitution in Zimbabwe, November 2011. http://www.hrforumzim.org/?s=item+5+%28e%29

54 For example on 9 October 2012 the Energy and Power Development Minister Elton Mangoma was arrested on charges of undermining President Robert Mugabe. http://www.newsday.co.zw/2012/2012/10/10/minister-mangoma-arrested/

55 Civil Society Monitoring Mechanism (CISOMM), Periodic Report, April to May 2011.

56 See K. Zigomo, 'A Community Based Approach to Sustainable Development: The Role of Civil Society in Rebuilding Zimbabwe' (Harare: Solidarity Peace Trust, 2012).

57 Ibid. p. 7.

58 Ibid. p.10.

59 N. Cheeseman and B-M. Tendi, 'Power Sharing in Comparative Perspective: The Dynamics of Unity Government in Kenya and Zimbabwe', *The Journal of Modern African Studies*, 48 (2), 2010.

60 This point came out in interviews with the NANGO Chairperson, Mr Cephas Zinumwe, February 2012.

CHAPTER 5

Politics behind Politics:
African Union, Southern African Development Community and the Global Political Agreement in Zimbabwe

SABELO J. NDLOVU-GATSHENI

Introduction

The mediation of the Zimbabwe crisis that deepened in the 2000s and the facilitation of the implementation of the Global Political Agreement (GPA) that was signed on 15 September 2008 became entangled in complex 'politics behind politics'. This form of politics is informed by questions of power playing itself out at the global, continental, regional, national levels as well as within the key political formations namely the Zimbabwe African National Union-Patriotic Front (ZANU-PF), Movement for Democratic Change (MDCs) and the African National Congress (ANC). ZANU-PF and the two MDC formations have turned the mediation and facilitation process into a site of struggle for state power. Political dynamics within the ANC as well as leadership changes have impinged on the nature and quality of mediation and facilitation.

Disputes over complex issues of sovereignty, democratisation, and redress of the land question have globalised the Zimbabwe problem to the extent that the question of removal of sanctions has been turned by ZANU-PF into an essential pre-requisite for full implementation of GPA. At the same time, legacies of anti-colonialism, histories of liberation struggle-solidarities and realities of personalities and clashes also inform decisions of the Southern African Development Community (SADC) as well as the politics of quiet diplomacy that dominated during President Thabo Mbeki's mediation of the Zimbabwe crisis.

This chapter, therefore, unpacks complex politics lying behind mediation, facilitation and implementation of the GPA covering the period from 2001 to 2012. The first section introduces the idea of 'politics behind politics' of third party mediation that was aimed at finding a solution to the Zimbabwe crisis. The second section briefly outlines the global context within which the Zimbabwe crisis unfolded and how this exacerbated the complexity of the problem that had to be mediated. It also explains the logic behind Thabo Mbeki's adoption of the policy of quiet diplomacy. The third section tracks the beginning of third party mediation that was provoked by the way the government of Zimbabwe went about resolving the land question. The fourth section is focused on formal SADC mediation that is traceable to 2007 when Mbeki was officially mandated to mediate between ZANU-PF and MDC political formations. The fifth section analyses politics that crystallised around the signing of the GPA itself, right up to the formation of the inclusive government in February 2009. The sixth section deals with problematic challenges of implementation of the GPA and the role of President Jacob Zuma who succeeded Mbeki as SADC facilitator. It also discusses the issue of the SADC Election Road Map and the prospect of another election, which is seen as a lasting solution to the Zimbabwe crisis. The last section is the conclusion.

'Politics behind politics' of mediation

The third party mediation process in Zimbabwe became imbricated in and intertwined with complex politics of regime survival on the one hand and regime change on the other at the national level. The equally complex 'politics behind politics' unfolding at the regional and continental levels added to the difficulties of resolving the Zimbabwe problem. The involvement of the African Union (AU) and SADC as guarantors and facilitators of the mediation process has not succeeded in resolving the Zimbabwe problem, partly due to difficulties associated with defining its core elements. These difficulties are compounded by entanglement of the Zimbabwe crisis within complex regional, continental, and international politics. The idea of 'politics behind politics' is intended to capture the multi-layered national, regional, continental and international politics that impinges on the Zimbabwe problem. In the first place, the concept helps in capturing the existence of complex histories of solidarities, camaraderie, and personal ties rooted in the tradition of an anti-colonial liberation struggle, ones which continue to influence current approaches to security and conflict issues as well as SADC mediation.[1]

In the second place, the notion of 'politics behind politics' speaks to how SADC approached and conducted the mediation process through 'closed door' sessions and on the sidelines of its summits. This made it difficult for analysts to understand the internal ructions taking place inside the regional body that were not reflected in its formal communiqués.[2] Perhaps due to the sensitivity and complexity of the Zimbabwe problem, SADC initially preferred the route of quiet as opposed to megaphone diplomacy. It is, however, not easy to establish the extent of the influence of Mbeki as president of South Africa and official SADC mediator on how SADC approached the Zimbabwe problem. What is clear is that SADC's quiet diplomacy only began to change since the time of the Livingstone Summit of the Organ on Politics, Defence and Security that took place on 31 March 2011 in Zambia. During this summit, President Zuma had taken over as the SADC mediator and he presented an openly critical report on the pace of implementation of the GPA and criticised ZANU-PF for continuing to pursue violent and unaccountable politics.[3] This change might have been influenced by MDC-T's lobbying as well as Zuma's efforts to break ranks with Mbeki's soft approach towards ZANU-PF's violations of the GPA. This summit also took place during a time when the Arab Spring was gathering momentum, thus a strong message had to be sent to the Harare disputants about the dangers of not resolving internal problems, if they were to avoid inviting popular uprisings.[4]

To a large extent, the idea of 'politics behind politics' also helps to capture how the internal dynamics within the main Zimbabwean political parties (ZANU-PF, MDC-T and MDC-N), impinged on their approaches to negotiations and interpretations of the GPA as well as its implementation. Across the border, internal dynamics within the ANC, and particularly the openness with which its partners, namely the South African Congress of Trade Unions (COSATU) and South African Communist Party (SACP), sided with the MDC political formations also played a role in shaping the nature and quality of mediation of the crisis and facilitation of the implementation the GPA. The untimely removal of Mbeki from power, and his replacement by Zuma provoked expectations of change in the nature and quality of mediation and facilitation. Zuma, unlike Mbeki, was expected by the opposition formations to take a tough line on ZANU-PF. Zuma's energies as mediator were compromised by internal ructions within the ANC. Now that he has secured ANC endorsement for a second term, there is an expectation that he will re-commit himself to the adherence of Zimbabwe to the SADC Road Map. The rumour that ZANU-PF was trying to use the ousted ANC Youth League leader, Julius Malema, to destabilise the ANC and work with forces opposed to Zuma, might also contribute to the latter taking a firmer stand against ZANU-PF.

What is emphasised in this chapter is that any serious study of mediation of the Zimbabwe crisis and the facilitation of the implementation of GPA must take into account the complex histories lurking behind and hovering above the mediation process. The complex and hidden histories impinged not only on inter-party relations but also on inter-state relations in the region. This is so mainly because the SADC region is still dominated by enduring solidarities among 'sister liberation movements' and 'brother presidents' at the helm of governments in Zimbabwe, South Africa, Angola, Mozambique, Namibia, and Tanzania.[5] This reality led Eldridge Adolfo to argue that:

> The liberation parties in the SADC region have gone through a very painful shared history, where they fought bloody wars together and for each other as brothers/sisters and comrades for many years (and even decades). It is important to acknowledge that these SADC states are still very young and the liberation wars they fought ended as recently as fifteen years ago. Most of the people who were engaged in the liberation struggle—including the peasantry that felt the wrath of both colonial and liberation forces—are still alive. Therefore, this history still holds some significance for the peoples of the SADC region and cannot just simply be swept away. The liberation parties within SADC have continued to develop and strengthen their relationships.[6]

But while it is important to emphasise the role of liberation wartime solidarities in shaping SADC's approach to the Zimbabwe crisis, there is a need to note that SADC is not a homogenous entity. Among its fifteen member states there are some that are more influential than others owing to the size of their economies. For instance, Angola and South Africa have the biggest economies together with strong liberation credentials. Namibia, Mozambique and Tanzania have small economies, but strong liberation credentials, which make them indispensable within the circle of former liberation movements. The Democratic Republic of Congo (DRC) owes its survival to Zimbabwe's military intervention in 1998 and its leader, Joseph Kabila, is therefore loyal to Mugabe. But relations between Zimbabwe and South Africa are more complex because ZANU-PF and the ANC were not close allies during the liberation struggle. ZANU-PF supported the Pan-African Congress (PAC), which split from the ANC in 1959. The ANC had a formal alliance with the Zimbabwe African People's Union (ZAPU), from which ZANU-PF emerged as a breakaway formation in 1963. So there are no strong liberation-war solidarities between the ANC and ZANU-PF.

This was clearly demonstrated during the ANC centenary on 12 January 2012 where a portrait of the veteran nationalist Joshua Nkomo who led ZAPU graced the occasion instead of that of President Robert Mugabe who often justifies his power by harking back to the liberation struggle. At another level, despite both ZANU-PF and ANC coming from a background of fighting protracted liberation struggles against settler and apartheid colonialism, they were not only not closely linked, but the ANC cherishes both its liberation credentials and its commitment to democratic governance. For ZANU-PF, it seems liberation credentials and an economic redistributive agenda have been allowed to overshadow the importance of democratic governance.[7]

At SADC, there seems to be no clear collective voice and message on Zimbabwe. For example, the president of Tanzania, Jakata Kikwete, increasingly became openly critical of President Mugabe and ZANU-PF's democratic and human rights. The same is true for the leader of Botswana, Ian Khama, who went to the extent of offering asylum to the leader of MDC-T, Morgan Tsvangirai, soon after the controversial elections of 2008. Zambia under Levi Mwanawasa was also very critical of Mugabe and ZANU-PF's political conduct. What is distinctive about all these states is that they have witnessed transitions at the presidential level from one leader to another in contradistinction to Zimbabwe which has been under one president since 1980.[8] On a lack of a common vision within SADC, Adolfo had this to say:

> *The emergence of the post-liberation states—Botswana, Malawi, and Zambia—bifurcates SADC's ideology and has contributed to the serious internal divisions that are not reflected in their of-*

> *ficial communiqués. This feature of two political camps within SADC—the liberation parties on one side and the post-liberation parties on the other—has meant that SADC has become a battle ground for politics as opposed to a regional organisation driving one common goal of socio-economic and political integration. [...] The lack of commitment by the SADC states to the common vision as well as the divide between the liberation parties and the post-liberation parties, has somewhat weakened SADC as an organisation in that it is not always pushing or pulling in the same direction.*[9]

But it is premature to categorise members of the SADC into clear-cut liberation parties and post-liberation parties because of similarities in ideology and styles of undemocratic governance in countries like Malawi and Zimbabwe. Malawi under Bingu wa Mutharika had degenerated into authoritarianism and intolerance of dissenting voices, reminding Malawians of the dark days of Kamuzu Banda's long dictatorship. But while the former was on open admirer of President Mugabe, the current president, Joice Banda, does not appear willing to associate her regime with dictators. Her stand became apparent when she refused to allow the president of Sudan, who is wanted at the ICC for crimes against humanity, to attend an AU meeting in Malawi in 2012. ON the other hand, Zambia, under its new President, Michael Sata, is harking back to the common anti-colonial nationalist ideology and is dismissive of the MDC-T leader as a puppet of the West.[10]

At the continental level, the AU has been, since its formation in 2002, a weak organisation, which is still undergoing construction. This weakness was amply demonstrated when it failed to apply its 'African solution to African problems' to the Libyan crisis, and over the fragmentation in the choice of AU chairperson between Jean Ping and Nkosazana Zuma. The Anglophone and Francophone divide has continued to weigh like a nightmare on its cohesiveness.[11] If, indeed, as put by Delphine Lecoutre, Mbeki's mediation in the Ivorian crisis raised question of how an Anglophone African could understand the particular cultural dynamics of a region still shaped by French influence, then the bulk of members of the AU could be asked the same question: how could they understand the dynamics of former settler colony like Zimbabwe, and the concerns of a former liberation movement (ZANU-PF).which had been radicalised by years of an armed liberation struggle?[12]

Posing these questions is meant to dramatise the lack of cohesion within the

AU. As with SADC, the AU has also not been able to speak with one authoritative voice. Some of the key members such as Libya under Colonel Muammur Gaddafi and others were considered sympathetic to ZANU-PF and President Mugabe's actions. The struggle for leadership of Africa between Nigeria and South Africa have also not enabled the AU to capitalise on the leadership role of the two states on conflict resolution. Nigeria and South Africa have competed over which country should represent Africa at the United Nations Security Council.[13] A combination of these weaknesses perhaps explains why the AU has been comfortable to allow SADC to deal with the Zimbabwe problem.

At the global level, Britain's open support for MDC-T and hostility towards ZANU-PF not only culminated in the imposition of 'smart sanctions' but also contributed in further complicating the resolution of the Zimbabwe problem. ZANU-PF added anti-Western politics as a key variable in local contestations over power and made efforts to mobilise SADC to approach the Zimbabwe problem as that of anti-colonial forces versus pro-Western reactionary forces represented by the MDC-T.[14] The net effect of this perception was that the MDC formations found it very difficult to dispel the negative representation as 'running dogs of imperialism' mainly because of their close links with the West. As such, it has also been difficult for liberation parties in SADC to welcome MDC as a legitimate political force of progress. Western powers have condemned ZANU-PF and President Mugabe's leadership on the basis of its failure to afford Zimbabweans democratic and human rights protection. ZANU-PF and Mugabe have hit back at the West accusing it of harbouring re-colonisation agendas in disregard for African countries' national sovereignty. In the SADC region, issues of national sovereignty are guarded jealously by those countries that received juridical independence in the period between 1980 and 1994, after protracted liberation struggles.

The smaller MDC, which was initially led by Professor Arthur Mutambara until 2011, has also been driven by its desire to remain relevant despite its few parliamentary seats. During the negotiations for power-sharing, MDC-M played its cards very well to the extent of being a power broker. It projected the issue of taking national interests seriously ahead of the size of a political following as the key determinant in the negotiations. It also increasingly embraced the discourse of the liberation struggle to set itself apart from MDC-T, which was accused of being a front for Western interests. Now under Professor Welshman Ncube, the smaller MDC (now MDC-N), has continued to play the role of power broker even, for example, during the elections for Speaker of Parliament. It has always strategically positioned itself between ZANU-PF and MDC-T, to the extent that its support is often solicited when it comes to crucial elections. While trying to create a support base on the ground, it has also tried to capitalise on the intellectual power of its leaders, mainly Professors Mutambara and Ncube, to present well-reasoned arguments during negotiations. Ncube, however, gained a new lease of political life when the SADC meeting in Angola refused to recognise Mutambara as a principal and endorsed Ncube. Ncube has also played a pivotal role in the drafting of the final COPAC draft constitution that is awaiting a referendum and its adoption is an essential prerequisite for new elections planned for 2013.

Context of Zimbabwe crisis and third party mediation

The Zimbabwe crisis unfolded within the context of post-Cold War dispensation that was dominated by triumphalism of neo-liberalism. Issues of multilateralism, governance, democracy, human rights, and human security became dominant global concerns. Western powers claimed these values as ethical norms that underpinned their foreign policies. The turn of the millennium also provoked millenarian optimism and dreams of a new and better world order in which democracy and equality of nations would be the norm. But the 9/11 debacle and its aftermath reversed this optimistic perspective as the 'war on terror' became a global issue. It heralded the securitisation of world politics, with the US foreign policy embracing the strategy of regime change as part of its fight against what it considered to be the 'axis of evil' and 'outposts of tyranny.'[15] Inversely, the ideas of, in particular, regime change 'heightened the sensitivities of African states to opposition movements on the continent viewed as the agents of such a strategy'.[16]

For the SADC region, which had experienced the dominance of settler colonialism and become the last part of Africa to gain political independence, the theme of redressing material inequalities left behind by colonial powers was interpreted as part of deepening democracy and social justice.[17] SADC, as an outgrowth and product of liberation struggles, sought to lead a new struggle for economic justice and development once apartheid in South Africa was defeated. Consequently, the nationalist ideology with its emphasis on the defence of national sovereignty and resolution of the national question was being relaunched in countries like Zimbabwe where the land question had remained unresolved. At the same time, opposition and civil society, supported by the

West, forcefully pushed for democratisation and respect for human rights. The SADC region as a whole was seized by the spirit of transformation and critical self-appraisal that was captured by Nelson Mandela's statement at the official opening of the SADC Summit on 8 September 1997:

> Our dream of Africa's rebirth as we enter the new millennium, depends as much as anything on each country and each regional grouping in the continent, committing itself to the principles of democracy, respect for human rights and the basic tenets of good governance.[18]

While the West emphasised the morality of intervention in those states that did not respect human rights, SADC remained resolute in safeguarding the hard-won national sovereignties of member states. As the West pushed the agenda of the 'right to protect' (R2P), African leaders began to toy with new principles of finding 'African solutions to African problems'.[19] The logic was that such an approach would guarantee an African agency in dealing with issues of the time, and foreclose external interference particularly from the ex-colonial powers.

But complexities of the Zimbabwe crisis presented the SADC with a daunting challenge. For the first time the region had to deal with the political fallout of the first liberation movement led by a veteran nationalist to lose an election to a political formation with no liberation credentials.[20] While the ability of the Movement for Multiparty Democracy (MMD) led by Fredrick Chiluba to defeat the United Independence Party (UNIP) led by the veteran nationalist Kenneth Kaunda set the precedent, no one expected that ZANU-PF would suffer the same fate because of its projection of extraordinary liberation credentials.

Such a situation sent political shockwaves down the spine of other former liberation movements in power in the SADC region, which understood and represented themselves as champions of democratisation. They expected to shepherd and control the concept rather than give way to new political formations without liberation struggle credentials. Regime change was not envisaged as part of the democratisation process. But the events in Zimbabwe complicated many issues. ZANU-PF as a former liberation movement exposed itself as an undemocratic force that survived by violence. As the party and Mugabe intensified violence it became hard for other former liberation movements to condone what was happening. But ZANU-PF's push for land reform, its anti-colonial rhetoric, and pan-African pretensions enabled it to continue claiming to be pursuing a decolonial and redemptive agenda. Zimbabwe became a site for contestations between decolonisation values of social and economic justice vis-à-vis the post-Cold War universal claims of good governance, human rights and liberal democracy.[21]

South Africa under Nelson Mandela upped the stake on issues of democracy and human rights in the region and continent. In his 1993 article in *Foreign Affairs*, Mandela stated that: 'Human rights will be the light that guides our foreign affairs'.[22] But his foreign policy soon confronted challenges in its dealings and reactions to the hanging of Ogoni civil rights activist, Ken Saro-Wiwa and his compatriots in 1995; the Lesotho debacle that witnessed deployment of the South African Defence Force (SADF) into a neighbouring state; and the DRC crisis that involved the military intervention of Zimbabwean, Namibian and Angolan forces on the side of Laurent Kabila's government in 1998.[23]

Mandela took a hard line on Nigeria, including calling for its suspension from the Commonwealth and imposition of sanctions. On the DRC crisis, Mandela pushed for dialogue and negotiations. These actions were at variance with other African leaders. On Lesotho, South Africa found itself accused of continuing the military bullying and unilateralism of the apartheid regime in dealing with regional issues in favour of South African business interests that benefitted from the US$4 billion Katse Dam Project.[24] It would seem that Mandela had pitched his foreign policy on too high a moral ground to the chagrin of a majority of African leaders who doubted its practicability.

Thus when Mbeki succeeded Mandela as president, he had to re-articulate the South African foreign policy away from accusations of bullying and unilateralism. South African foreign policy became predicated on the precept of African Renaissance. It was informed by the ideas of 'Africa, define yourself'.[25] Under Mbeki, South Africa had to act in concert with other African states to avoid being accused of being a white state led by black leaders who are hostage to white power and interests. Multilateralism occupied the centre of South African foreign policy. Promotion of peace and security and pursuit of sustainable development and poverty reduction became South African foreign policy's foremost goal, without necessarily shedding concerns about democracy and human rights.[26]

Mbeki assumed a leading role in the process of building pan-African institutions such as the African Union (AU); the New Partnership for Development of Africa (NEPAD), African Peer Review Mechanism (APRM) and construction of 'a robust continental peace and security architecture anchored in regional mechanisms and linked to the United Nations' infrastructure of global peace'.[27] All these initiatives were informed by the positive spirit of multilateralism whereby African problems had to be solved through African concert cascading from the AU and regional communities. The Zimbabwe problem became one of the tests for SADC's emerging multilateral approach to the resolution of contemporary African problems. The test took the form of how to balance the imperatives of liberal democracy and human rights on the one hand, and those of distributive justice (accompanied by violence, militarisation, and authoritarianism), on the other.

Beginning of the third party mediation and the land question

The land question and how ZANU-PF and Mugabe sought to resolve it through the controversial Fast-Track Land Reform Programme (FTLRP) became the first development that provoked regional and international concerns about the Zimbabwe issues. The Blantyre SADC Summit of 2001 became the first attempt by the regional body to resolve the Zimbabwe crisis.[28] At this time, the crisis was defined as an issue to do with land redistribution, which had to be done urgently but in an orderly fashion. The problem was also understood as a bilateral one involving Zimbabwe and the former colonial power, Britain. This is why the Blantyre SADC Summit welcomed the initiative of President Olusegun Obasanjo of Nigeria to mediate between Zimbabwe and the United Kingdom. A task force comprising of the then SADC Troika, Botswana, Mozambique and South Africa was established, to work with the government of Zimbabwe on economic and political issues affecting the country.[29] The SADC and South Africa pledged to assist Zimbabwe by persuading the international community in general, and the United Kingdom in particular, to honour the financial pledges that were made at the Lancaster House Conference in 1979 and at the Donor Conference of 1998.

At the same time, SADC made it clear that it was against disorderly land reform involving farm invasions and violence.[30] This early SADC mediation initiative did not succeed because of a combination of a lack of co-operation from the Western powers, which failed to release funding, and ZANU-PF and Mugabe who decided to go ahead with FTLRP. By then, there was no official mediator to deal consistently with the Zimbabwe problem. South Africa could not take a tough stance on how Zimbabwe was handling the land issue partly because the country is sitting on an even worse situation regarding the land question and partly because ZANU-PF and Mugabe had deferred its radical land reform in the early 1990s in order to allow the South African transition from apartheid to take place unencumbered by a racial flare-up related to land redistribution on the other side of the border.³¹

Obasanjo's mediation initiative that preceded the SADC Summit of August 2001 resulted in the Abuja Agreement of 6 November 2001. The Agreement stated that:

> Land is at the core of the crisis in Zimbabwe and cannot be separated from other issues of concern to the Commonwealth such as the rule of law, respect for human rights, democracy and the economy. A programme of land reform is, therefore, crucial to the resolution of the problem.³²

The Abuja Agreement was consummated as part of the Commonwealth initiative informed by its principles enshrined in the Harare Declaration of 1998.³³ The Abuja Agreement recognised historical injustices informing ZANU-PF and Mugabe's agenda of land distribution and called for a transparent and equitable rectification of unequal landownership. Britain re-affirmed its commitment to a significant financial contribution to the land reform programme and its undertaking to encourage other international donors to do the same.³⁴ But while the Abuja Agreement had identified the land question as the key problem in Zimbabwe, other debates were raging which doubted this and interpreted the Zimbabwe problem as a crisis arising out of misgovernance, mismanagement of the economy, lack of democracy and a political struggle to retain power by an unpopular regime. In this discourse, land reform was nothing but a political gimmick.³⁵ The Abuja Agreement failed due to lack of compliance by the Zimbabwe government which did not make any meaningful efforts to restore political sanity through the restoration of rule of law, stop violence, or prevent new farm invasions. On the other hand, Britain and the international community also failed to comply with pledges to provide finance for an orderly land reform.³⁶

South Africa was concerned about the consequences of a political and economic implosion in Zimbabwe. Therefore, Mbeki actively worked with Obasanjo in trying to mediate on the sidelines of the Commonwealth but met with a combination of obduracy and belligerence from ZANU-PF.³⁷ Mbeki and Obasanjo's attempts to facilitate dialogue between ZANU-PF and MDC also failed because the ruling party insisted on being the only guardian of a sacred, sacrosanct, and non-negotiable legitimacy that did not derive from any electoral victory but on its huge sacrifices during the liberation struggle. It went further to deliberately distort the essence of any dialogue with the MDC as an act of negotiating away Zimbabwe's sovereignty and compromising on the sacred tenets of the liberation struggle.[38] Such arrogance from ZANU-PF closed the doors for any breakthrough by Mbeki and Obasanjo in 2002. At the same time, MDC was equally committed to the belief that it was possible for it to win elections and form the next government. In short, what can be said about early attempts at mediation is that they took place at a time when the situation in Zimbabwe was not ripe for any successful third party intervention. The Harare disputants had not yet reached what Ira Zartman termed 'a hurting stalemate' capable of facilitating the transformation of a zero-sum mentality into 'positive mentality.'[39]

But between the 2002 and 2005 elections, SADC and South Africa tried to persuade the Harare disputants to adhere to the SADC Principles and Guidelines Governing Democratic Elections. The MDC also tried to push for the creation of an environment in which free and fair elections would be possible. This pressure led to some piecemeal reforms in 2004 taking the form of the establishment of a five-person Zimbabwe Electoral Commission (ZEC); establishment of an ad hoc electoral court/tribunal within six months of elections; reduction of polling days from two to one, as well the as abolition of mobile polling stations; use of visible and indelible ink; and replacement of wooden ballot boxes with transparent ones.[40] The result was the relatively free and fair elections of 2005. The SADC observer team deemed the elections credible. But it did not resolve the Zimbabwe crisis, as the MDC continued to cry foul and to claim that it had again been cheated of victory through a combination of the use of violence, repressive legislation and outright rigging by ZANU-PF. The pursuit of free and fair elections as a solution for the Zimbabwe crisis therefore intensified after 2005.

It was in 2005 that the AU also tried to intervene in Zimbabwe through the appointment of former Mozambican President Joaquim Chissano as its special representative to Zimbabwe. Chissano's mission was to try and persuade President Mugabe and ZANU-PF to open negotiations with the MDC formations. Chissano did not make any headway as he was rebuffed by the ZANU-PF government which had calculated that its best chance was to put the Zimbabwe question into the SADC court, where there was a greater possibility of Mugabe and his party influencing decisions in its favour.[41] Since then, the AU has had only a limited role in the internal affairs of Zimbabwe beyond sending election observer teams at elections and currently by acting as the guarantor of the GPA. The AU seems comfortable with SADC assuming direct involvement in the resolution of the Zimbabwe question, while playing a supportive role and retaining Zimbabwe within its radar as evidenced by its occasional featuring in the agendas and communiqués of the Peace and Security Council and the AU Assembly of Heads of State and regular Government reports.[42]

On 1 July 2008, the eleventh Summit of the AU Assembly of Heads of State and Government took place in Sharm el-Sheik in Egypt where the Zimbabwe question was part of the agenda. This Summit took place soon after Mugabe had organised a sham presidential run-off marred by extreme violence that led MDC-T leader Morgan Tsvangirai to withdraw from the race. Mugabe went ahead with the election and declared himself winner and was quickly sworn-in as president of Zimbabwe. While MDC formations expected the AU to take a stern position including suspending Zimbabwe from the AU and barring Mugabe from attending its summits, the AU allowed Mugabe to attend, and then simply acknowledged that the elections had not been free and fair. The AU, however, went further to push for negotiations among the Harare disputants to reach an agreement, one which they hoped would result in stabilisation of the country. The AU also endorsed Mbeki as SADC mediator on Zimbabwe.[43] In summary, the Egypt Summit produced three points: that violence negated the credibility of the June 27 election; the election did not reflect the will of the people; and consequently, the outcome was not legitimate.

On the basis of this, the AU recommended further mediation for a power-sharing arrangement. For ZANU-PF and Mugabe, who had lost the elections, it was a political breakthrough; the AU recommendations allowed him to remain in power despite this. Thus, on 11 February 2009 the AU Commission Chairperson Jean Ping came to Harare to participate in the inauguration of Robert Mugabe as president and Morgan Tsvangirai as prime minister in line with the GPA. This solution gave ZANU-PF and Mugabe a new lease of political life despite having lost elections to MDC-T on 29 March 2008.

Thabo Mbeki's quiet diplomacy and SADC mediation

While Mbeki has been active as a mediator on Zimbabwe since 2002, he was only formally endorsed by SADC in 2007. This followed the embarrassing violence that was unleashed by the Zimbabwe government on opposition leaders on Sunday, 11 March 2007.[44] The SADC decision to intensify mediation commenced with an Extraordinary SADC Heads of State Summit in Tanzania held on 28-29 March 2007, when Mbeki was officially endorsed to continue dialogue between the Harare disputants. The same summit appealed to Britain to honour its pledges to provide finance for an orderly land reform. Finally, the SADC summit also voiced opposition to the imposition of sanctions on Zimbabwe by the Western powers.

What must be noted is that during this time, Mbeki, as an African leader, espoused a broad African grand design that crystallised around the philosophy of African Renaissance. His foreign policy had an expansive scope beyond South Africa's immediate national interests. It included a determination to show that Africa was able to take charge of her destiny and use African solutions to solve African problems. Mbeki's grand vision encompassed a delicate balancing of the strategic imperatives of South Africa, the West, Africa, the Global South and the wider global world.[45] Mbeki's mediation of the Zimbabwe crisis, therefore, had to be done in such a way that it did not tarnish South Africa's continental ambitions and without sacrificing Western support.[46] Africa's support was desperately needed to bolster South Africa's claim for a middle-power position in global politics. Re-articulation of the ideology of pan-Africanism was Mbeki's pre-occupation as he campaigned for the reform of the asymmetrical global order. To Chris Landsberg Mbeki's foreign policy stood on these legs: consolidation of the African agenda, South-South co-operation, North-South dialogue, strengthening bilateral relations, and promotion of global governance in areas of political and security and socio-economic issues.[47] Even the recent white paper on South Africa's foreign policy, emphasises pan-Africanism, South-South solidarity informed by the spirit of the Bandung Conference of 1955, opposition to colonialism and *ubuntu* as its core tenets.[48]

The policy of quiet diplomacy was a cog in Mbeki's grand design intended to prevent alienation of some African regimes from his plans. Quiet diplomacy did not arise out of a vacuum. It was informed partly by attempts to bury the foreign policy mistakes that were noticeable under the Mandela regime. It was also Mbeki's way of dealing with strong undercurrents of African solidarity and avoiding the risk of South Africa being isolated by other African states. Stephen Chan noted that Mbeki's approach to the Zimbabwe problem was also informed by experiences of South African mediation in Burundi, the DRC, and other parts of Africa.[49]

Quiet diplomacy allowed space for respect for the camaraderie that emanated from politics of liberation. It enabled Mbeki to stave off the perception of him being used by the West as its 'point man' to solve Zimbabwe's problems. It also facilitated Mbeki's working behind the scenes to prevent Zimbabwe from degenerating into a failed state.[50] Mbeki made it clear that his aim regarding Zimbabwe was 'to ensure that Zimbabwe does not end up in a situation of isolation, confronted by an array of international forces it cannot defeat, condemned to sink into an ever-deepening social and economic crisis that would result in the reversal of so many of the gains of the national democratic revolution'.[51]

Other factors also informed the logic of quiet diplomacy. These included the ANC's suspicious view of the MDC to the extent of seeing it as nothing but a symptom of the weaknesses and errors committed by ZANU-PF, which, in their view, could be corrected. The ANC tried to support those it identified as reformers within ZANU-PF who would avoid violence as they worked to win a credible election. What the ANC sought to prevent was what it considered to be the danger of a regime change via the ballot box in which MDC won elections outright. The ANC also doubted whether the MDC would have the capacity to run a successful state. The closeness of the MDC to the West also contributed to increasing anxieties about its future role in the region.[52] But when the MDC performed very well in the 2000 general elections, the ANC changed its thinking and accepted that the party could not be easily dismissed despite its fear that the Zimbabwean military and security sectors would not accept an elected MDC government.

It was within this context that Mbeki's mediation emphasised the need for national dialogue between the major parties. The mediation was aimed at developing an understanding of the differences among the Harare disputants in order for them to reach a political compromise and to persuade them to commit to resolution of the Zimbabwe crisis through democratic means including free and fair elections in 2008.[53] The process which began in mid-2007 soon yielded agreement on a package of constitutional, electoral and other reforms aimed at securing freedom of speech, assembly, and expression and these were quickly passed by the Zimbabwe Parliament in December 2007.

But ZANU-PF resolved to have harmonised parliamentary, presidential, and council elections in March 2008, without a new constitution in place. Their logic was that the opposition formations would be unable to campaign effectively in such a short time. The lack of agreement on the date for elections and ZANU-PF's unilateral decision to declare that they would be held on 29 March 2008 resulted in a deadlock,[54] though eventually the MDC conceded to the declared date. The MDC-T political formation won the general election and its presidential candidate got more votes than Mugabe who stood for ZANU-PF: for the first time since 1980, the ruling party and its leader lost elections to an opposition party.

SADC and Mbeki must be credited for steering Zimbabwe into credible elections. However, they both failed to defend the outcome from being spoiled by the losers who were still in control of the state's coercive instruments of violence. This plunged Zimbabwe into a deeper political/legitimacy crisis. Zandile Bhengu argued that 'power politics is what informed the SADC mediation at the expense of the electorate and democracy in Zimbabwe. As a result, the future of democracy in this country and region at large could be a fragile one'.[55]

Election crisis, SADC and the bumpy road to the GPA

The crisis that befell Zimbabwe following the post-29 March elections is well captured by Eldred V. Masunungure who correctly characterised ZANU-PF's political behavior as a form of 'defying the winds of change'.[56] On realising that the MDC-T had won, ZANU-PF, as the losing party, did everything in its power to confuse the situation, testing the electorate's patience and power, testing the opposition's ability to move from electoral victory to state power, and testing the international and regional bodies' preparedness to intervene in Zimbabwe in support of democracy.

This test took the form of delaying announcement of the results of the presidential poll for over five weeks. When they were finally announced the MDC-T candidate had won but without meeting the 50% plus one threshold required by the new electoral law to make one an outright winner. In such a situation, a presidential run-off had to be held.[57] The presidential run-off turned out to be nothing but 'electoral cleansing' that culminated not only in an election crisis but also a political legitimacy logjam.[58]

SADC and Mbeki had to respond to the crisis. On 12 April 2008, the late Zambian President Levy Mwanawasa in his capacity as SADC chairperson convened an extraordinary summit of Heads of State and Government. Surprisingly, Mbeki did not consider this summit necessary as he denied there was any crisis in Zimbabwe. This view further discredited him as a mediator among opposition circles. It is still not clear whether Mbeki's denial of the existence of a crisis in Zimbabwe was consistent with the tenets of quiet diplomacy. At the SADC summit, Mwanawasa argued that the solution to the Zimbabwe crisis was to hold another election that would be conducted in strict accordance with SADC Principles and Guidelines Governing Democratic Elections. But the post-29 March situation in Zimbabwe had proven that conducting elections according to SADC Principles and Guidelines without a strategy of enforcement was as good as useless in situations where entrenched dictatorships had the will to subvert the people's choice.[59] The post-29 March election-crisis exposed the weaknesses of SADC as it failed to put pressure on ZANU-PF and Mugabe to desist from subverting the election results and stop the violence. The open condemnation of ZANU-PF and Mugabe came from Botswana whose president (Ian Khama) refused to recognise Mugabe as president. Botswana's Vice-President, Lieutenant General Mopati Merafhe, denounced Mugabe at the AU Summit in Egypt and called for Mugabe's exclusion from attending SADC and AU meetings.[60]

While the opposition formations expected Mbeki to openly denounce the presidential run-off and to fully recognise the results of the 29 March 2008 polls as the only basis for negotiations, the reality is that Mbeki lacked any coercive power vis-à-vis Mugabe and ZANU-PF despite being endorsed as mediator by SADC, the United Nations (UN) and the AU – three powerful multilateral institutions. Mbeki engaged in post-29 March mediation as a weakened politician who was also fighting for survival back home. In the first place, the ANC, which has never been a homogeneous political formation with a common view on Zimbabwe, was sending mixed signals that further discredited Mbeki.[61] By this time, Zuma openly criticised ZANU-PF and Mugabe for violation of human rights, and denying the people of Zimbabwe democracy.

As Mbeki was busy mediating in Zimbabwe, his party was experiencing unprecedented intra-party divisions that culminated in the Polokwane Conference in December 2008 where his presidency of the party was challenged and won by Jacob Zuma. The ANC eventually recalled him as state president. There is no doubt that the Harare disputants were closely observing the decline of Mbeki's power, and this made it more difficult for him to maintain much credibility.[62]

The negotiations and mediation took a new twist after the June 2008 presidential run-off. Previously, the mediation was all about creating conditions for free and fair elections. Now Mbeki was faced with trying to resolve the problems of a country that had had no legitimate government since the elections of March 2008 and was engrossed in the inferno of massive post-election violence involving regular and irregular military sectors. The thrust of the negotiations and mediation was thus towards the creation of a government of National Unity in preparation for another free and fair election. Kenya, after the violent 2007 elections, had set a precedent for Zimbabwe to follow. The politics of power-sharing had become fashionable in situations where political formations, which were entrenched but experiencing diminishing popularity and legitimacy, refused to leave power.[63] Throughout their participation in the mediation process the MDC political formations insisted that the negotiations be premised on the results of the 29 March elections, which they considered credible. They also insisted that the results of the 29 March elections reflected the will of the electorate and hence must form the benchmark for negotiations.

ZANU-PF on the other hand, wanted MDC formations to recognise it as a legitimate government based on the botched June presidential run-off. What led the political formations to negotiate were the stark political realities facing them: despite emerging victorious in the 29 March 2008 elections, the MDC political formations were prevented by ZANU-PF from ascending to power and its support base was exposed to unprecedented and unbearable violence. ZANU-PF clung to power by violence but its legitimacy was completely eroded.[64] Added to this, the Zimbabwean economy continued to degenerate to its lowest ebb and international, continental, and regional pressure together with sanctions, contributed to ZANU-PF's decision to accept negotiations as the only game in town if it was to survive politically.

It is within this context that the Harare disputants agreed to sign a Memorandum of Understanding (MOU) on 21 July 2008, as a first step to epitomising their commitment towards the resolution of the crisis. The issues that ZANU-PF put down as pre-conditions to continue negotiations included removal of sanctions, acceptance of irreversibility of the land question, and an end to external interference amongst others. On the MDC formations' side, the question of violence, hate speech, protection of civil and political rights, and the rule of law were of immediate concern.[65] Symbolically, the MOU placed the concerns of the key political parties on an equal footing and allowed all of them to be legitimate issues that needed to be negotiated.[66] To that extent, it was a breakthrough for the next step in negotiations.

But because the Harare disputants across the political divides sought to use the negotiations to secure state power, moving from the MOU to the GPA became intractable. ZANU-PF, which was facing what Brian Raftopoulos terms 'an organic political and economic crisis' has used 'the space to reconfigure and renegotiate the terms of its existence with the opposition, civil society and international community.'[67] Raftopoulos' argument is reinforced by Richard Bourne who suggests that the GPA 'represented a desire by ZANU-PF to retain power, in the face of electoral defeat and international skepticism, while seeking some economic revival and the removal of individual sanctions and asset freezes which inconvenienced 200 of its own elite.'[68]

The consummation of the GPA was delayed as key political parties jostled for government posts and as they calculated the amount of power each party would enjoy in a future unity government. Finally, it was on 15 September 2008 that the GPA was signed as a basis for a power-sharing arrangement that would reflect the balance of political power in the country.[69] The signing of the GPA marked Mbeki's success as a mediator though he was criticised for bias for taking a soft approach towards Mugabe and ZANU-PF's political transgressions. What is often ignored by his critics is that he was dealing with a very complicated situation where legitimate issues of land redistribution became entangled with the politics of regime survival as well as an opposition force that sought to oppose anything that had to do with ZANU-PF.

What must also be noted is that dealing with ZANU-PF and Mugabe, and trying to convince them to take a different political trajectory from their chosen one was not an easy task. This is a point articulated by Daniel Compagnon who notes that 'South Africa's "quiet diplomacy" was not rewarded with a more loyal cooperation from the Zimbabwean authorities. On several occasions since 2000, a high profile meeting between Mbeki and Mugabe, either in Harare or during an SADC summit, would lead to the announcement by Mbeki's office of a breakthrough, only to be contradicted a few days or weeks later by Harare's actions such as a new repressive law or Mugabe's inflammatory speeches.'[70] Mbeki was dealing with typically irascible political actors who were difficult to convince to commit to anything except what they considered would give them political mileage and enhance regime security. ZANU-PF and Mugabe have enjoyed a long period of purporting to be the model of a progressive liberation movement in the SADC region. Mugabe has enjoyed being considered a nationalist icon until his thunder was stolen by Nelson Mandela in the 1990s. He is still one of the senior veteran nationalists in the region who finds it hard to be tutored by Mbeki on his political behaviour.[71]

But what is often ignored is that Mbeki actually achieved two key important results that changed the course of the Zimbabwean political trajectory and content of political conversations among the Harare disputants. The first is that Mbeki's skillful mediation was responsible for the relatively credible harmonised elections of March 2008. Secondly, as Richard Bourne argues, Mbeki also worked behind the scenes to stimulate the emergence of a breakaway ZANU-PF candidate in Simba Makoni, which according to him 'set the stage for a fairer election, and one that Morgan Tsvangirai could win'.[72]

Thus when Mbeki exited the political scene as mediator, he had managed to negotiate the GPA. Bourne argues that the process of actually 'converting the GPA into a working, if sometimes dysfunctional, government took almost five months of arduous negotiation over portfolios, with an enfeebled Thabo Mbeki trying to assist as SADC facilitator, though no longer South African president.'[73] All this proves Mbeki's commitment to see Zimbabwe return to stability even without the achievement of democratisation, which needs a long-term political paradigm shift that can only be done by Zimbabweans actively participating in the political process and forcing their leaders to be accountable to the citizens. The inclusive government was installed in February 2009, with the mandate to drive economic recovery, set the country on a course of democratisation including facilitating the making of a people-driven constitution and creating the conditions for the return of Zimbabwe to full political legitimacy underpinned by free and fair elections. To an extent, Mbeki succeeded in his mediation role.

But when President Jacob Zuma took over as the new mediator, there were expectations especially among opposition and civil society circles that Mbeki's departure as mediator marked an end to the era of South Africa's quiet diplomacy. This was based on Zuma's open criticism of ZANU-PF and Mugabe before he assumed the national presidency of South Africa. Zuma's strong ally COSATU was also openly critical of the situation that was obtaining in Zimbabwe and was often seen as sympathetic to the MDC formations because of their roots in the Zimbabwe Congress of Trade Unions (ZCTU). This expectation has not yet been fully realised though Zuma continued to voice criticism of Mugabe and ZANU-PF's political behaviour.

Jacob Zuma, implementation of GPA and Election Road Map for Zimbabwe

President Zuma continued with a series of talks initiated by Mbeki. His first change was to appoint a facilitation team comprised of Mac Maharaj, Lindiwe Zulu, and Charles Ngqakula to assist him with facilitation of the implementation of the GPA. This action was hailed by many people as a sign that Zuma meant serious business on resolving the Zimbabwe problem. Zuma also brought the South African Department of International Relations and Co-operation (DIRCO) to play the instrumental role of providing the technical support for the intervention by the presidency and the facilitation team.[74]

SADC and President Zuma were expected to facilitate the implementation of the GPA within the different conditions described in chapter one. The Joint Monitoring and Implementation Committee (JOMIC) that was established under the GPA to be the internal mechanism of conflict and dispute resolution during the implementation of the GPA has not been effective, having been sidelined by the political parties in preference for SADC. But so far, the latter has also not been effective in pushing harder for the Harare disputants, who are now partners in the inclusive government, to fully implement the GPA to the letter. What has happened is that between 2009 and 2011 a number of SADC Summits of Heads of State and Government as well as the Troika of the Organ on Politics, Defence and Security Co-operation, have been called, and have subsequently issued a series of communiqués urging the parties in the inclusive government to implement the GPA, on occasion even giving timelines. However, these communiqués were simply ignored by the Harare disputants. Moreover, ZANU-PF and Mugabe in particular, and to a much lesser extent MDC-T and Tsvangirai, have added new conditions for the implementation of GPA. At one time the so-called outstanding issues ballooned to 27 areas of concern.[75]

Indeed, the political formations in the inclusive government have failed to implement 24 out of 27 areas of dispute, which they reported to the SADC Troika in August 2010 as having been agreed upon. Prior to the August SADC Troika Summit held in Namibia, the political parties in the inclusive government reported that they had agreed on an 'implementation matrix', but a few days after the summit, Mugabe made it clear that he would not implement any of the GPA issues unless sanctions were removed. The failure by the political parties to implement the GPA finally led the SADC Troika Summit held in Livingstone in Zambia on 31 March 2011 to take a more openly critical view towards Mugabe and ZANU-PF as the major stumbling block to the full implementation of the GPA and the general smooth functioning of the inclusive government.

This critical communiqué was informed by Zuma's presentation of a frank and critical report on the negative political behaviour of Mugabe and ZANU-PF for the first time. The communiqué called for an immediate end to violence, intimidation, hate speech, harassment and any other action that contradicted the letter and spirit of the GPA.[76] The Troika pledged to appoint a team of officials to join the facilitation team and to work with JOMIC to ensure monitoring, evaluation and implementation of the GPA.[77] For the first time as argued by Murithi and Mawadza, 'It was a moment of truth in which SADC read the riot act to Mugabe.'[78] The Extraordinary Summit of SADC Heads of State and Government held in Sandton in South Africa on 11-12 June 2011 did not dispute Zuma's report and the decisions of the Troika taken at the Livingstone Troika Summit; rather it 'noted' them.[79]

What is presently pre-occupying SADC is the roadmap to fresh elections in Zimbabwe. SADC and South Africa are insisting that there can be no elections without clear criteria ensuring their credibility premised on their 'freeness and fairness'. The political parties in the inclusive government are under pressure to prepare for elections that meet the SADC Principles and Guidelines Governing Democratic Elections. There seem to be consensus among SADC members that only elections can resolve the Zimbabwe crisis, one which has preoccupied SADC since the time of the controversial land reform programme. Internally, ZANU-PF and Mugabe have been trying to push for early elections ever since 2010 whereas MDC-T has been pushing for institutional reforms, including the adoption of a new constitution and security sector reform, before any new elections can take place in Zimbabwe. Similarly, MDC-N is warning against any rush to elections without the necessary reforms being completed.

Conclusion

One can conclude that at the centre of the mediation has been shifting definitions of core issues that constituted the Zimbabwe problem and that needed resolution. Prior to 2002, the problem was defined as a bilateral one involving Zimbabwe and Britain over the land question that needed to be urgently resolved. Between 2002 and 2008, the search was for how to end violence and how to create conditions for credible elections. After 2008, the problem shifted from pushing for credible elections as a solution to the Zimbabwe problem to a search for a power-sharing arrangement in a context where there was no legitimate government in Harare. Currently, the Harare disputants have gone full circle to the issue of elections as a resolution of the Zimbabwe problem. This push for elections is taking place within a context in which SADC mediation and facilitation has lost momentum. The key facilitator is pre-occupied with local problems rocking the ANC, and ZANU-PF is taking advantage of the situation to push for elections before the completion of key reforms. There is nothing that indicates any change for the better in implementation of the GPA and the reform process is protracted and slow as ZANU-PF seems not keen to continue even with the constitutional reform exercise. The present remains murky and the future looks precarious as long as there is no political paradigm shift on the side of Harare disputes to save Zimbabwe from another botched election, whose consequences are too appalling to contemplate.

ENDNOTES

1 S. J. Ndlovu-Gatsheni, 'Reconstructing the Implications of Liberation Struggle History on SADC Mediation in Zimbabwe' (SouthAfrican Institute of International Affairs (SAIIA) Occasional Paper No. 94, September 2011).
2 E. Adolfo, 'The Collision of Liberation and Post-Liberation Politics within SADC: A Study on SADC and the Zimbabwean Crisis', (Stockholm: Swedish Defence Research Agency (FOI) Research Paper, June, 2009), p. 14.
3 SADC Communiqué Summit of the Organ Troika on Politics, Defence and Security Cooperation, Livingstone, Republic of Zambia, 31 March 2011; B. Raftopoulos, 'STP-Zimbabwe Update No. 3, June 2011: Beyond Livingstone', 24 June, Solidarity Peace Trust: http://www.solidaritypeacetrust.org/1079/spt-zimbabwe-update-no-3/ Accessed on 20/12/2011; J. Moyo, 'Unmasking SADC Troika Circus in Zambia', in http://www.newzimbabwe.com/blog/index.php/2011/04/jmoyo/unmasking-sadc-troika-circ Accessed 8/11/2011.
4 On the Arab Spring, see F. Manji and S. Ekine (eds), *African Awakening: The Emerging Revolutions* (Oxford: Pambazuka Press, 2012).
5 W. C. Reed, 'International Politics and National Liberation: ZANU and the Politics of Contested Sovereignty in Zimbabwe', in *African Studies Review,* 36 (2), (1993), pp. 36-67; N. James, 'When "Messiahs" Turn "Persecutors": Reflecting on the Blocked Transition of Liberation Movements in Africa: Case Study of ZANU-PF'

(Unpublished Master of Laws Dissertation, Faculty of Law, Universidade Eduardo Mondlane, 30 October 2009); S. Badza, 'Zimbabwe's 2008 Harmonized Elections: Regional and International Reaction', in E. V. Masunungure (ed.), *Defying the Winds of Change: Zimbabwe's 2008 Elections*, (Harare: Weaver Press and the Konrad Adenauer Foundation, 2009), pp. 149-175; Sabelo J. Ndlovu-Gatsheni, 'Angola-Zimbabwe Relations: A Study in the Search for Regional Alliances', in *The Roundtable*, 99 (411), (December 2010), pp. 631-653.

6 E. Adolfo, 'The Collision of Liberation and Post-Liberation Politics within SADC', p. 7.

7 S. J. Ndlovu-Gatsheni, *Do 'Zimbabweans' Exist? Trajectories of Nationalism, National Identity Formation and Crisis in a Postcolonial State*, (Bern: Peter Lang AG, 2009) and S. J. Ndlovu-Gatsheni, *The Zimbabwean Nation-State Project: A Historical Diagnosis of Identity and Power-Based Conflicts in a Postcolonial State*, (Uppsala: The Nordic Africa Institute, 2011).

8 S. J. Ndlovu-Gatsheni, 'Reconstructing the Implications of Liberation Struggle History on SADC Mediation in Zimbabwe'.

9 Adolfo, 'The Collision of Liberation and Post-Liberation Politics within SADC,' pp. 24-25.

10 President Michael Sata, 'Tsvangirai Is a Stooge, Won't Stop the Country Holding Elections', in http://allafrica.com/stories/printable/201201260247.html Accessed on 29/01/2012.

11 D. Lecoutre, 'South Africa's Mediation Efforts in Francophone Africa: Assessment of the Case of Côte d'Ivoire in the Context of a Stylistic Divide Between Anglophone and Francophone Africa', in K. Shillinger (ed.), *Africa's Peacemaker? Lessons from South African Conflict Mediation* (Johannesburg: Jacana Media, 2009), pp. 153-163.

12 Ibid., pp. 161-162.

13 J. Campbell, 'South Africa and Nigeria's Edge Relationship', in http://blogscfc.org.cambell/2012/03/12/south-africa-and-nigerias-edge-relationship/ Accessed on 26/05/2012.

14 S. Badza, 'Zimbabwe's 2008 Harmonized Elections: Regional and International Reaction', p. 153.

15 B. Buzan, *People, States and Fear: An Agenda for International Security Studies in the post-Cold War Era*, 2nd edn (Boulder: Lynne Rienner, 1991); R. Abrahamsen, 'Blair's Africa: The Politics of Securitization and Fear' in *Alternatives: Global, Local, Political*, 30, 1 (2005), pp. 55-80; R. I. Rotberg, 'Failed States in a World of Terror', *Foreign Affairs*, 81 (4), (2002), pp. 127-140; S. E. Rice, 'The New National Security Strategy: Focus on Failed States', *Brookings Policy Brief*, 1, (2003), pp. 116-130.

16 B. Raftopoulos, 'The Global Political Agreement as a "Passive Revolution":

Notes on Contemporary Politics in Zimbabwe', *The Round Table*, 99 (411), (Dec. 2010), p. 710.

17 Ibid., pp. 709-710.

18 Opening Statement by President Nelson Mandela speaking as Chairperson of SADC at the Official Opening of the Summit of SADC Heads of State and Government, Blantyre, Malawi, 8 September 1997 in http://www.sahistory.org.za/print/article/statement-opening-sadc-summit Accessed 29/01/2012.

19 A. Mlambo and B. Raftopoulos, 'The Regional Dimensions of Zimbabwe's Multi-Layered Crisis: an analysis' (Paper presented at the Election Processes, Liberation Movements and Democratic Change in Africa Conference, Maputo, Mozambique, 8-11 April 2010), p. 7.

20 Ibid., pp. 6-7.

21 T. Ranger, 'Introduction to Volume Two' in T. Ranger (ed.), *The Historical Dimensions of Democracy and Human Rights in Zimbabwe: Volume Two: Nationalism, Democracy and Human Rights* (Harare: University of Zimbabwe Publications, 2003), pp. 1-37; S. J. Ndlovu-Gatsheni, 'Putting People First: From Regime Security to Human Security: A Quest for Social Peace in Zimbabwe, 1980-2002', in A. G. Nhema (ed.), *The Quest for Peace in Africa: Transformations, Democracy and Public Policy* (Addis Ababa and Amsterdam: OSSREA and International Books, 2003), pp. 297-322; I. Phimister and B. Raftopoulos, 'Mugabe, Mbeki and the Politics of Anti-Imperialism', *Review of African Political Economy*, 31 (101), (2004), pp. 385-400; M. Neocosmos, 'Thinking the Impossible? Elements of a Critique of Political Liberalism in Southern Africa', *Identity, Culture and Politics*, 5 (1/2), (2004), pp. 207-234; B. Raftopoulos, 'The Zimbabwean Crisis and the Challenges for the Left', *Journal of Southern African Studies*, 32 (2), (2006), pp. 197-223; S. J. Ndlovu-Gatsheni, 'Making Sense of Mugabeism in Local and Global Politics: "So Blair, Keep Your England and Let Me Keep My Zimbabwe"', *Third World Quarterly*, 30 (6), (2009), 1139-1158.

22 N. Mandela, 'South Africa's Future Foreign Policy', *Foreign Affairs*, 72, (1993), pp. 86-94.

23 L. Freeman, 'South Africa's Zimbabwe Policy: Unraveling the Contradictions', *Journal of Contemporary African Studies*, 23 (2), (May 2005), p. 149; M. van Aardt, 'A Foreign Policy to Die For: South Africa's Response to the Nigerian Crisis', *Africa Insight*, 26 (2), (1996), pp. 114-135.

24 Ibid. pp. 149-152.

25 *Financial Gazette*, 4 December 2003; T. Mbeki, *Africa: Define Yourself* (Cape Town and Johannesburg: Tafelberg and Mafube, 2002); P. Kagwanja, 'Power and Peace: South Africa and the Refurbishing of Africa's Multilateral Capacity for Peacemaking', *Journal of Contemporary African Studies*, 24 (2), (May 2006), p. 159.

26 G. Evans, 'South Africa's Foreign Policy after Mandela: Mbeki and his Concept of an African Renaissance', *The Round Table*, 352 (1), (1999), pp. 621-628 (8).
27 P. Kagwanja, 'Power and Peace', op.cit. p. 159.
28 Z. Bhengu, 'The Role of SADC Mediators in Zimbabwe – Exploring the Process Behind the Breakthrough', (Unpublished M. A. thesis, University of the Witwatersrand, 2010), pp. 50-51.
29 SADC Heads of State and Government Summit Communiqué, 'The Summit of Heads of State and Government of the Southern African Development Community (SADC),' Blantyre, Malawi, 12-14 August 2001.
30 Ibid.
31 This point is well articulated in B. M. Tendi, *Making History in Mugabe's Zimbabwe: Politics, Intellectuals and the Media* (Bern: Peter Lang, 2010), p. 73-74. Tendi indicates that it was through the appeal of Emeka Anyaoku, the Commonwealth Secretary-General, that Zimbabwe had to postpone its radical land reform in the 1990s.
32 Full text of the Abuja Agreement on Zimbabwe in http://www.zimbabwemetro.com/945/full-text-of-the-abuja-agreement-on-zimbabwe/ Accessed on 13/01/2012.
33 International Crisis Group (ICG), 'Zimbabwe: The Politics of National Liberation and International Division', *Africa Report* No. *52,* (17 October 2002); Z. Bhengu, 'The Role of SADC Mediators in Zimbabwe' op.cit.
34 Ibid.
35 Zimbabwe Human Rights NGO Forum, 'Zimbabwe, the Abuja Agreement and Commonwealth Principles: Compliance or Disregard?' (Relief Web Report, 8 September 2003).
36 P. Chigora, 'On Crossroads: Reflections on Zimbabwe's Relations with Britain at the New Millennium', *Alternatives: Turkish Journal of International Relations,* 5(3) (Fall 2006), pp. 61-76.
37 International Crisis Group (ICG), 'Zimbabwe: Danger and Opportunity', *Africa Report,* 60 (10 March 2003).
38 P. Chinamasa, Opening Remarks by Patrick Chinamasa, Head of the ZANU-PF Team to the ZANU-PF-MDC Dialogue (Harare: Parliament Building, 8 April 2002).
39 I. W. Zartman (ed.), *The Negotiation Process: theories and applications* (Beverly Hills, CA: Sage Publications, 1978); H. Saunders, 'We Need A Larger Theory of Negotiation: The Importance of Pre-Negotiation Phases', *Negotiation Journal*, 1 (3), (1985), p. 249-62.
40 K. Matlosa, 'The Role of SADC in Mediating Post-Election Conflict: Case Studies of Lesotho & Zimbabwe', (Paper presented at the EISA Symposium, Johannesburg, South Africa, 17-18 November 2009).
41 T. Murithi and A. Mawadza, 'Voices from Pan-African Society on Zimbabwe: South Africa, the African Union and SADC', in T. Murithi and A. Mawadza (eds), *Zim-*

babwe in Transition: A View from Within (Johannesburg: Jacana Media, 2011), p. 292.
42 Ibid.
43 African Union, 'AU Executive Council Decision on Current Political Situation in Zimbabwe', (Sharm el-Sheikh, Egypt, 1 July 2008).
44 M. Tsvangirai, 'I Will Soldier on Until Zimbabwe is Free', *New African* (January, 2007).
45 T. Mbeki, 'The African Renaissance, South Africa and the World', (South African Deputy President Thabo Mbeki Speaks at the United Nations University, 9 April 1998) in http:/www.unu.edu/unupress/Mbeki.html Accessed 20/11/2011.
46 L. Freeman, 'South Africa's Zimbabwe Policy', op.cit. p. 156.
47 C. Landsberg, 'New Powers for Global Change: South Africa's Global Strategy and Status,' *FES Briefing Paper* (16 November 2006), p. 2.
48 Department of International Relations and Cooperation, 'White Paper on South African Foreign Policy – Building a Better World: The Diplomacy of Ubuntu', (draft paper, 13 May 2011).
49 S. Chan, *Old Treacheries, New Deceits: Insights Into Southern African Politics* (Johannesburg and Cape Town: Jonathan Ball Publishers, 2011).
50 C. Landsberg, *The Quiet Diplomacy of Liberation: International Politics and South Africa's Transition*, (Johannesburg: Jacana Media, 2004); S. Field, 'When Neighbours Stray: Political Implications for the SADC Region of the Situation in Zimbabwe', in K. Colvard and M. Lee (eds), *Unfinished Business: The Land Crisis in Southern Africa*, (Johannesburg: African Century Publications, 2003); P. Kagwanja, 'Power and Peace',op. cit. pp. 166-167.
51 T. Mbeki, 'The Mbeki-Mugabe Papers: What Mbeki told Mugabe', *New Agenda*, 30, (2008), pp. 56-72.
52 B. Raftopoulos, 'The Global Political Agreement as a "Passive Revolution"', op.cit. pp. 710-711.
53 Z. Bhengu, 'The Role of SADC Mediators in Zimbabwe', op.cit. p. 71.
54 Ibid., p. 75.
55 Ibid., p. 77.
56 E. V. Masunungure (ed.), *Defying the Winds of Change: Zimbabwe's 2008 Elections* (Harare: Weaver Press and Konrad Adenauer Foundation, 2009).
57 E. V. Masunungure, 'A Militarized Election: The 27 June Presidential Run-Off,' in E. V. Masunungure (ed.) , ibid. pp. 79-97.
58 M. Bratton and E. Masunungure, 'Zimbabwe's Long Agony', *Journal of Democracy*, 19 (4), (2008), p. 51.
59 Z. Bhengu, 'The Role of SADC Mediators in Zimbabwe', op.cit. p. 78.
60 J. Borger, 'African Union Calls for National Unity Government in Zimbabwe', *The Guardian*, 2 July 2008.
61 P. Kagwanja, 'Power and Peace', op.cit. p. 162.

62 Z. Bhengu, 'The Role of SADC Mediators in Zimbabwe', op.cit. p. 81.

63 A. C. LeVan, 'Power Sharing and Inclusive Politics in Africa's Uncertain Democracies', *Governance: An International Journal of Policy, Administration, and Institutions,* 24 (1), (January 2011), pp. 31-53; I. S. Spears, 'Understanding Inclusive Peace Agreements in Africa: The Problems of Sharing Power', *Third World Quarterly,* 21 (1), (2000), pp. 105-118; N. Cheeseman and B. M. Tendi, 'Power-Sharing in Comparative Perspective: The Dynamics of "Unity Government" in Kenya and Zimbabwe', *Journal of Modern African Studies,* 48 (2), (2010), pp. 203-229.

64 Z. Bhengu, 'The Role of SADC Mediators in Zimbabwe', op.cit. pp. 85-86.

65 S. Mpanyane, 'The First Step Towards a Deal in Zimbabwe', *ISS Today,* (24 July 2008).

66 S. Touval, *Mediation in the Yugoslav Wars: The Critical Years 1990-95* (New York: Palgrave Macmillan 2002), p. 11.

67 B. Raftopoulos, 'The Global Political Agreement as a "Passive Revolution"', op.cit. p. 707.

68 R. Bourne, *Catastrophe: What Went Wrong in Zimbabwe?* (London and New York: Zed Books, 2011), p. 208.

69 Full Text of Agreement between the Zimbabwe African National Union-Patriotic Front (ZANU-PF) and the Two Movements for Democratic Change (MDC) Formations, on Resolving the Challenges Facing Zimbabwe, 15 September 2008.

70 D. Compagnon, *A Predictable Tragedy: Robert Mugabe and the Collapse of Zimbabwe,* (Philadelphia: University of Pennsylvania Press, 2011) pp. 248-249.

71 S. J. Ndlovu-Gatsheni, 'Bob Is Peerless: Zimbabwe and the Quest for an African Peer Review Mechanism', in H. Melber (ed.), *Governance and State Delivery in Southern Africa: Examples from Botswana, Namibia and Zimbabwe* (Uppsala: Nordic Africa Institute, 2007), pp. 43-65.

72 R. Bourne, *Catastrophe*, op.cit. pp. 200-201.

73 Ibid., p. 211.

74 T. Murithi and A. Mawadza, 'Voices from Pan-African Society on Zimbabwe'op. cit. , p. 296.

75 D. Matyszak, *Law, Politics and Zimbabwe's Unity Government,*(Harare: Konrad Adenauer Stiftung and Research and Advocacy Unit, 2010) p. 176.

76 Southern African Development Community Summit of the Troika Organ on Politics, Defence and Security Cooperation, 'Communiqué', Livingstone, Republic of Zambia, 31 March 2011.

77 Ibid.

78 T. Murithi and A. Mawadza, 'Voices from Pan-African Society on Zimbabwe', op.cit. p. 297.

79 Ibid, p. 298.

CHAPTER 6

Sanctioning the Government of National Unity:
A Review of Zimbabwe's Relations with the West in the Framework of the Global Political Agreement

MUNYARADZI NYAKUDYA

Introduction

The impasse that has characterised Zimbabwe's political landscape since the turn of the millennium has been as much a struggle between ZANU-PF and the MDC as it has been a confrontation between ZANU-PF and the West. Relations between the newly independent government of Zimbabwe under the control of the ruling ZANU-PF and the western world started on a promising note as the country enjoyed flourishing donor support, particularly from the Scandinavian countries,[1] for its health provision and educational programmes. The internal racial differences of the colonial period seemed a thing of the past after the new government embarked on a policy of 'moderation and reconciliation'.[2] However, while signs of racial tension began to resurface in the mid-1980s, relations generally remained fairly amicable until 2000 when ZANU-PF embarked on a violent process of land repossession from the white commercial farmers.³ Relations between the government and a large section of the black community also frayed as the former failed in its mandate of service delivery. There were serious accusations of lack of respect for the rule of law as the government employed heavy-handed tactics to pacify its citizens and relations between the two became so tenuous that they sucked in the western world. In 2001, the United States of America imposed a raft of targeted sanctions on the ZANU-PF government; the European Union did similarly in 2002, and several other western governments followed suit. These sanctions have remained in place despite the fact that the feuding Zimbabwean political parties signed the Global Political Agreement (GPA) in September 2008 – a step that culminated in the formation of a Government of National Unity (GNU) in February 2009.

Since then, the sanctions have provided the pivot around which the relationship between ZANU-PF (and by extension, Zimbabwe) and the West has been defined. Indeed, ZANU-PF has accused its nemesis, the MDC, of fronting western interests at the expense of national ones. The former now refuses to implement key reforms, which it agreed to in the GPA, until the sanctions have been removed. The West, however, maintains that sanctions were imposed to force ZANU-PF to respect the rule of law, institute democratic practices and honour property rights. As such, they cannot be lifted until ZANU-PF complies. Consequently, the GNU's operations have been largely hamstrung and it has failed to deliver a new constitution, a prerequisite for the country to conduct democratic general elections that will establish a proper government committed to peaceful coexistence and tolerance.

This chapter thus attempts to explain why the West steadfastly refuses to lift sanctions and discusses how the GNU could have benefited if these strictures had been eased. The conclusion is that while the West's concerns about ZANU-PF repression, abuse of state power and total disrespect for human rights and democracy are legitimate, it is arguably more preoccupied with the economic fortunes of its kith and kin, the white population in Zimbabwe, and post-Cold War imperialist interests in general. Arguably, softening sanctions would have enabled the GNU to operate more effectively by removing the excuse for stubborn inaction with which they have provided ZANU-PF, and which it has so skillfully instrumentalised in its battle against the West. On the other hand, the MDC formations have either wittingly or unwittingly allowed themselves to be placed in various invidious positions by the West,⁴ thereby weakening their struggle for democratisation and sustainable development.

The West refers to the western world, characterised by a common race, culture and civilisation of European origin. It includes the countries of western Europe, America, Australia and New Zealand. It is not by any means a homogenous entity, certainly not in terms of geographical space, language, interests and policy. In terms of their dealings with both ZANU-PF and the MDC formations, there are both soft-liners and hard-liners among the western powers. Each individual country in the West has distinctive interests. The European Union, for example, acts for the collective interests of its member states, and has its own arrangement, the Cotonou Agreement, which governs its relations with the African, Caribbean and Pacific countries.[5] Its members, nonetheless, sometimes act in their own individual right. This has resulted in the West sometimes failing to act in unison on Zimbabwe. While conscious of the West's heterogeneity, however, this discussion does not always dwell on the different individual concerns of western countries, but focuses more on their common interests and how these have impacted on the fulfillment of the GPA objectives in general and the effectiveness of the GNU in particular. The rationale for this approach lies in the post-modern imperialism conceptual framework used to analyse the West's relationship with Zimbabwe's GNU, a paradigm which basically revolves around the West's collective imperial interests.

Theoretical Framework

Zimbabwe's relationship with the West can best be conceptualised within the context of post-Cold War politics. The Cold War had pitted the communist-oriented Soviet Union and her allies against the capitalist world dominated by the USA and her allies, notably Britain, and the generality of the countries that constitute the West, as defined above, as they battled for control of the world. With the disintegration of the colonial system, the above superpowers strove to ensure that the newly independent African countries championed their interests. Since the Marxist-Leninist ideology asserted the right of nations to self-determination, it was inevitable that the Soviet Union appeared attractive to most African countries. This naturally alarmed the anti-communist ruling elites of the USA and her western allies, causing them to employ various interventionist tactics and strategies. According to Thabo Mbeki, these included:

> ...the establishment of the system of neo-colonialism, the overthrow of governments which resisted this, support for the white minority and colonial regimes in Southern Africa..., the assassination of such leaders as Patrice Lumumba, Thomas Sankara

and Eduardo Mondlane, sponsorship of such instrumentalities as UNITA in Angola and Renamo in Mozambique, support for predatory and client regimes... and even such major catastrophes as represented by the 1994 genocide in Rwanda.[6]

Mbeki's expose succinctly sums up the leftist neo-colonialism paradigm expounded by Kwame Nkrumah,[7] Walter Rodney[8] and others[9] on how the West perpetuated its stranglehold over its erstwhile colonies, keeping them within its 'sphere of influence' for economic and strategic gain during the Cold War. However, the demise of the Soviet Union and the end of the Cold War meant the Americans became free to exercise their will, and interests, in the new unipolar world over which they dominated. Some analysts have argued that in the absence of 'a countervailing force against imperialist domination', Africa's strategic significance to the West declined, especially in the light of low income per capita, which restricted the market for western goods.[10] Africa was thus left to herself, except in cases of 'humanitarian crises', hence reducing the continent to 'a recipient of charity'.[11]

However, with the emergence of India, Brazil and particularly China as competing economic global forces, America, and the West in general, have been forced to adopt a new strategy, with advocates for a post-modern imperialism coming to the fore. Bruce Anderson has declared that Africa lacks the capacity and ability to end its own woes and, as such, the USA, UK and their allies should implement a new form of imperialism in which they install puppet leaders whom they guide towards free markets, the rule of law and democracy.[12] According to Robert Cooper, post-modern imperialism is premised on the ground that '...the weak still need the strong and the strong still need an orderly world. A world in which the well governed and efficient [*read the West*][13] export stability and liberty, and which is open for investment and growth'.[14] Cooper postulates that post-modern imperialism exists in two forms, namely, 'voluntary imperialism of the global economy' and 'imperialism of neighbours'.[15] The former hinges on the tying of aid to governance issues. The idea is that 'if states wish to benefit, they must open themselves up to the interference of international organizations and foreign states'. Similarly, the 'imperialism of neighbours' is premised on the notion that 'instability in your neighbourhood poses threats' and in this era of globalisation, the entire world is potentially our neighbour.[16]

Achin Vanaik echoes the same sentiments by stating that:

> The 'internationalist' segment of capital has a major interest in global stability and a minimization of the kind of inter-imperialist rivalry that might lead to competing protectionist blocks. It exercises influence both within and outside governments and through multilateral institutions like IMF, WB, EBRD and MTO/GATT though these bodies ... must pay due attention to the interests of their major governmental underwriters'.[17]

In pursuit of the above, the USA has adopted a more proactive role as it seeks to reclaim its dominance. Hillary Clinton's comment is quite instructive:

> ... part of what I have tried to do as Secretary of State is to reassert American leadership, but to recognise that in 21st century terms we have to lead differently than the way we historically have done.... [M]y goal is to assert our leadership in the most value-centered way... using so-called smart power, to build more durable coalitions and networks... into which we are imbedded. We have to be looking for ways that America can expand our economic presence, exercise our influence ... (and) exercise our power for the advancement of American security, interests and values ...[18]

Clinton's assertion exposes a mixture of neo-liberalism and realism as part of the post-modernist imperialism. Realism stresses the advancement of national interests and an emphasis on national security as the guiding principle in international relations while neo-liberalism is more concerned with the common interests of global societies, hence its emphasis on the promotion of human rights, democracy and respect for the rule of law.[19] This is reiterated by Jennifer G. Cooke and Richard Downie who argue that 'US diplomacy is at a crossroads' in the wake of 'new challenges and opportunities [that] are emerging in Africa that require new approaches'. They cite the strengthening of democracy and governance, promotion of economic development and prevention of conflict as the core of US global objectives. They argue that this calls for a 'dedicated military command for Africa, focused on building African military capacities ... and respect for civilian authorities and the rule of law'.[20]

When these schemes either fail to achieve the desired goals or are threatened, punitive measures are taken against the errant states. One common measure is the application of sanctions against the state perceived to be errant with the view of coercing it to comply.[21] While sanctions have a long history, they have become an integral part of the grand objective of the West's post-modern imperialism to advance their interests. Sanctions are viewed as a genuine instrument to pressure rogue regimes to adopt democracy, respect human rights and enforce good governance practices that ensure liberty, freedom and sustainable development for their countries. The pain wrought by sanctions is perceived as inducing compliance by the sanctioned regime.[22] Kurebwa concurs, arguing that the purpose of sanctions is to bring delinquent states under check so as to achieve collective security.[23]

Scholars have, however, never been able to reach a consensus on the effectiveness of economic sanctions to induce the target country to yield. While the likes of Kimberly Ann Elliot[24] and Gary Clyde Hufbauer et al[25] concede that sanctions are only moderately effective, scholars of Johan Galtung,[26] Margaret P. Doxey[27] and Robert A. Pape's[28] persuasion are almost unequivocal in dismissing sanctions as ineffective. Out of the 116 cases they analysed, Hufbauer et al concluded that the sanctions success rate was 34%.[29] This figure was however drastically reduced by Pape who re-analysed the same cases and concluded that only 4% of these resulted in meaningful concessions by the sanctioned countries.[30] Echoing the same pessimism, Baldwin has concluded that, '[i]t would be difficult to find any proposition in the international relations literature more widely accepted than those belittling the utility of economic techniques of statecraft.'[31]

Several reasons have been advanced to explain why sanctions are often ineffective. These can be summed up as follows:
 i. 'sanctions busting' (smuggling)
 ii. resort to alternative customers and suppliers
 iii. stockpiling, import substitution and rationing
 iv. the elite passing on the costs of sanctions to other segments of the population
 v. sanctions may significantly hurt the sanctioned country's neighbours
 vi. sanctions may arouse defiance, patriotism and popular support for the political leadership in the sanctioned country
 vii. the sanctions may not be credible
 viii. there is no incentive to yield – the target country knows sanctions will be maintained even after yielding to the given demands
 ix. the effects of defiance may be a lesser evil than compliance
 x. compliance may be more costly politically.[32]

ZANU-PF has tried to discredit the sanctions and explain the 'Zimbabwe Crisis'[33] in general within the framework of post-modern imperialist politics, arguing that the West is besieging Zimbabwe through its local puppets in retaliation at the country's implementation of a land redistribution programme, which challenged the West's interests by dispossessing nearly 4,500 commercial farmers of their farms.[34] ZANU-PF sees itself as waging a war for sovereignty and self-determination, a war against imperialist forces. It is a war not primarily against the MDC, but the West. The war represents the third phase of the struggle against white hegemony, hence the tag, 'Third Chimurenga', to describe this struggle against the western forces of imperialism.[35] The ZANU-PF argument is that the raft of travel and economic sanctions imposed on it by the West, allegedly for human rights abuses and lack of democracy, are simply a punitive measure for its anti-imperialist policies and assertion of its sovereignty. Instead, the party has insisted on the need for 'African solutions to African problems' with its leader spearheading a vanguard of African leaders who are championing the drive for an 'African renaissance' in the aftermath of the Cold War.[36]

On the other hand, the two MDC formations have embraced support from the West as legitimate assistance by well-meaning friends. Their thinking is apparently that international relations are about 'the internationalization of domestic conflict and the domestication of international conflicts'.[37] While the effective domestication of international conflicts may still be way beyond the dreams and expectations of African countries, save for participation in United Nations' structures and activities, the internationalization of domestic disputes has been universalised by the West as an integral part of the post-modern imperialist politics. In this vein, the West has sponsored UN-sanctioned invasions of, notably, Iraq and Libya, among others, resulting in the ultimate dethronement and execution of their long-time dictators, Saddam Hussein and Muammar Gadhafi, respectively. It has also sponsored a spirited anti-nuclear and disarmament crusade against Iran. More significantly, however, the West has championed the promotion of human rights democracy and good governance in numerous countries to the point of applying punitive measures against perceived rogue states.

In light of the above, in seeking to unbundle the West's relationship with Zimbabwe in the context of the GPA, this discussion examines the impact of sanctions and explains their role in the dynamics of Zimbabwe's socio-political and economic landscape since the inauguration of the GNU. The question is, 'if sanctions are generally so ineffective, why then is the West so obsessed with them?' Zimbabwe's relations with the West, particularly in the context of the GPA, have to be analysed within the framework of the sanctions debate highlighted above as an integral aspect of the post-modern imperialism paradigm employed by the West at the instigation of the USA. However, a word on the history of Zimbabwe's relations with the West should provide the background knowledge to aid our appreciation of the current dynamics.

Historicising relations between the West and Zimbabwe

This section analyses the trends in Zimbabwe's relations with the West from colonial times through to the GPA in 2008. While these have always fluctuated in response to political circumstances, they became severely strained during the 'decade of crisis' (1998-2008) whose dynamics had a direct bearing on the signing of the agreement and therefore in shaping the nature of the socio-political and economic developments that have characterised the tenure of the GNU, itself a direct outcome of the GPA.

Several factors helped shape relations between Zimbabwe and the West during the colonial era, chief among them being economic interests and the race question. Throughout the colonial period, the relations between blacks and the white settlers could be described as the relationship 'between a horse and a rider'.[38] Until the mid-1960s, the latter regarded themselves as 'fully-fledged members of the British Empire'[39] since most had roots in Britain or its dominions and also because Rhodesia was a British colony. What this meant is that Rhodesia's blacks saw their plight as a British responsibility. Indeed, as Mlambo posits, up to the mid-1950s, Rhodesia's Africans generally saw themselves as British citizens.[40] Relations were therefore characterised by African disgruntlement not just with the white settlers but with the British government itself for its failure to reign in the settlers. Africans felt Britain had a kith and kin relationship with the settlers and would therefore not 'abandon' them to the fate of African nationalism for purely racist and imperialist reasons.

As the 'winds of change' blew across Africa from the late 1950s, and the greater part of sub-Saharan Africa attained independence, it became apparent that the status quo of white hegemony on the continent could no longer be sustained. However, a reverse process, which seriously compromised race relations, was taking place in Rhodesia. Through the Rhodesia Front, the white settlers unilaterally declared independence from Britain in 1965,[41] thereby thwarting African hopes of achieving majority rule, as had occurred on the rest of the continent. The Unilateral Declaration of Independence (UDI), together with the 1972 Pearce Commission and the 1979 Lancaster House Agreement, were critical benchmarks, which underlined the turbulent race relations in the colony, at a time when the greater part of Africa had fallen under African majority rule. UDI was meant to safeguard white minority interests, 'Christian Civilization and its values and standards' against Communism,[42] described by a Rhodesian Minister of Foreign Affairs as the 'Russian colossus'.[43]

Interestingly, Britain responded to Rhodesia's rebellion by cutting diplomatic ties and imposing a raft of economic sanctions. These included terminating trade ties with Rhodesia and denying her access to London's capital markets. The United Nations added its weight by imposing an oil embargo in 1966 and then, two years later, placed the country under comprehensive mandatory sanctions.[44] With all due respect to these efforts, however, Africans still deemed these measures half-hearted. The British, they noted, refused to use force of arms to bring their errant subjects to book, even when it became apparent that the Rhodesia Front would not move an inch without force. More significantly, as Mtisi, Nyakudya and Barnes argue, the international community showed a 'general lack of commitment' to the effective implementation of the sanctions.[45] Several western nations such as West Germany and Switzerland refused to ratify them, while, as Kapungu observes, Denmark and the Netherlands adopted a non-interventionist stance.[46] In the same vein, the *New York Times* noted that even at the United Nations, sanctions received lip-service; Britian and most of her allies did little or nothing to curb their trade with Rhodesia.[47] The French and the Americans both passed legislation, which exempted from the sanctions list strategic products available in Rhodesia.[48] It is clear, therefore, that individual interests meant that the West, always heterogeneous by nature, never acted in unison, thereby undermining the effectiveness of the sanctions.

The ability of the sanctions to force the Rhodesia government to yield has remained a subject of debate among scholars. The 'pro-sanctions' scholars credit the sanctions for forcing Smith to agree to negotiate. Baldwin argues that the sanctions weakened the government's ability to withstand the guerrillas[49] and also strengthened the resolve and morale of the opposition within the country.[50] On the other hand, a second school of thought argues that the Rhodesia government finally agreed to a settlement not as a result of sanctions but due to pressure from the guerrilla onslaught and the abdication of South Africa in its traditional support of the Rhodesia government. In these scholars' estimation, sanctions were actually a blessing for the country. They are credited with the massive growth – 212% – in secondary industries, while production volumes rose by 160% between 1966 and 1974.[51] Such phenomenal growth came about as the government increased emphasis on import-substitution industries and the diversification of those already in existence.[52] This unintended effect on the Rhodesian economy was made easy by the international community's unenthusiastic attitude to the sanctions.

Faced with such a negative attitude to their plight, Rhodesia's Africans intensified the armed struggle to seek the redress that the British, without any meaningful support from their western allies,[53] apparently reneged on instituting. It is on this fundamental aspect of the half-hearted attitude of the western powers to the African nationalists' aspirations that relations between the two sides revolved. True, the western powers did offer Rhodesia's Africans non-military support in the form of education scholarships, food, clothing and medicines for the thousands of refugees who streamed into the neighbouring countries.[54] The West saw this support as '[t]he most effective way to counter Soviet influence'.[55] However, the African nationalists insisted that this *welfarist* support was not capable of dislodging the unjust racist regime. Indeed, throughout the 1970s, British efforts to broker peace were perceived as lukewarm and not radical enough to force the Rhodesians to accede to demands for Black majority rule.[56] For instance, the British even had the temerity to propose a new so-called liberal constitution through the Pearce Commission that would have seen Africans attaining majority rule no earlier than 2035.[57] Thus, while acknowledging the humanitarian assistance generously rendered by Scandinavia, for example, Africans felt the military assistance (in the form of arms, ammunition, training and expertise) they received from the communist nations was more decisive in waging the war against the Rhodesian settlers.[58]

The protracted negotiations to end the war in Rhodesia add further credence to the 'conspiracy theory' of British complicity alluded to above. As the principal actor, Britain's handling of the results of the 1972 Pearce Commission and the 1976 Geneva Conference left the Africans convinced beyond any measure of doubt that the western powers were guided by racial considerations. After the Africans had rejected – through a referendum instituted by the Pearce Commission – the British proposals to allow limited concessions to blacks in the constitution, Rhodesia's UDI government found ample excuse to continue, and with impunity, to disregard the black interests.[59] On the other hand, the Geneva Conference was called by the British as an attempt to be more involved in the resolution of the Rhodesian crisis after the détente initiative[60] had finally convinced Smith to concede to the idea of majority rule for the first time.[61] However, as with the Victoria Falls Conference,[62] held the previous year, negotiations collapsed due to Smith's intransigence and Britain's failure to coerce him to comply.

Ultimately, the Lancaster House Constitution, brokered by Lord Carrington, the then Conservative British Foreign Secretary, ushered in independence aided by the coercive pressure exerted on the Patriotic Front by the Frontline States, and on Ian Smith by apartheid South Africa,[63] is a clear example of how western interests shaped relations with the Africans. This constitution's primary feature was how it safeguarded white interests, chiefly private property. Among other privileges, whites had 20 out of 100 seats reserved for them in Parliament for seven years[64] while their property rights were protected through clauses that prevented the new state from arbitrarily appropriating land except on a willing-buyer willing-seller basis.[65] This racially crafted constitution simply became an albatross for the new government's nation-building efforts, and Muzondidya aptly observes that it 'hampered the progress towards justice and political reconciliation'[66] because the white farmers, '[c]onscious of the racial protection guaranteed by the constitution..., were generally reluctant to relinquish their colonially inherited privilege'.[67] The situation was compounded by the West's seemingly deceitful offer to pay for land appropriated for resettlement, deceitful because there was apparently no written commitment and this was to become a subject of conflict with Tony Blair's Labour government.[68]

Juxtaposed against this was the nascent state's own intolerance of political diversity and penchant for using force against opponents. This saw an estimated 20,000 civilians in the Matabeleland and Midlands Provinces perishing at the hands of the security forces[69] as they sought to thwart a handful of armed rebels in a manner described as 'unwarranted and disproportionate to the security threat posed.'[70] However, despite the brutal and callous nature of the atrocities committed during the Matabeleland crisis, the western world chose to turn a blind eye. Heidi Holland notes that 'Gukurahundi[71] was barely noticed, let alone condemned, by the West.[72] Timothy Scarnecchia has explained this apparent tolerance of Gukurahundi by the West as part of the dynamics of Cold War politics. Since ZANU received the bulk of its war-time support from China rather than the Russians, the Americans perceived independent 'Zimbabwe as a non-Soviet southern African state'. The West thus believed that financial and other support for Zimbabwe would 'help maintain a balance against Soviet and Cuban influence in Angola, Mozambique and to a certain extent in Zambia'.[73]

Censoring Mugabe was therefore certainly not then in the West's interests. In the early 1980s, having adopted a policy of reconciliation on romping to victory in the independence elections, contrary to fears that he would take the country down the communist path, Mugabe clearly became the West's blue-eyed boy. The former white settlers' property interests and the western corporations and conglomerates' investments were all safe and it was business as usual. In fact, the bulk of Zimbabwe's trade was with the West, prompting the Indigenous Business Women's Organisation (IBWO) to accuse the government of cushioning multinationals and white-owned businesses against outside competition without doing the same for black businesses.[74] Clearly, the West was willing and ready to do business with Mugabe's Zimbabwe as long as their interests were safe, irrespective of the abuses being meted out against Zimbabweans.

The relationship between Zimbabwe and the West began to experience some episodic tensions around the mid-1980s. These centred primarily on the Zimbabwe government's own relations with the white community. Feeling protected by the provisions of the Lancaster House Constitution, the whites failed to reciprocate the hand of reconciliation extended by the new government. The majority of the whites 'maintained conservative attitudes with racial undertones'[75] and 'abdicated from actively engaging in the process of nation building'.[76] Instead, they found comfort in retreating into what Godwin has termed, 'racial enclaves'.[77] The Zimbabwe government was particularly peeved by the whites' continued support of the racist Rhodesia Front, now named the Conservative Alliance of Zimbabwe, which they overwhelmingly voted for in the 1985 parliamentary elections.[78] Holland postulates that Mugabe perceived this as 'betrayal' and 'racial rejection', and was so 'deeply hurt' that he was 'hell-bent on revenge'.[79] In fact, Dennis Norman, a former president of Rhodesia's Commercial Farmers' Union who became Zimbabwe's first Minister of Agriculture, argues that this marked 'the beginning of the Zimbabwean tragedy'.[80]

However, relations between the West and the ZANU-PF government began to diminish more seriously in the early 1990s, after the expiry of the ten-year moratorium on amendments to the Lancaster House Constitution, when the Zimbabwe government began to make changes detrimental to white interests. In 1992, the government passed the Land Acquisition Act (No. 3 of 1992) to allow it to compulsorily acquire resettlement land.[81] However, the success of land acquisition rested on western funds, but as alluded to previously,[82] the British cut off such support in 1994 alleging that most of the farms acquired with the £44m they had already advanced for the programme were allocated to 'Mugabe's cronies in a generally corrupt exercise'.[83] Indeed, this marked the beginning of a cataclysmic decline in relations between Zimbabwe and the West, which worsened after the 1998 United Nations Development Programme-sponsored Donor Conference when no western country was willing to contribute to the targeted £145m earmarked for purchasing land to resettle 35,000 landless rural households.[84]

The West's abandonment of the critical Zimbabwe land redistribution programme coincided with the beginning of the collapse of the Zimbabwean economy. The *welfarist* policies that had seen huge improvements in social services delivery in the 1980s began to backfire in the early 1990s. A mixture of skewed policies and a series of droughts caused a decline in agricultural production and exports, forcing the government to grudgingly implement western-inspired austerity measures, termed the Economic Structural Adjustment Programme (ESAP).[85] By late 1997, the country's economy was straining under the weight of these measures. Holland quotes Father Mukonori, a Mugabe confidante, stating that Mugabe's view was that ESAP 'was imposed by northern hemisphere bigwigs… who would refuse to work with you – and make sure that nobody worked with you either – if you didn't.' So, in Mugabe's book, ESAP marked the beginning of Zimbabweans' dissatisfaction with ZANU-PF.[86] Indeed, the meltdown largely contributed to the emergence of a much stronger opposition than seen before,[87] the MDC, whose first taste of victory against the ZANU-PF regime was its successful campaign for a 'No' vote in the February 2000 referendum for a new constitution. This development angered ZANU-PF who accused the MDC of championing western interests, especially after the press splashed pictures of Morgan Tsvangirai, the MDC President, surrounded by several white farmers signing cheques to fund his new party. Holland notes that Father Mukonori posits that the footage, taken by an American network, convinced Mugabe that it was only out of the support by white farmers and some western countries, notably Britain and some Scandinavian countries, that the MDC had come so close to defeating him.[88]

Feeling beleaguered, especially in the face of impending parliamentary elections in June 2000, ZANU-PF launched a vicious land repossession and redistribution exercise that saw white commercial farmers lose their farms to a coalition of landless peasants, war veterans and many other disgruntled people.[89] At the twentieth independence celebrations, Mugabe had labeled the white farmers 'enemies of Zimbabwe'.[90] The farm invasions were justified as a genuine movement to empower disadvantaged blacks who were in desperate need of land. The argument was that 'the land was the economy and the economy was the land' and as such, as a sovereign people, indigenous Zimbabweans had to own their most important resource.[91] This position once again brought to the fore one of the major questions that had caused turmoil during the colonial era, the question of who qualifies to be a citizen. On the other hand, the West argued that the invaders disregarded human rights and shunned democratic principles as they unleashed a reign of terror on the farms under the directorship of ZANU-PF. Thus, in 2001, the West imposed a range of sanctions. Since then, relations between the two sides have revolved around the legitimacy or illegality, and the lifting or maintenance, of the said sanctions.

The above historical exposé shows that the white settler regime in Rhodesia freely defied muted calls for black majority rule by their western masters, particularly the British, because the calls were half-hearted and guarded. It is also patently clear that while Rhodesia was a British colony, other western powers, notably the USA, took a direct interest and initiative to resolve the crisis when their strategic interests were threatened. The Scandinavian countries, which offered humanitarian assistance, did so to avert wholesale Soviet dominance of the region; their hypocrisy was exposed by their adamant refusal to arm the guerrilla movements, even though, ironically, they claimed to believe they were fighting for a just cause.[92] When their economic interests were threatened, the same powers refused to adopt comprehensive sanctions against apartheid South Africa until as late as 1986 when Denmark became the first western country to do so while Sweden, Norway and Finland followed suit in 1987.[93]

After Zimbabwe's independence, it was also apparent that for as long as their interests were safe, the West maintained mutual relations with the Mugabe regime. Thus, it was little wonder that Jim Sinclair, the then Commercial Farmers' Union president, justified the Gukurahundi atrocities, arguing that the government had a 'legitimate right to rule the country as it saw fit'[94] while Roger Martin, the then British Deputy High Commissioner, found Gukurahundi 'comprehensible, (as) it has a certain rationality other than mere brutishness'.[95] The British media mogul and mining magnate, Tiny Roland, in appreciation of mining and other rich business concessions, even fired journalist Donald Trafford for reporting on the security forces' Gukurahundi excesses and labeling them a crime against humanity.[96] In 1994, Mugabe received royal endorsement when the queen knighted him with the Order of Bath.[97] Gukurahundi was perceived to be a manifestation of ethnic differences in Zimbabwe and as long as they did not affect western interests, the West maintained fairly cordial relations with the governing elite in Zimbabwe, lending weight to the post-modern imperialist theory in explaining the West's relations with Zimbabwe.

Sanctions

However, as the socio-economic and political conditions in Zimbabwe began to spiral into a catastrophic decline and the West's interests became seriously compromised, relations between the two sides severely deteriorated. On 21 December 2001, George W. Bush, the then US President, signed the Zimbabwe Democracy and Economic Recovery Act (ZDERA) into law, ostensibly to pave the way for a transition to democracy and to promote economic recovery in Zimbabwe. The purported philanthropic justification for the sanctions is captured in the Act's Statement of Policy that reads; 'It is the policy of the US to support the people of Zimbabwe in their struggle to effect peaceful democratic change, achieve broad-based and adequate economic growth, and restore the rule of law'.[98] The Americans cited the breakdown in the rule of law, lawlessness and lack of respect for property and ownership rights as reasons for instituting the law. This came in the wake of the violent land repossession exercise, later renamed the Fast Track Land Reform Programme (FTLRP), which accelerated in the aftermath of the February 2000 Constitution Referendum. The programme saw the number of commercial white farmers drastically reduced from about 4,500 in the late 1990s to less than 500 by 2002, in a manner characterised by 'criminality' in the form of 'looting and vandalism of farm property, tree-cutting, poaching and gold-panning'.[99] Another common feature of the FTLRP was the displacement of some 200,000 farm workers, two-thirds of the entire farm-worker population at the start of the FTLRP.[100] More significantly, the disturbances were characterised by fatalities, reportedly in the region of about 1,000 deaths between 2000 and 2008.[101] It is in the context of this breakdown in law and order that ZDERA was instituted.

ZDERA particularly obliged the US executive director to each international financial institution 'to oppose and vote against any loan, credit or guarantee to, as well as any cancellation or reduction of indebtedness by, the Government of Zimbabwe from any financial institute'.[102] Significantly, the act further implored the US President to immediately consult with the EU member states' governments, Canada and other allies for a concerted effort in applying the sanctions. Thus, on 18 February 2002 – following the expulsion of the Swedish diplomat, Pierre Schori, the EU head of the election monitoring mission in Zimbabwe, allegedly for interfering with the elections – the EU introduced restrictive measures on Mugabe and some of his senior government officials barring them from travelling in and around Europe and freezing their personal assets and bank accounts. Australia followed suit in September 2002 with its own set of restrictive measures, ranging from an arms embargo to travel bans and financial sanctions. The Howard administration went a step further by excluding children of sanctioned Zimbabweans from their Australian institutions of learning.[103] The sanctions have been renewed annually ever since, with Canada also imposing sanctions as late as 2008.[104]

The West has conscientiously renewed the sanctions every year on the grounds that conditions for their removal have not been met. These have been stipulated as: an end to the widespread political and election violence that has characterised the Zimbabwe electoral landscape, respect of property-ownership rights and the rule of law, and a transition to unfettered democracy. Meantime, the Zimbabwean economy experienced a cataclysmic decline of unprecedented proportions. Life became characterised by shrinking incomes, 'starvation wages', dramatic levels of unemployment, and a worthless currency as inflation reached 'dizzying' levels. Homelessness for about 700,000 people in the wake of Operation Murambatsvina, which destroyed so-called unplanned shelters and informal businesses, exposed the government's vindictiveness against an allegedly unpatriotic urban population. A deadly cholera outbreak was manifestation of a collapsed health sector while a crumbling education sector signalled the government's general failure to deliver services.[105]

In the face of such hardships, opposition to ZANU-PF intensified, but was met with increased repression. This reached its zenith in March 2007 when opposition and civic leaders were brutalised by the police as they attended a prayer meeting. Embarrassed by the international (read western) coverage of the incident, the Southern Africa Development Community (SADC) sprang into action by initiating a mediation process.[106] This culminated in the signing of the GPA on 15 September 2008 by the principals of ZANU-PF and the two MDC parties.[107] The agreement committed the signatory parties to instituting a range of reforms and called for the removal of sanctions.

The West and the GPA: Sanctioning the GNU

The inauguration of the GNU signalled the end of ZANU-PF's uncontested grip on state power since independence in 1980, and, after a decade of turmoil, marked a significant watershed in the country's political history. While the new dispensation had several critics,[108] Marc Lizoain argues that the GNU had the support of the generality of the people of Zimbabwe[109] as it provided a chance for the country to move towards a democratic dispensation and economic stability and growth. Even the Commercial Farmers' Union (CFU) noted through their President, Charles Toffs, that there was a 'new sense of hope for the CFU farmers after the GPA'.[110] Indeed, within two months, a 100-day Short Term Economic Recovery Plan (STERP), the product of all key stakeholders, was put in place while SADC pledged a US$8 billion assistance package for the country's economic turnaround. Several European countries, notably Sweden and Denmark, advanced some money for the inclusive government to kickstart its operations, specifically paying civil servants. Very soon the economy showed tangible signs of recovery, with the inflation rate remarkably falling to an impressive 3% in March 2009 after the suspension of the then worthless Zimbabwean currency and the adoption of a multi-currency regime. Goods became abundantly available in the shops while the black market completely disappeared. The crafting of a new constitution for the country was initiated with the consent and participation of all the parties in the inclusive government, heralding prospects of a more democratic Zimbabwe where the rule of law and human and economic rights are observed.

In the light of these early positive developments, MacDermott proffered the opinion that the GPA and, indeed, the GNU, offered 'a window of opportunity' for the international community to re-engage with Zimbabwe.[111] However, almost four years into the GNU, this has not happened. Sanctions remain solidly in place. In this section, I therefore discuss the West's failure or refusal to re-engage, and explain how this has not only handicapped the GNU as it attempts to grow the economy, but has also drastically weakened the MDC in its efforts to usher in an environment conducive for the holding of free and fair elections which many believe will bring an end to the excesses of Mugabe's reign.

The West was apparently caught on the wrong foot by the political truce that ushered in the GNU. This is evidenced by the paradoxical ambivalence of the West as it instituted punitive sanctions against Zimbabwe (more specifically against Mugabe and his allies) but continued to provide humanitarian assistance. While the direct impact of sanctions on the Zimbabwean socioeconomic landscape may be difficult to quantify, it is clear that the restrictions on access to funding have been disastrous. The economy has faltered through lack of capitalisation, and this, in turn, has had ripple effects on social services. The West is certainly aware of the effects of its measures on the generality of Zimbabweans. Geoffrey Van Orden, a member of the European Parliament and Defence and Security spokesman, has categorically stated that '...Zimbabweans will have to suffer for the actions of a wayward leader'.[112] Ironically, the West, having contributed to the suffering, has offered humanitarian assistance. The EU alone channelled close to €1.5billion between 2002 and 2010, supporting mainly the agriculture, education and health sectors.[113] In 2009, the EU contributed 25% of Zimbabwe's communal farmers' fertiliser needs and 80% of the country's vital medicines, textbooks to 820,000 primary school children, i.e. almost 100% of the country's total needs. The European Commission provided €80 million to support social services between 2009 and 2010 alone, while a total of €365 million has been committed to services prioritised by the GNU since 2009.[114]

The West has grappled with two scenarios: either to engage Mugabe, lift sanctions and support the GNU, or to shun him completely and maintain, if not tighten, the sanctions. The latter scenario has largely prevailed. It must be conceded that the US, EU and their allies' various Sanctions Bills all stipulate the need for tangible progress in terms of establishing democracy, respecting human rights and upholding the rule of law before re-engaging. There has simply been no such progress, with the reform deficit clearly still outstanding. ZANU-PF has persistently and consistently refused to implement critical electoral, judicial, media and security sector reforms necessary before new elections can be held. Mugabe unilaterally renewed the respective terms of office of the ZANU-PF aligned Attorney General and Reserve Bank Governor contrary to the spirit of the GPA, which stipulates that this be done in consultation of other GPA principals. A façade of media 'reforms' was instituted when two broadcasting licenses were issued to ZANU-PF sympathisers, Zimpapers and AB Communications.[115] At the same time, the local broadcasting houses have upped the tempo in churning out pro-Mugabe jingles *ad nauseum*,[116] while the state newspapers continue to spew out hate speech against Mugabe's opponents, particularly Morgan Tsvangirai, leader of the larger MDC party. The highly maligned Zimbabwe Electoral Commission, largely accused of fixing previous elections, has not been significantly restructured and remains largely intact in its old discredited form. Worse still, it suffers from serious funding constraints.[117]

MacDermott has identified several risks of engaging the GNU. He argues that doing so before fulfillment of the various reforms agreed to in the GPA is tantamount to legitimizing the oppressive and repressive Mugabe regime. This in turn subjects whoever legitimizes Mugabe to accusations of abetting the abuses and crimes of which he is accused. There is also the danger of losing the support of home taxpayers.[118] These are legitimate concerns, particularly in the face of intransigence on the part of the ZANU-PF section of the GNU cited above.

In view of these considerations, the West has therefore apparently shunned the option of re-engaging, opting instead to steadfastly maintain sanctions. But what has been the cost? Certainly, the 'window of opportunity' MacDermott saw in the GPA has been lost. Zimbabwe is again fast descending into another cycle of organised violence. Critics argue ZANU-PF wishes to frustrate the other parties to the GNU into quitting so that new elections can be held under the current Lancaster House Constitution whose structures now clearly favour them[119] after instituting a staggering eighteen amendments to it before the nineteenth that ushered in the GNU. The sanctions have ironically provided ZANU-PF with a useful ace up its sleeve. The party has simply refused to implement important reforms, arguing that the MDC has to first see to it that sanctions are removed. In terms of media reforms, the ZANU-PF aligned Minister of Media, Information and Publicity, Webster Shamu, was reportedly tasked by the three GPA principals to complete media reforms by 11 March 2012, but to date, neither have the reforms been implemented nor any explanation proffered for his non-compliance.[120]

Similarly, on the issue of the security sector, the ZANU-PF Congress of December 2009 passed the following critical resolution: 'ZANU (PF) as the party of revolution and the people's vanguard shall not allow the security forces to be the subject of any negotiation for a so-called security sector reform,' ostensibly because the 'security forces are a product of the national liberation struggle'.[121] The party thus argues that 'calls for security sector reform violate Zimbabwe's sovereignty'.[122] This simply throws spanners in the GPA implementation process: the MDC formations have vowed not to accept that general elections be held before security sector reforms are instituted, maintaining that the latter have been politicised, as revealed in their proclamations not to accept any leader without liberation war credentials.[123] Indeed, it is commonly acknowledged that ZANU-PF survival has rested on the control of state power through this sector. In view of the apparent power and influence of the security sector in the country's governance, whose legacy is in the liberation struggle era, it is imperative that, as Hendricks and Hutton suggest, a delicate balancing of the critical question of amnesty and retribution be worked out.[124] Only when there is this reassurance may there be a change of mindset on the part of the security sector. Assured of unequivocal backing by the security sector, Mugabe and his party have stated that they will no longer entertain any further reforms until sanctions are removed.[125]

According to Raftopoulos, the West's rigidity on sanctions has provided ZANU-PF and Mugabe with 'the pretext for a persistent contestation',[126] alleging a more sinister motive for the sanctions. They now argue that the sanctions are meant to bring about regime change in Zimbabwe. Evidence on the ground seems to support these fears. To start with, the injunction in ZDERA imploring US officials in international financial institutions not to support any loan, credit or guarantees to the Zimbabwe government was immediately followed by 'a formal declaration by the IMF of non-cooperation with Zimbabwe' and suspension of all technical assistance.[127] The idea was certainly to cripple Mugabe's government and not only coerce it to comply with democratisation and general reform processes, but certainly cause it to fall. Mamdani notes that further US legislation authorised the government 'to fund an independent and free press and electronic media in Zimbabwe and to allocate six million dollars for democracy and governance programmes'.[128] In this respect, there has been an injection of funds purportedly to assist with the capacity building of the office of the Prime Minister, raising accusations of sponsoring a parallel government in Zimbabwe and giving credence to accusations of regime change.

However, even more instructive is the EU's categorical statement that Zimbabwe would be 'better off without Mugabe' and only then would it be authorised to apply for a share of the €13.5bn available to African, Caribbean and Pacific States under the 9th European Development Fund.[129] Geoffrey Van Orden has openly stated that the EU is 'completely fed up with Mugabe' who they claim remains an albatross on the country's economic progress.[130] Such hard talk has in turn evoked a hard-line stance on the part of Mugabe's regime. Responding to Van Orden, George Charamba, Mugabe's spokesman, reduced the debate to one of racism, arguing that Van Orden 'is part of the conservative side of the EU that wants to equate land redistribution to the quest for democracy. *To them democracy should exist to the whites only and not to blacks*' (my emphasis).[131] Speaking in similar vein, an anonymous commentator has argued that' [t]he trouble with British foreign policy, especially under Labour, is that it has always been influenced by kith and kin i.e. the white farmers. It was so under Harold Wilson and remains so under Brown'.[132]

Indeed, some radical leftist commentators have seen the sanctions through the lenses of post-modern imperialist politics, stating that '[t]hey are meant to weaken and remove the regime of President Robert Mugabe. Like other sanctions imposed by institutions such as the International Monetary Fund and the World Bank, they seek to pressure and impose a government on the people of Zimbabwe in the name of 'democratic elections'.[133] Others have seen the western rigidity on sanctions as a declaration of war: 'Sanctions are war without guns and bloodshed…'[134] Connie White concurs, claiming that ZDERA 'sends the message that the U.S. Government is at war with the Southern African nation of Zimbabwe'.[135] ZANU-PF itself has also adopted this defensive line, arguing as way back as 2002 that '[w]e are at war. … it is a war going on in Zimbabwe]. The war goes back to 1999-2000'.[136]

Still others see the western siege of Zimbabwe as a broad-based attack on the entire region's former liberation movements. As R. W. Johnson argues:

> *In Mbeki's and Mugabe's minds Western imperialism is engaged in a struggle to overthrow the NLMs (national liberation movements) and restore, if it can, the preceding regimes – apartheid,*

colonialism or white settler rule. In so doing it will use various local parties as lackeys: Inkatha and the Democratic Alliance in South Africa, Renamo in Mozambique, Unita in Angola – and the MDC in Zimbabwe.[137]

This certainly gives ZANU-PF the much needed regional solidarity that has largely sustained Mugabe in the face of mounting internal and international pressure.

The seeming double standards applied by the West have given some semblance of credibility to the above views. Claims that the sanctions are targeted do not seem to be backed by the reality on the ground. The past year or so has seen restrictions being visited on all and sundry. For instance, a Chinhoyi University of Technology student was refused computer software for her studies by a US-based company while Africa University was denied certain software and programmes by Microsoft on the grounds that Zimbabwe is under sanctions.[138] Similarly, the US Treasury Department reportedly blocked the transfer of a UK-based couple's US$30,000 to Chinhoyi Municipality allegedly because US financial institutions are obliged to 'block all wire transfers in which a sanction's target has an interest'.[139] This targeting of seemingly apolitical individuals and institutions seems to go beyond the restrictions stipulated in the series of Executive Orders (EOs) from the US President.[140] As MacDermott observes, the first two EOs targeted specific persons, their families, businesses and accomplices while the latter was concerned with government personnel.[141] Nowhere in these EOs is the US obliged to extend restrictions to persons and institutions outside the stipulated parameters. This, therefore, smacks of US vindictiveness and double standards. It is not clear what the West wishes to achieve by targeting innocent citizens when they claim sanctions are not meant to punish ordinary Zimbabweans.

Further double-dealing that exposes the West's insincerity in its relations with the GNU includes the issue of the Marange Diamonds. The Marange Diamond fields, discovered at the height of the Zimbabwe crisis in 2006, soon became the centre of controversy as the Mugabe regime was accused of using the proceeds from the diamond sales to fund repression in Zimbabwe. There were unsavory reports of massive killings and abuse by the country's security forces[142] leading to suspension of Zimbabwe from the Kimberley Process, the body that governs global trade in diamonds.[143] However, even in the face of a damning BBC report on the abuses by Zimbabwean troops,[144] the EU spearheaded a secret campaign to have some banned diamonds from Zimbabwe back on the market. The BBC reported that an internal document it saw stated that the 'EU was confident that two mines in the area now meet international standards and it wanted diamonds from those areas to be immediately approved for export...'.[145] The reason is easy to see. According to Rajiv Jain, President of India's Gem and Jewellery Export Promotion Council, Zimbabwe diamonds are '40-50 per cent cheaper than diamonds from other sources'.[146] Eventually, Zimbabwe got permission to sell its diamonds. This attracted the ire of many, with Farai Muguwu, Director of the Centre for Research and Development positing that:

> *The permission to resell is ok, but does not protect the Marange community from abuse. The deal is silent on human rights, nor does it call on the Zimbabwe authorities to protect the Marange community. The deal sweeps under the carpet the failure by Zimbabwe to implement earlier agreements reached in Namibia and St Petersburg recently.*[147]

This poses serious questions about the West's sincerity. It would appear the talk about concerns over human rights abuses is merely expedient. The main interest remains economic, giving legitimacy to the arguments of proponents of the post-modern imperialist theory.

While the West may project a sense of oneness in imposing sanctions on Zimbabwe, the reality on the ground portrays a totally different picture. The West has certainly not always acted in unison. For instance, the EU had to grapple with the embarrassment of trying to explain how Air Zimbabwe allegedly managed to acquire two airbus planes from France amid sanctions. The planes were apparently purchased through China Sonangol, 'a Chinese-controlled oil company based in Angola roped in to circumvent sanctions'.[148] According to the same report, Air Zimbabwe pilots were sent to several European countries for expert training on handling the airbuses, clearly exposing western double standards through which sanctions-busting has apparently taken place. Equally revealing was Anglo America's desire to inject US$400 million in Zimbabwe to safeguard access to platinum mines in 2008,[149] again exposing the West's pre-occupation with economic interests. Such a lack of unity certainly undermines not only the effectiveness and ultimate success of the GNU, but the efforts of the MDC. As Judy Smith-Höhn argues, 'In the case of Zimbabwe, it appears that the effectiveness of smart sanctions has been limited by inconsistencies in their implementation as well as by their selective nature'.[150] This is clearly shown by the lack of co-operation between the US and the EU over the Marange Diamonds. After secret EU support for their readmission into the Kimberley Process, the US on the other hand recently banned the sale of the diamonds by two Zimbabwean companies, Mbada Diamonds and Marange Resources.[151] A third company operating in Marange, Anjin, has not been placed on the sanctions list. It is Chinese-owned. This is certainly a case of not wanting to jeopardise global economic relations with the Chinese. Interestingly, Anjin is the only mining company not remitting anything to the treasury 'despite generating more than US$72 million in sales from the beginning of the year'.[152]

The West's lack of tact and diplomacy has also weakened the operations of the GNU through inadvertently undermining a key player in the GNU, the MDC-T. Shari Eppel aptly observes that '[t]he nature and outspokenness of western support for the democratic movement has not been unproblematic for MDC, making it possible for ZANU-PF to declare Tsvangirai a stooge of the West carrying out its regime change agenda...'[153] An example of this reckless outspokenness was when the then British premier, Tony Blair, bluntly confessed in the House of Commons that the British government was collaborating with Tsvangirai to replace the government of Zimbabwe.[154] This was followed by a general furore that damaged Tsvangirai's standing as he struggled to brush off the 'sell-out' tag, that, as Wifred Mhanda notes, Mugabe is 'skilled' at employing against his 'African rivals'.[155] Another example is that after sixteen western nations met in Ottawa, Canada, in October 2008 to discuss Zimbabwe, they reported that they had had little influence on breaking the Zimbabwe stalemate. They resolved, however, that they stood 'to be guided by what the MDC was willing or able to achieve through negotiations and to facilitate the MDC's effectiveness'.[156]

Mugabe certainly finds such western posturing consistent with his long held fears that the West has always wanted him out. In an interview with Holland, Rajan Soni, a consultant in international development working for Overseas Development Administration, reported that he had reached the conclusion that 'Labour's strategy was to accelerate Mugabe's unpopularity by failing to provide him with funding for land redistribution. 'They... wanted him out and they were going to do whatever they could to hasten his demise'.[157]

Some scholars have noted that sanctions compliance is normally encouraged by putting pressure that is laced with incentives, the 'carrots and sticks' approach.[158] However, as Cameron observes, in the case of western sanctions on Zimbabwe, no incentives were offered. What is in place are only 'negative sanctions'. Instead, the incentives ('carrots') have been offered 'exclusively to the regime's opponents', thereby further exposing 'a policy preference for regime change'.[159] All western aid now flows into Zimbabwe through third parties as Article 96 of the Cotonou Agreement prohibits aid payment through government structures, a direct snub of Mugabe. This refusal to give aid directly to the government started with the British when in 2000 they announced a £5 million injection for land resettlement projects through non-governmental structures, making Mugabe livid at the apparent rebuff.[160] This also certainly helps explain his current intransigency.

It may not be easy to accurately predict how western softening on sanctions could have influenced the democratisation process in Zimbabwe considering the risks of doing so discussed earlier on, but several commentators are convinced of the retrogressive consequences of maintaining a hard line stance. Brilliant Mhlanga, a London-based Zimbabwean political analyst argues that '[m]aintaining sanctions only harden Mr. Mugabe's anti-reform position'.[161] As Raftopoulos implies, western influence in the Zimbabwean crisis has enabled the Mugabe regime to articulate 'a repressive national politics to a broad anti-imperialist, pan-Africanist appeal, with essentialist notions of race as the central markers of the conflict'.[162] This stance has found sympathy regionally. For instance, leaders of liberation movements in Southern Africa described the sanctions as 'subversive acts intended to economically sabotage Zimbabwe'.[163] True to Hovi et al's analysis,[164] these sanctions have aroused Mugabe's defiance for several reasons: they do not offer any incentive for compliance and in Mugabe's estimation, the cost of compliance is unquestionably much more severe than resisting dethronement. The West has acted in a manner that leaves no doubt that they are for outright regime change as shown in the discussion above.

Why the West's policies have affected the operations of the GNU can best be summed up in Gatsheni-Ndlovu's words. While acknowledging that the 'Zimbabwe crisis' exposes how the state wasted all opportunities to pursue sound socio-economic policies in the 1980s and 1990s, he argues that '…it is difficult for a weak African state to pursue radical development in an environment dominated by neo-liberal forces that are quick to discipline and decimate that which appears to deviate from neo-liberal orthodoxy'.[165] The West is simply obsessed with punishing the deviant and defiant Mugabe regime for self-serving interests. Otherwise, how does one explain the fact that countries with worse human rights records like Afghanistan and Rwanda in 1994, for example, have not been subjected to similar restrictions and sanctions?

Recent posturing by the EU and Australia in which they have respectively removed 51 and 82 members from their sanctions lists only exposes indecision. The EU's stated criteria for removing some members from the list and retaining others is unconvincing. EU Ambassador to Zimbabwe, Aldo Dell'Ariccia, stated:

> As for us, we perform our yearly assessment of these measures and our criteria were based on the activities of the individuals in as far as their involvement in human rights abuses is concerned. It was seen that the delisted people and companies were no longer actively or indirectly participating in gross human rights abuses hence the decision to remove them.[166]

This claim sounds hollow when we consider that the 51 members removed from the list include six state media journalists[167] at a time the state broadcasting enterprises have gone into overdrive in spewing vitriol against opponents of ZANU-PF in the same manner observed, and aptly described by Chitando way back in 2005, as 'saturation of the communication environment with propaganda'.[168] Worse still, there is a blatant disrespect for the rule of law in the heart of Harare. Chipangano, a wing of the ZANU-PF Youth League, invaded Parliament and beat up MPs, banned the MDC from holding rallies in Mbare suburb and took over several City of Harare facilities, depriving the city of income for service provision.[169] The ZANU-PF aligned law enforcement authorities have either been powerless or unwilling to act against these unlawful deeds.

The two MDC formations have not helped matters either. While they certainly have no power to remove the sanctions as ZANU-PF insists they should do, they can surely speak unequivocally on the issue. It appears neither party has had a clearly principled policy position on the matter, at least until about March-April 2012. Granted, the Minister of Finance, Tendai Biti, who is the MDC-T Secretary General, occasionally acknowledged that sanctions were crippling the economy, but his party president, Morgan Tsvangirai, has prevaricated on the matter. Speaking at the London Business summit in March 2012, he echoed the West's position when he urged the world to 'insist on the necessary reforms to create an environment conducive for free and fair elections and a lasting solution to the crisis in Zimbabwe'.[170] However, speaking in the House of Assembly in the same month, he acknowledged that sanctions had harmed the economy and wanted 'every individual and entity on the sanctions list removed'.[171] Tsvangirai's MDC-N counterpart, Welshman Ncube, has rarely spoken on the matter in public, but was quite forthright against sanctions in an obscure publication, *Green Indaba*, where he attacked them as 'an albatross around our necks' as they negate 'the very democracy they were meant to serve'. He argued that with sanctions in place, the chances of free and fair elections were impossible as 'they give ZANU-PF a pretext for refusing to accept the verdict of the people...'[172] While every ZANU-PF functionary has taken every opportunity to lambast sanctions, as of March 2012, only Tsvangirai, Ncube and Biti from the two MDC formations had spoken for their removal.

In the final analysis, the general consensus is that sanctions have been stalling progress, exacerbating polarisation and strengthening the position of hardliners who have used them as a tool against instituting reforms. Even the highly respected International Crisis Group, while insisting that the arms embargo against Zimbabwe must be maintained, recently observed that the sanctions cum restrictive measures have not achieved the desired objectives and have instead been responsible for the current 'reform stalemate'. It lamented the lack of co-ordination of the measures adopted by the US, the EU and their other allies and general inconsistency in implementing the restrictive measures.[173] The group has suggested two possible options: either suspending 'the ban on government to government development co-operation' as a goodwill measure, or if it is deemed inappropriate to lift the ban, then conduct a study of the impact of sanctions and seek ways to negotiate with the EU to end the ban and also ensure more rigorous SADC facilitation.[174]

Developments in May 2012 offer the false impression that the West is softening its stance on Zimbabwe. A Zimbabwe three member inter-party ministerial delegation met the EU in Brussels to agitate for the removal of sanctions. The group, however, met with little success as there was no tangible commitment by the EU to remove the sanctions, save for a pledge to review the situation in July 2012, but insisting through Amabassador Aldo Dell'Ariccia that sanctions can only be lifted if Zimbabwe holds free and fair elections.[175] In fact, the UK Ambassador to Zimbabwe soon after reiterated that GNU reforms are 'key to credible elections'.[176] Ironically, this came at a time that a key EU ally, the US, through Charles Ray, its then Ambassador to Zimbabwe, was hailing Zimbabwe as 'a peaceful country, rich in wildlife and with friendly people'. He further noted the efforts of politicians, stating that '... Zimbabwe is open to business. They are coming from political challenges, that might have made leaders fail to implement certain projects but *let us give them a chance* (my emphasis) because reconciliation takes quite some time.'[177] Such contradictory posturing from the West has simply been detrimental to the operations of the GNU.

Thus, as things stand, the ball is certainly in the West's court. While it is not given that the removal of sanctions would result in the implementation of reforms,[178] only an unwavering decision to suspend sanctions/restrictive measures and engage the security sector through SADC for a change of mind set is the key to unlocking the current deadlock in Zimbabwe as it will leave ZANU-PF groping for alternative non-existent alibi for not instituting reforms.

Conclusion

When Zimbabwe's belligerent political parties signed the Global Political Agreement in September 2008 paving the way for the formation of the Government of National Unity in February 2009, critics believed this marked the opening of a 'window of opportunity' to end nearly a decade of bloody feuding. The feuding revolved around two distinct issues. ZANU-PF was rapped for its disrespect for human rights, abuse of state power and disregard of property rights bordering on dictatorship characterised by repressive practices. On the other hand, the MDC was accused of being sell-outs and stooges who front western interests in total disregard of the country's sovereignty. While evidence of ZANU-PF misrule and repression abounds as shown in this chapter, western complicity is equally apparent. Western sanctions were imposed beginning in 2001 and they have been in existence ever since. Calls for their easing in the wake of the GPA and GNU have fallen on deaf ears. In the words of Baroness Catherine Ashton, Vice President of the European Commission and High Representative of the Union for Foreign Affairs and Security Policy, the sanctions on Mugabe and his colleagues would be maintained until democratic reforms are instituted.[179] The argument is that sanctions were imposed to pressure Mugabe's government to undertake radical improvements in its human rights record, governance practices and an end to economic cronyism in the form of lawless land expropriation, shady diamond mining practices and company take-overs under the guise of economic black empowerment.

While these are legitimate concerns given the ZANU-PF regime's disastrous human rights and governance records, critics have argued that the West could certainly have afforded the GNU an unstifling operating environment by lifting the sanctions. This could have disarmed ZANU-PF by denying it what has proved to be an ace in the pack. ZANU-PF has courted regional sympathy by invoking the neo-colonialism argument on the basis of the sanctions. When we also consider that sanctions have been shown not to be as effective as they were meant to be, one cannot help but agree that they are merely self-serving. Where it has suited them, the western powers have invested in Zimbabwe. Indeed, according to the EU Ambassador to Zimbabwe, Mr Aldo Dell'Ariccia, trade between Zimbabwe and the EU, for instance, doubled between 2010 and 2011, totaling US$860 million,' with a positive trade balance of US$270 million in favour of Zimbabwe'.[180]

Worse still, it has not been uncommon to see individual western countries acting unilaterally as they pursue national interests. This failure to always act in unison has undermined the effectiveness of the sanctions, hence thwarting the democratisation efforts that the GNU is supposed to be pursuing. Regimes with equally bad, if not worse, human rights records and disregard for democratic practices have not been subjected to similar treatment. Thus, while the articulated reasons for imposing sanctions are legitimate, it is not easy to totally discount the post-modern imperialist theory as the West's continued refusal to give the GNU an opportunity to succeed exposes ulterior motives for the sanctions. Mugabe and his hard-line supporters have simply been emboldened by the sanctions, giving them the high moral ground to refuse to implement critical reforms required for a transition to democracy and justice because the West has openly shown an unrelenting determination to 'get rid' of him more than they are keen to see reforms. The situation has been compounded by the MDC formations' failure to show principled positions and shake off the 'sell-out' label ZANU-PF has placed on them.

What the Zimbabwe stalemate calls for is the implementation of all reforms agreed upon, the suspension of sanctions and the removal of the ban on government to government development co-operation.[181] There should be a concerted effort by SADC and the West in engaging the security sector in Zimbabwe to persuade them to desist from dabbling in politics and let the will of the electorate prevail.

Endnotes

1 J. Muzondidya, 'From Buoyancy to Crisis: Zimbabwe 1980-1997' in B. Raftopoulos and A. Mlambo (eds), *Becoming Zimbabwe: A History from the Pre-colonial Period to 2008* (Harare: Weaver Press, 2009) p. 167.

2 J. Alexander, *The Unsettled Land: State-making and the Politics of Land in Zimbabwe, 1893-2003* (Harare: Weaver Press, 2006) p. 106.

3 The fairly cordial relations can be explained within the politics of the post-Cold War dynamics. See endnote 74.

4 See endnote 88 for an example of the MDC's self-defeating shortcomings.

5 The Cotonou Agreement, signed between the European Community and the African, Caribbean and Pacific (ACP) states in June 2000 and entered into force in 2003, is a partnership treaty that aims at, among other goals, achieving sustainable development for the ACP states and also helping them to enter the world economy. Significantly, a revised treaty in 2005 now includes the issue of good governance as an 'essential element' whose violation leads to the suspension of development cooperation with the violating country. See Stephen Kingah, 'The Revised Cotonou Agreement Between the European Community and the African, Caribbean and Pacific States: Innovations on Security, Political Dialogue, Transparency, Money and Social Responsibility', *Journal of African Law,* 50 (2006), 59-71, p. 64.

6 Thabo Mbeki, Address at the Makerere Institute of Social Research Conference on the Architecture of Post-Cold War Africa between Internal Reform and External Intervention, 19 January 2012.

7 Kwame Nkrumah, *Neo-Colonialism: The Last Stage of Imperialism* (London: Thomas Nelson & Sons, Ltd, 1965)

8 Walter Rodney, *How Europe Underdeveloped Africa* (Washington: Howard University Press, 1974)

9 See, for instance, Amilcar Cabral, 'The Weapon of Theory'. Address delivered to the first Tricontinental Conference of the Peoples of Asia, Africa and Latin America, held in Havana, Cuba, in January 1966.

10 Steven A. Holmes, 'The World: Africa From The Cold War To Cold Shoulders', *New York Times*, 7 March 1993, cited in Mbeki, Address at the Makerere Institute of Social Research Conference.

11 Mbeki, Address at the Makerere Institute of Social Research Conference.

12 *The Independent* (UK), 2 June 2003, cited in ibid.

13 My emphasis.

14 Robert Cooper, 'The New Liberal Imperialism' http://www.guardian.co.uk/world/2002/apr/07/1.

15 Ibid.
16 Ibid.
17 Achin Vanaik, 'Imperialism, Soviet Collapse and Implications for Post-Colonial World', *Economic and Political Weekly*, 28 (5) January 30, 1993, p. 39.
18 Hillary Rodham Clinton, Secretary of State, USA, *TIME Magazine*, 27 October 2011.
19 See David McCraw, 'New Zealand Foreign Policy Under the Clark Government: High Tide International Liberalism?' *Pacific Affairs*, 78 (2) (Summer 2005), pp. 217-18.
20 J. G. Cooke and R. Downie, 'African Conflicts and US Diplomacy: Roles and Choices', A Report of the Center for Strategic and International Studies Africa Program and the American Academy of Diplomacy, January 2010.
21 J. Hovi, R. Huseby and D. F. Sprinz, 'When Do (Imposed) Economic Sanctions Work?' *World Politics,* 57 (4) (July 2005), p. 480.
22 Ibid.
23 Joseph Kurebwa, 'The Politics of Multilateral Economic Sanctions on Rhodesia During the Unilateral Declaration of Independence Period, 1965-1979' (D.Phil thesis, University of Zimbabwe, 2000) p.3.
24 Kimberly Ann Elliot, 'The Sanctions Glass: Half Full or Completely Empty?' *International Security,* 23 (1) (1998).
25 Gary Clyde Hufbauer, Jeffrey J. Schott and Kimberly Ann Elliot, *Economic Sanctions Reconsidered: History and Current Policy*, 2nd ed. (Washington D.C.: Institute for International Economics, 1990).
26 Johan Galtung, 'On the Effects of International Economic Sanctions with Examples from the Case of Rhodesia', *World Politics* 19 (3) (April 1967).
27 Margaret P. Doxey, *International Sanctions in Contemporary Perspective* (Basingstoke: Macmillan, 1987).
28 Robert A. Pape, 'Why Economic Sanctions Do Not Work', *International Security* 22 (2) (1997) and Robert A. Pape, 'Why Economic Sanctions Still Do Not Work', *International Security* 23 (1) (1998).
29 Hufbauer et al., *Economic Sanctions Reconsidered,* cited in Hovi et al., 'When Do (Imposed) Economic Sanctions Work?' p. 481.
30 Pape, 'Why Economic Sanctions Do Not Work', and Pape, 'Why Economic Sanctions Still Do Not Work', both cited in Hovi et al, 'When Do (Imposed) Economic Sanctions Work?' p. 481.
31 David A. Baldwin, *Economic Statecraft* (Princeton: Princeton University Press, 1985), p. 57.
32 See Hovi, et al., 'When Do (Imposed) Economic Sanctions Work?' pp. 481-485.
33 This refers to the upheaval in Zimbabwe in the period from the late 1990s to late 2008 when the country's main political parties signed the Global Political Agreement. See B. Raftopoulos, 'Crisis in Zimbabwe, 1998-2008' in Raftopoulos and Mlambo (eds)

Becoming Zimbabwe, footnote 1, p. 201, for the rich literature on the 'Crisis in Zimbabwe'. While the socio-political and economic situation in Zimbabwe stabilised at the onset of the GPA, the current impasse among the GPA principals may warrant extending the term 'Crisis in Zimbabwe' to the time when a new constitution is agreed upon, free and fair elections are held, and the results do usher in a new democratically elected government.
34 http://www.irinnews.org/ 30/08/12.
35 See R. G. Mugabe, *Inside the Third Chimurenga: Our Land is Our Prosperity* (Harare: Government of Zimbabwe, 2001)
36 See Olaf Bachmann, 'The African Standby Force: External Support to an "African Solution to African Problems"?', Institute of Development Studies Research Report 67, University of Sussex, April 2011, for this general viewpoint..
37 See Vanaik, 'Imperialism, Soviet Collapse and Implications', p. 37, for a detailed analysis of this concept.
38 This phrase was used by Godfrey Huggins, Prime Minister of Southern Rhodesia and the Central African Federation, to describe the Federation. See J. Mtisi, M. Nyakudya and T. Barnes, 'Social and Economic Relations During the UDI Period' in Raftopoulos and Mlambo (eds) *Becoming Zimbabwe*, p.116. The phrase, however, applies quite aptly to black-white relations under colonialism. See Charles van Onselen, *Chibaro: African Mine Labour in Southern Rhodesia, 1900-1933* (London: Pluto Press, 1976) and also T. H. Mothibe, 'Zimbabwe: African working class nationalism, 1957-1963,' *Zambezia*, 23 (2), 1996 .
39 A.S. Mlambo, 'From the Second World War to UDI, 1940-1965' in Raftopoulos and Mlambo (eds) *Becoming Zimbabwe*, p.113.
40 Ibid.
41 Ibid., p. 110.
42 'Rhodesian Christian Group Pamphlet, March 1977' cited in Bruce Moore-King, *White Man, Black War* (Harare: Boabab Books, 1988) p. 51.
43 P. K. van der Byl, Rhodesia Minister of Foreign Affairs, 1977, speaking at the National Rehabilitation Centre for the Wounded, cited in J. Frederikse, *None But Ourselves: Masses vs Media in the Making of Zimbabwe* (Harare: Zimbabwe Publishing House, 1982) p.57.
44 H. R. Strack, *Sanctions: The Case of Rhodesia* (Syracuse, NY: Syracuse University Press, 1978) pp. 16-20. See also Kurebwa, 'The Politics of Multilateral Sanctions on Rhodesia' and W. Minter and E. Schmidt, 'When Sanctions Worked: The case of Rhodesia re-examined', *African Affairs*, 87 (347), 1988, for a more nuanced discourse on the Rhodesia sanctions.
45 Mtsi et al., 'Social and Economic Developments', p.133.
46 L. Kapungu, *The United Nations and Economic Sanctions Against Rhodesia* (Lexington, Lexington Press, 1973) pp. 86-8.

47 Quoted in ibid., pp. 9-10.
48 Mtisi et al., 'Social and Economic Developments', pp. 133-35.
49 Baldwin, *Economic Statecraft*, pp.197.
50 Hovi, et al., 'When Do (Imposed) Economic Sanctions Work?' p. 488.
51 E.S. Pangeti, 'The State and Manufacturing Industry: A Study of the State as Regulator and Entrepreneur in Zimbabwe, 1930-1990' (D.Phil. thesis, University of Zimbabwe, 1995), p. 110.
52 Mtisi et al., 'Social and Economic Developments', p 132.
53 This is not to imply that only Britain's allies failed to act against Rhodesia. Many countries, including even some of Rhodesia's independent African neighbours like Malawi, Botswana and Zambia, lacked the economic stamina to impose and execute sanctions on Rhodesia. See Kurebwa, 'The Politics of Multilateral Sanctions,' for details on sanctions 'busting'.
54 In fact, Scandinavia provided 'approximately 70%' of all the humanitarian aid that went to southern Africa's liberation movements. See Piero Gleijeses' Review Article, 'Scandinavia and the Liberation of Southern Africa', *The International History Review*, 27, (2) (June 2005), p. 326. The article also provides a review of the literature that discusses and evaluates the assistance rendered to the region's liberation movements by Scandinavia (pp. 324-331).
55 Gleijeses, 'Scandinavia and the Liberation of southern Africa', p. 325.
56 In the 1970s, and prior to 1979, there were a plethora of initiatives to end the civil war. These ranged from conferences that provided platforms for negotiations to offers of more 'liberal' constitutions. Some of these include the Anglo-Rhodesia Agreement and the Malta, Victoria and Geneva Conferences. See J. Mtisi, M. Nyakudya and T. Barnes, 'War in Rhodesia, 1965-1980' in Raftopoulos and Mlambo (eds) *Becoming Zimbabwe*, pp. 141-166.
57 R. C. Good, *U.D.I.: The International Politics of the Rhodesia Rebellion* (Princeton: Princeton University, 1973), p. 306.
58 See Gleijeses, 'Scandinavia and the Liberation of Southern Africa', for comments on this issue by Luis Cabral, first president of Guinea-Bissau (p. 330) and Nelson Mandela, first president of independent South Africa (p. 331).
59 See Judith Todd, *The Right to Say No* (London: Sidgwick and Jackson, 1972) on the politics of the Pearce Commission.
60 Détente refers to the period between December 1974 and January 1976 when tensions between the white minority regimes of Southern Africa (Rhodesia and South Africa) on the one hand and the independent African states on the other relaxed as a result of diplomatic manoeuvres by the former in the wake of the collapse of Portuguese power in Angola and Mozambique. See Mtisi et al., 'War in Rhodesia', pp. 145-6.
61 Mtisi et al., 'War in Rhodesia', p. 148.

62 See D. Martin and P. Johnson, *The Struggle for Zimbabwe: The Chimurenga War* (Harare: Zimbabwe Publishing House, 1981), pp. 158-65 and also M. Meredith, *The Past Is Another Country: Rho*desia 1890-1979 (Chicago: Chicago University Press, 1979), p. 195.

63 See E. Sibanda *The Zimbabwe African Peoples' Union, 1961-87: A Political History of Insurgency in Southern Rhodesia* (Trenton, NJ: Africa World Press, 2005), p. 218, for an explanation of the pressures exerted on the PF by Presidents Kaunda and Machel to accede to the unsatisfactory terms of the Lancaster House Constitution.

64 L. Tshuma, *A Matter of (In)Justice: Law, State and the Agrarian Question in Zimbabwe* (Harare: SAPES Books, 1997). See also F. Chung, *Re-Living the Second Chimurenga: Memories from Zimbabwe's Liberation Struggle* (Uppsala: The Nordic Africa Institute; Harare: Weaver Press, 2006) p. 146, and Muzondidya, 'From Buoyancy to Crisis, 1980-1997', p. 172.

65 S. Moyo, The 'Land Question' in I. Mandaza (ed.) *Zimbabwe: The Political Economy of Transition, 1980-86* (Dakar, CODESRIA, 1986), p. 72.

66 Muzondidya, 'From Buoyancy to Crisis', p. 173.

67 Ibid., p. 172.

68 In 1997, Clare Short, the British International Development Secretary, wrote a letter to Zimbabwe clearly defying International law by claiming her government was not obliged to pay for land in Zimbabwe because they were not party to the agreement. See H. Holland, *Dinner with Mugabe: The untold story of a freedom fighter who became a tyrant* (Johannesburg: Penguin Books, 2008), pp. 95-8.

69 Catholic Commission for Justice and Peace in Zimbabwe and Legal Resources Foundation, *Breaking the Silence, Building True Peace: A Report on the Disturbances in Matabeleland and the Midlands, 1980-1989* (Harare: CCJP, 1997).

70 Muzondidya, 'From Buoyancy to Crisis', p. 179.

71 *Gukurahundi*, meaning 'clearing the chaff', refers to the massacres that characterised the anti-rebel military activities of the Fifth Brigade during the Matabeleland and Midlands crisis.

72 Holland, *Dinner with Mugabe*, p. 66.

73 Timothy Scarnecchia, 'Rationalizing Gukurahundi: Cold War and South African Foreign Relations with Zimbabwe, 1981-1983', Kronos [online], 2011, 37 (1) p. 89.

74 R. Saunders, 'Zimbabwe: ESAP's fables', cited in Muzondidya, 'From Buoyancy to Crisis,' p. 191.

75 A. Selby, 'Commercial Farmers and the State: Interest Group Politics and Land Reform in Zimbabwe' (D. Phil. thesis, Oxford University, 2006), p. 242

76 K. Alexander, 'Orphans of the Empire: An analysis of elements of white identity and ideology construction in Zimbabwe', in B. Raftopoulos and T. Savage (eds)

Zimbabwe: Injustice and Political Reconciliation (Cape Town: Institute for Justice and Reconciliation, 2004), p. 194.

77 P. Godwin, 'Whose Kith and Kin Now? Black Africa's White Dilemma', *The Sunday Times* (London), 25 March 1984, accessed at http://www.maryellenmark.com/text/magazines/london/sundaytimes/904G-0.

78 See M. Sithole and J. Makumbe, 'Elections in Zimbabwe: The ZANU-PF hegemony and its incipient decline', *African Journal of Political Science*, 2 (1), 1997, for details of the election results.

79 Holland, *Dinner with Mugabe*, p.115.

80 Ibid., p. 114.

81 Muzondidya, 'From Buoyancy to Crisis,' p. 190.

82 See endnote 68.

83 Holland, *Dinner with Mugabe*, p. 98.

84 Ibid.

85 For the decline of the Zimbabwe economy under ESAP, see, among others, Kanyenze, 'The Performance of the Zimbabwean Economy, 1980-2000' in S. Darnolf and L. Laakso,(eds), *Twenty Years of Independence in Zimbabwe: From Liberation to Authoritarianism* (Basingstoke and New York: Palgrave Macmillan, 2003); A. S. Mlambo, *The Economic Structural Adjustment Programme: The Zimbabwean Case, 1990-1995* (Harare: University of Zimbabwe Publications, 1997) and also 'Zimbabwe: Economic Structural Adjustment Programme', Project Performance Evaluation Report, Operations Evaluation Department, African Development Bank, 9 December 1997, available on http://www.afdb.org/fileadmin/uploads/afdb/Documents/Evaluation-Reports/06050223.

86 Holland, *Dinner with Mugabe*, pp. 136-7

87 Since the hounding of PF ZAPU into a unity arrangement in 1987, the next formidable opposition to face ZANU-PF was Edgar Tekere's Zimbabwe Unity Movement which garnered 18 percent of the vote in the 1990 elections. See Sithole and Makumbe, 'Elections in Zimbabwe', p. 128.

88 Holland, *Dinner with Mugabe*, p. 139.

89 W. Z. Sadomba, 'Movements within a Movement: Complexities within the Land Occupations', in S. Moyo, K. Helliker and T. Murisa (eds) *Contested Terrain: Land Reform and Civil Society in Contemporary Zimbabwe* (Pietermaritzburg: S & S Publishers, 2008) pp. 159-60, identifies 'lower classes of peasants, farm workers, the urban unemployed and poor war veterans who participated in the liberation struggle' as the chief protagonists in the land invasions.

90 Ibid., p. 138.

91 Mugabe, *Inside the Third Chimurenga*.

92 Gleijeses, 'Scandinavia and the Liberation of Southern Africa', p. 328.

93 Ibid., p.329.
94 Sowetan, 'Mugabe's Pan-Africanist Status Questionable', *Daily News*, 30 November 2011.
95 Ibid.
96 Ibid.
97 Ibid.
98 Zimbabwe Democracy and Economic Recovery Act.
99 J. Alexander, *The Unsettled Land*, pp. 191-192.
100 L. M. Sachikonye, 'The Situation of Commercial Farm Workers after Land Reform in Zimbabwe'. A report prepared for the Farm Community Trust of Zimbabwe', May 2003, cited in ibid. p. 191.
101 Sharri Eppel, 'The Global Political Agreement and the Unity Accord', Solidarity Peace Trust, February 2009, p. 2.
102 J. MacDermott, *Breaking the Mould in Zimbabwe: Pragmatic Engagement at a Critical Juncture* (Stockholm: Swedish Defence Research Agency, 2009), p. 38.
103 Heather Chingono, 'Zimbabwe Sanctions: An analysis of the "Lingo" guiding the perceptions of the sanctioners and the sanctionees', *African Journal of Political Science and International Relations*, Vol. 4 (2), February 2010, p. 66.
104 Heather Cameron, 'Sanctioning Zimbabwe: Comparing the European Union and Canadian Approaches' (MA Public Policy Dissertation, King's College, London, August 2009), p. ii.
105 See Raftopoulos, 'The Crisis in Zimbabwe', pp. 219-227, for a broad outline of the economic decline and political impasse in Zimbabwe between 1998 and 2008.
106 Ibid., p. 227.
107 The MDC, formed in 1999, split in 2005 over policy differences. See B. Raftopoulos, 'Reflections on opposition politics in Zimbabwe: The politics of the Movement for Democratic Change (MDC)' in B. Raftopoulos and K. Alexander (eds), *Reflections on Democratic Politics in Zimbabwe* (Cape Town: Institute of Justice and Reconciliation, 2006), pp. 6-29, for an in-depth discussion of the dynamics of the split.
108 The Zimbabwe Congress of Trade Unions, out of which the MDC emerged, rejected the deal while most civic groups would reportedly have preferred an all-inclusive Transitional National Authority. See Jon Lunn and Gavin Thompson, Zimbabwe since the Global Political Agreement, (International Affairs and Defence Section and Economic Policy and Statistics Section, House of Commons, London) p. 3.
109 Marc Lizoain, 'Zimbabwe sanctions weaken democracy' (http://www.guardian.co.uk/commentisfree/2010/apr/13).
110 http://www.radiovop.com 05/09/11.
111 MacDermott, *Breaking the Mould*, p. 12.

112 'EU fed up with Mugabe's ruinous policies' http://www.thezimbabwean. co.uk/50784/eu-fed-up-with-mugabe 11/07/11.
113 'Beyond the Sanctions Stand-off', Zimbabwe Briefing Note, No. 86, Johannesburg/Brussels, 6 February 2012.
114 Ibid.
115 'New Broadcasting Licences a "Farce" and "Unacceptable"- Tsvangirai' http://www.thezimbabwemail.com/zimbabwe/9761-zimbabwe-new-radio-licences,25/11/12
116 The Mbare Chimurenga Choir jingles extolling the virtues of Mugabe and ZANU-PF and denigrating Tsvangirai are repeatedly played on radio and television on a daily basis. See also Eric Worby, 'The End of Modernity in Zimbabwe? in Amanda Hammar, Brian Raftopoulos, and Stig Jensen (eds), *Zimbabwe's Unfinished Business: Rethinking Land, State and Nation in the Context of Crisis* (Harare: Weaver Press, 2003), p. 52, for a similar observation on how the state media has utilised songs and jingles to reinforce the issue of sovereignty.
117 'Elections: ZEC's independence critical', *Zimbabwe Independent*, 13 to 19 January, 2012.
118 MacDermott, *Breaking the Mould*, p. 13.
119 Douglas Mwonzora, MDC–T spokesman, cited in 'Reform efforts in Zimbabwe move slowly as tensions rise', (http//www.monstersandcritics.com, 25/12/11).
120 'No Sign of Changes as Information Minister Defies Media Reform Deadline', http:www.voazimbabwe.com, 9 March 2012.
121 http//www.nation.co.ke 20/12/2009
122 Rugare Gumbo, ZANU-PF National Spokesperson, http://www.voanews.com 15/08/11.
123 'Army general, Nyikayaramba vows not to salute Tsvangirai' http://www.thezimbabwean.co.uk/news/40016/army-general/nyikayaramba-vow,29/05/11.
124 C. Hendricks and L. Hutton, 'Providing Security and Justice for the People: Security Sector Reform in Zimbabwe', ISS Paper 199, September 2009, p.11.
125 'No land audit until sanctions are lifted' http://www.insiderzim.com/stories/3583-no-land-audit-until-sanctions-are-lifted.html 29/02/12.
126 B. Raftopoulos, SPT-Zimbabwe Update No. 4, March 2012, 'The Shadow of Elections', 9 March 2012, Solidarity Peace Trust: http://www.solidaritypeacetrust.org/1150/stp-zimbabwe-up-date-no-4-the-shadow-of-elections/
127 Mahmood Mamdani, 'Lessons of Zimbabwe', *London Review of Books*, 30 (23), 4 December 2008, p. 9.
128 Ibid.
129 'EU fed up with Mugabe's ruinous policies' http://www.thezimbabwean.co.uk/new/zimbabwe/50784/eu-fed-up-with-mugabers 11/07/11)
130 Ibid.

131 Ibid.
132 Quoted in Marc Lizoain, 'Zimbabwe sanctions weaken democracy', p.3.
133 'No Sanctions on Zimbabwe', AfricanPerspective.com, Issue 51, 3 February 2002,) cited in Connie White, 'Sanctions on Zimbabwe: Africa Under Attack', http://www.nathanielturner.com/sanctionszimbabwe.htm.
134 Working Paper 1997 of the Institute for International Economics, cited in White, 'Sanctions on Zimbabwe: Africa Under Attack'.
135 White, 'Sanctions on Zimbabwe: Africa Under Attack'.
136 Cited in ibid.
137 R. W. Johnson, 'Where do we go from here?' *London Review of Books*, 30 (9), 8 May 2008.
138 *The Herald*, 7 September 2011.
139 Ibid.
140 Executive Orders (EOs) are legally binding orders issued by the US president (http://www.thisnation.com>Home, 01/01/12). The EOs in question are 'Blocking Property of Persons Undermining Democratic Processes or Institutions in Zimbabwe' (EO 13 288, 10 March 2003), 'Blocking Property of Additional Persons Undermining Democratic Processes or Institutions in Zimbabwe' (EO 13 391, 25 November 2005, and EO 13 469, 25 July 2008).
141 MacDermott, *Breaking the Mould*, p. 39.
142 Human Rights Watch accused the Zimbabwe security forces of killing more than 200 people, raping women and forcing children to search for gems in the fields http://www.timeslive.co.za 05/11/11.
143 The Kimberley Process was set up in 2002 following brutal wars in Sierra Leone and Liberia that were fueled by 'blood diamonds'. Nations that participate in the Process are obliged to certify the origins of their diamonds to ensure that they are not used to fund wars and human rights abuses http://www.timeslive.co.za 05/11/11.
144 Hilary Anderson, 'Marange Diamonds Field: Zimbabwe torture camp discovered' (http://bbc.co.uk/news/world-africa-143777215 8/8/11).
145 'Marange Diamonds: Zimbabwe denies "torture camp"', (http://www.zimbabwesituation.com,10/08/11).
146 http://www.timeslive.co.za Accessed on 05/11/11.
147 (http://www.radiovop.com 5/11/11).
148 'Air Zimbabwe trying to secure French planes amid sanctions', (http://www.theafricareport.com, 26/10/11).
149 Timothy Scarnecchia, Jocelyn Alexander and 33 others, Responses to Mahmood Mamdani's 'Lessons of Zimbabwe', *London Review of Books*, 31 (1). 1 January 2009.
150 Judy Smith-Höhn, 'Zimbabwe: Are targeted sanctions smart enough?' Institute for Security Studies Situation Report, 4 June 2010, cited in Lunn and Thompson,

'Zimbabwe After the Global Political Agreement', p. 17.
151 'US bans Marange diamonds', *Daily News*, 11 December 2011.
152 Tendai Biti, Minister of Finance, speaking at the Centre for Research Development workshop on Diamond Mining, Harare, 22 May 2012, http://www.theindependent.co.zw 24/5/12.
153 Shari Eppel, 'The Global Political Agreement and the Unity Accord in Zimbabwe', Solidarity Peace Trust, February 2009 (http://www.africalegalbrief.com).
154 Holland, *Dinner with Mugabe*, p.139.
155 Wilfred Mhanda, *Dzino: Memories of a Freedom Fighter* (Harare: Weaver Press, 2011) p. 231.
156 *Daily News*, 23 May 2011.
157 Holland, *Dinner with Mugabe*, p. 105.
158 A. L. George and W. E. Simons, *The Limits of Coercive Diplomacy*, 2nd edition (Boulder: Westview Press, 1994), p.16. See also Canadian Centre for Foreign Policy Development, 'UN Sanctions: Policy Options for Canada', Background Paper (Ottawa: Canadian Centre for Foreign Policy Development, 1998), p. 20, cited in Cameron, 'Sanctioning Zimbabwe', p. 39.
159 Cameron, 'Sanctioning Zimbabwe', p. 39.
160 Holland, *Dinner with Mugabe*, pp. 99-100.
161 (http://www.voanews.com 16/09/11).
162 B. Raftopoulos, 'The Zimbabwean Crisis and the Challenges for the Left', *Journal of Southern African Studies*, 32 (2), June 2006, p. 212.
163 http://www.voanews.com, 12/08/11.
164 Hovi et al., 'When Do (Imposed) Economic Sanctions Work?' pp. 481-485.
165 S. J. Ndlovu-Gatsheni, *The Zimbabwean Nation-State Project: A Historical Diagnosis of Identity and Power-Based Conflicts in a Postcolonial State* (Uppsala: Nordic Africa Institute, 2011), p. 83.
166 'There are no sanctions on Zimbabwe-EU Envoy', the *Zimbabwe Independent*, 15 March, 2012.
167 These journalists are *The Herald*'s editor-in-chief and his assistant editor, Sunday Mail political editor and the ZBC boss and two of his reporters. See 'Sanctions Lifted on Reutenbach [sic] and Bredenkamp', http://www.newzimbabwe.com,17/02/12.
168 Ezra Chitando, '"In the Beginning Was the Land": The Appropriation of Religious Themes in Political Discourses in Zimbabwe', *Africa: Journal of the International African Institute*, 75 (2) (2005), p. 233.
169 See 'Chipangano must be stopped and disbanded', http://www.swradioafrica.com,29 March 2012 and also 'Mugabe's pleas for peace falling on deaf ears?' http://www.thezimbabwean.co.uk/28 March 2012.

170 'Stop Mugabe from Rigging: Tsvangirai', *NewsDay*, 20 March 2012.
171 'PM wants sanctions to go', *The Herald*, 14 March 2012.
172 'Zimbabwe sanctions are not only short sighted but unstrategic – Ncube', http://greatindaba.com/issue/february-2012-volume-40/article Accessed 28/3/12.
173 'Zimbabwe's Sanctions Stand-off', Africa Briefing No. 86, Johannesburg/Brussels, 6 February 2012. Also entitled 'Beyond the Sanctions Stand-off'.
174 Ibid.
175 'EU Notes Progress in Zimbabwe But Says Wont Lift Sanctions Yet', http://www.voanews.com 11 May 2012.
176 'GNU reforms key to credible elections-UK Ambassador', http://www.independent.co.zw 24 May 2012.
177 Charles Ray, US Ambassador to Zimbabwe, Speech at the 37th Annual Africa Travel Association Congress, Victoria Falls, 19 May 2012.
178 In the past both ZANU-PF and the MDCs have moved the goalposts when it comes to the implementation of decisions unfavourable to their political objectives. ZANU-PF is currently pushing for elections without a new constitution ostensibly because, as Mugabe put it on 8 March 2012 at the Chiefs' Conference in Bulawayo, the GPA 'was never about a new constitution. The main issue was about violence and fresh elections without that violence'. See 'GPA was never about writing a new constitution – Mugabe', http://www.radiovop.com 9 March 2012. Secondly, the party has pledged to block Parliament from debating important legislative bills, including the Human Rights and Electoral Amendment Bills, arguing these are not covered by the GPA, yet they are already at the second reading stage. On their part, the MDC formations belatedly brought up the issue of security sector reform as an important prerequisite for holding elections when it suited them. It is also generally believed the two MDC formations had initially agreed with ZANU-PF to adopt the Kariba Draft as a springboard for a new constitution, but the two later backtracked after heavy criticism from other stakeholders. See 'Constitution: GPA exposes Mugabe's poll duplicity', *Zimbabwe Independent*, 15 March 2012.
179 www.dailynews.co.zw 27/10/2011
180 'Zimbabwe-EU trade doubles', *The Herald*, 30 March 2012.
181 This position has been reiterated by the SADC Troika on Defence, Politics and Security meeting in Luanda, Angola, 1 June 2012. See 'Ball in your court, SADC tells Zim', *The Sunday Mail*, 3 June 2012 and also 'Mugabe faces end of political career', *The Standard*, 3 June 2012.

CHAPTER 7

Repairing a Fractured Nation:
Challenges and Opportunities in Post-GPA Zimbabwe

SHARI EPPEL

The epidemic of state-driven violence that prevailed from April to June 2008, during the months between the harmonised elections and the presidential run-off, played a key role in deciding the political future of Zimbabwe. Most immediately, the violence rendered the run-off election a tragic farce, with the main contender Morgan Tsvangirai, who had won the first round of the elections with 47% of the vote, withdrawing in June from the second poll. He did so on the justifiable grounds that levels of violence and intimidation against his supporters were so high that a free and fair vote was impossible. Secondly, the undeniable scale of violence, and the effective way in which images, stories and victims themselves were placed into the international domain,[1] resulted, for the first time, in heads of state in the SADC region refusing to endorse Mugabe as the legitimate President of Zimbabwe. One could say that the torture of 2008 denied Tsvangirai electoral victory, and simultaneously denied Mugabe legitimacy, thus feeding directly into the creation of the Global Political Agreement (GPA) as the only political way forward. Victims were therefore hopeful that their needs would be taken into account by the GPA.

Yet the most uneasy and tentative clause in the GPA document is that which relates to the political crimes of the past. The GPA binds all parties to:
> give consideration to the setting up of a mechanism to properly advise on what measures might be necessary and practicable to achieve national cohesion and unity in respect of victims of pre- and post-independence political conflicts...[2]

From this, it can be seen that the GPA approaches the issue of transitional justice (TJ) as obliquely as possible – this clause is a promise to 'give consideration' to what would be merely an *advisory mechanism* on what 'might' be needed with regard to past violence. Those close to the negotiations that resulted in the GPA have commented that it was the facilitator, Thabo Mbeki, who promoted the need for a clause on dealing with past political violence, rather than the political parties themselves.[3] Nor was there any talk of a Ministry of Healing in the original prolonged arguments during 2008/9 about government ministries and who should run them. The Organ of National Healing, Reconciliation and Integration (ONHRI), with its three ministers, one from each signatory party, only surfaced several months after the signing of the GPA, possibly in part as a way of including more ministers in the government.[4] The three Ministers of ONHRI do not attend Cabinet, as they head an 'organ', not a ministry: they inherited no enabling legislation, no bureaucratic framework or staff, and no budget to speak of. The staff of the President's Office – who are members of the Central Intelligence Organisation, well known for its perpetration of violence and repression over the decades – have been seconded to carry out much of the bureaucratic work of the organ.

This chapter seeks to give a review of TJ processes over the last four years, and also to broaden the Zimbabwean TJ discussions by raising aspects of international debates about this still-developing genre. The chapter begins by situating the ONHRI and its activities within the current political context. Conceptual ambiguities and various models of TJ currently in the Zimbabwe domain are touched upon. The possibility of including corruption and cultural and socio-economic rights more centrally in local TJ debates is considered, as are reflections on individual versus community reparations. The need to avoid the pitfall of reducing 'truth-telling' to the collection of thousands of individual accounts that could ignore the underlying structural causes of violence is considered. To date, some eras of violence have been given more 'legitimate' space by the state, with some memories being allowed into the public domain and others not – this is typified in the state reaction to mass graves of different eras. The chapter concludes by looking at some practical experiences in the last few years in the implementation of peace-building and healing programmes in Zimbabwe, and the need for NGOs to develop a more considered position on 'theories of change' in the realm of conflict resolution, as they develop practical intervention strategies.

Current context and TJ

For TJ and peace-building mechanisms to gain traction, the country needs to have achieved a moment of real transition, and the GPA has not evolved into this moment. Control of the security sector is still firmly within the grip of ZANU-PF, and any mention of security sector reform has been vociferously attacked. Selective arrests for political violence, and impunity for security sector perpetrators, still predominate; the state media remains partisan, often viciously so.

Political party support for any process of accountability during the lifespan of the GPA has clearly been hesitant at best. There are good reasons for this – ZANU-PF fears the spectre of its own lengthy and grim history of violence. With the revolutions in North Africa in 2011, including the gruesome death of Gaddafi, and International Criminal Court (ICC) proceedings at various stages in Kenya, Uganda, Central African Republic, Sudan, Dafur, Côte d'Ivoire and now Libya, fear of accountability is a strong motivator for ZANU-PF to remain in power in Zimbabwe, and to resist any meaningful transitional justice processes.[5] Consequently, the MDCs realistically fear destabilising the fragile coalition if they demand truth or justice too firmly at this stage.[6] Ominously for the future, MDC-T has since 2000 also opted routinely for secrecy around its own violence.[7]

Zimbabwe has a hundred-year history of politically motivated violence that has aimed at entrenching the government of the day, accompanied by impunity for that violence. Colonial injustices were legalised by unjust laws, and the excesses of the liberation war were amnestied in 1979 and 1980. After independence in 1980, there were an estimated 10,000 civilians murdered in the west of the country, as ZANU-PF sought to establish its political hegemony and destroy ZAPU's support base. These murders and other violations during what is known as *Gukurahundi*,[8] were amnestied in 1988.[9] There were further amnesties in 1995 and 2000 in the wake of election-related violence. Breaking this cycle of violence with impunity – which has served all previous governments so well – will not be a simple task.

Indeed, it would be unrealistic to expect any profound government-driven advances in the domain of TJ during the lifespan of the GPA, whose continued existence has faced multiple threats – not least from continuing political violence and repression.[10] For ZANU-PF, the ONHRI exists as a pragmatic mechanism that can be gestured to whenever the issue of accountability is raised; it might even be said that the organ's primary reason for existing has been to prevent any meaningful, official developments in the TJ arena. Any decisions made by the ONHRI have to be referred back to the three political principals, and approved by all three.

The Organ of National Healing, Reconciliation and Integration

The ONHRI ministers have themselves publicly acknowledged that the GPA was a document of political compromise and has left unresolved issues which undermine their power to act.[11] The ONHRI has nonetheless undertaken some activities over the last three to four years, although on a diminishing basis as time has passed. A series of five countrywide consultations in 2009-2010 resulted in a report that summarised the transitional justice demands that had been raised by the public, and civil society organisations.[12] Meetings also took place with traditional leaders and churches separately in all provinces. At all these meetings, the ministers of the ONHRI articulated their mission to be:

> To heal the wounds caused by generations of injustice, intolerance, exclusion and impunity so as to reconcile Zimbabweans to become 'One Nation' focused on social, political, cultural, and economic development in order to improve the quality of life for all.[13]

It is noteworthy, and not surprising considering the current fragility of Zimbabwe's democratic space, that TJ is currently officially defined in Zimbabwe as being purely about 'healing' and 'reconciling', with no mention of the word 'justice', or the other word usually integral to TJ processes – 'truth'.

The ONHRI refers to itself as having a mandate to oversee a 'history programme', in which consultants will research the trends of past violence in Zimbabwe and how it has been resolved using local mechanisms, as well as making use of psychologists to offer counseling and healing to victims.[14]

The three ministers have attended gatherings and conferences both nationally and internationally and have contributed to the national debate on TJ. However, by the end of 2011 the ONHRI was conspicuous by its almost total invisibility. The arrest of ONHRI Minister Moses Mzila Ndlovu of the MDC after he attended a rural prayer service for Gukurahundi victims in April 2011, underlined the position of the ZANU-PF that in Matabeleland, 'healing' should take place without 'revealing'![15] The perceived lack of support for Minister Ndlovu by his fellow ONHRI ministers in the wake of this arrest drove a wedge between them, and by the end of 2011 the three ministers were seldom undertaking public activities together.[16] The ZANU-PF Minister of Healing, John Nkomo, was appointed Vice-President of Zimbabwe after the death of Joseph Msika in August 2009, yet retained his role in the ONHRI. The demands of balancing multiple commitments, combined with his own failing health, has meant less time for the ONHRI. The MDC-T Minister, Sekai Holland, has also stepped back from her once vocal position in the organ. In 2009, she incurred the wrath of activists in Matabeleland after stating at a workshop that the Ndebeles and Mzilikazi introduced torture into Zimbabwe in the nineteenth century.[17] While she made efforts to make amends in the wake of this, some activists in Matabeleland continue to regard her with suspicion and distrust.

During the closing months of 2011, the ONHRI promoted the adoption of a Code of Conduct by the three parties to the GPA. The executive councils of the parties met and agreed , and 2012 began with the suggestion that the three political principles should address joint rallies of their supporters, calling for an end to political violence. However, by May 2012, no such rally had taken place.[18]

'Ubuntu' versus 'truth and justice'

One of the dilemmas facing the ONHRI has been the tension about what 'healing' entails and what route TJ should take, with the predominant TJ paradigm of the truth commission/justice model standing in juxtaposition to a notion of home-grown 'ubuntu', or reconciliation. Although the two are not necessarily contradictory,[19] there has been a strong call from ZANU-PF to deal with reconciliation in terms of African conflict resolution practices, avoiding 'western' justice systems. ZANU-PF has been happy to use 'western' laws and courts to deliver justice to the political opposition since independence, but now that the issue of its own accountability is reaching centre stage, justice through the courts has suddenly become 'western' in a derogatory sense, with 'ubuntu' being said to provide the true African solution. ZANU-PF's position reflects a greater – and in many ways justifiable – perception among African leaders that there is a double standard when it comes to international justice, typified by the International Criminal Court (ICC) and its decisions as to which leaders should be indicted for crimes against humanity. Currently, all their proceedings are in relation to African nations: President Paul Kagame of Rwanda has condemned the ICC as 'part of colonialism, slavery and imperialism'.[20] In 2011, Robert Mugabe pronounced:

> We in Africa are also duly concerned about the activities of the International Criminal Court which seems to exist only for alleged offenders of the developing world, the majority of them Africans. The leaders of the powerful Western States guilty of international crime, like Bush and Blair, are routinely given the blind eye. Such selective justice has eroded the credibility of the ICC on the African continent.[21]

Civic society, while fairly uniformly agreeing that Zimbabwean community healing mechanisms must be identified and strengthened as part of a TJ approach, has nonetheless emphasised the more recognised and established truth-telling/justice/reparations model in their discussions, surveys and papers.[22] A nationwide survey done by Human Rights NGO Forum in 2010 is clearly biased towards this internationally familiar TJ model, with its questions and terminology based in this paradigm.[23] Alongside this, is the acknowledgement by civics of the need for peace building and conflict resolution skills to be imparted across the country. TJ and peace building are considered more or less as a continuum in civic programmes, as part of a greater endeavour to repair a damaged nation.

In 2011, the United Nations Development Programme (UNDP), funded a consultant to begin developing a way forward for the ONHRI. The resulting paper from the UNDP consultant, entitled 'National Policy Framework for National Healing and Reconciliation',[24] has clearly been deeply influenced by what could be called the 'ubuntu' model preferred by ZANU-PF. This document acknowledges that there have been calls within Zimbabwe for truth telling, justice and reparations. Yet, remarkably, the outlined policy – which is referred to as a long-term policy that will outlive the GPA – makes no mention whatsoever of a truth commission and has no policy directives at all in the arenas of reparation, retributive justice, lustration or institutional reform – which have all been very widely accepted, at least as discussion points, in TJ programmes elsewhere. The idea of memorialisation, which would open the way for monuments, exhumations and reburials of the dead, is also never mentioned. Instead, the document focuses on the setting up of Peace and Reconciliation Councils nationwide, down to the district and ward level, and on implementing training of traditional leaders, women and youth in reconciliation skills.

The words 'reconciliation' and 'national cohesion' are used repeatedly and without definition in the document. Yet the intolerance of political diversity that is so familiar to Zimbabweans is at one level, a manifestation of ZANU-PF's desire for 'national cohesion'. Reference to the acceptance of diversity of opinion and cultural background would be preferable in a 'healing and reconciliation' policy document, bearing in mind that in the last 40 years in Zimbabwe there has been a narrow line between 'national cohesion' and 'national coercion'. Additionally, a recommendation that these government-funded committees should 'supervise' all peace-building programmes on the ground is likely to meet with protests from civics and churches, and could be seen as government interference in civic space.

It is clear from this policy document that a chasm still exists between various models being put forward for Zimbabwe's TJ policy framework. The idea in the UNDP proposal that these processes should be driven by a council of independent, politically neutral individuals is commendable, as is the idea of supporting structures across the provinces. But the bureaucratic burden of structures down to ward and village level, and the centralising of control of all peace-building activities under these structures, could simply serve to introduce new hierarchies of power and state interference across the country. It is curious that a policy document on TJ at this time could fail to mention the possibility of a truth commission – even if only to advocate against it, considering that this issue has been raised repeatedly by other voices in the country including all opposition political parties and many civic groupings. The document reads as a sop to ZANU-PF, but under the constraints of the GPA, which as already noted has provided a very partial TJ space, this is to be expected: it is only the most non-threatening of TJ policies that could possibly be adopted and advanced by the unity government. Indeed, this UNDP policy paper was approved by Cabinet in April 2012.[25]

'Healing' and 'reconciliation'

Neither the civics TJ/peace-building model, nor the UNDP, 'ubuntu', Cabinet-approved model have to date interrogated the concepts of healing and reconciliation in very much detail, yet these are highly contentious ideas in this arena generally. In the first instance, victims should have the freedom to choose whether they wish to be 'healed' and 'reconciled' or not. The South African model of TJ has been criticised for placing too much emphasis on healing and forgiveness – ostracizing the relatives of murdered activist Steve Biko, for example, who insisted that they wanted justice and did not wish to forgive his murderers.[26]

The famous mothers of the Plaza De Mayo in Buenos Aires, have met and marched every week since April 1977: their children were disappeared during the military repression in Argentina, and the mothers, more than thirty years later, still demand nothing less than their children back alive – or to know what happened to them and who gave the orders for them to be disappeared.[27] They have refused compensation: their marching is a political statement, a choice to remain unaccepting of what happened, and to make the point that nothing can replace the lost children. To remain 'un-reconciled' is a legitimate choice.

What it means to be 'reconciled' can vary dramatically from one family or community to another. For example, 'reconciliation' can offer a choice of coming to terms with past injustice, so that the victim's life can move forward without daily bitterness; but without necessarily forgiving the perpetrators.

'Healing' too, is a process, not an event. It can present a long and varied path, one that victims can choose to journey on, or not. Healing does not often happen as the result of one workshop, or one truth commission testimony, or a few counselling sessions – although for some this might suffice. A victim could feel that s/he has healed at one point, and then feel a few years later that s/he has not done so. This has happened with many who testified to the South African truth commission, for example.[28] This chapter will not dwell on these issues at further length, as they are major topics in their own right, but herewith the words 'healing' and 'reconciliation' are used with diffidence, and with the recommendation that civics needs to seriously interrogate these terms in Zimbabwe in their TJ and peace-building debates.

Plunder and corruption: TJ and social injustice

It is evident that the push for TJ at this time will have to come largely from outside of the political parties themselves, from the churches, civil society and the grassroots. Furthermore, while policies can be discussed and developed now, the effective implementation of many aspects of TJ will have to wait for a different political space to that provided by the GPA.

Since 2000 and before, Zimbabwe's civic groups have taken on board, fairly uncritically, that what is needed in terms of TJ is a 'package deal of the usual' – a truth commission, reparations, healing, institutional reform, lustration, and a mixture of restorative and retributive justice – while recognition has also been made of the need to consult and include the rural citizens who make up 70% of Zimbabwe's population. Victims are seen as having to play a central role in the process. Most recommendations by civics have referred to individual reparations, including access to mental and physical health care and remuneration for lives and properties lost, as well as for permanent disabilities. Expectations are at times high as to what might be achieved if this 'package' becomes a reality, and the plethora of workshops, conferences and surveys now taking place in this field in Zimbabwe (and beyond) indicate a commitment among civics to this model going forward. There are scores of Zimbabwe NGO policy documents now in the public domain on TJ.[29]

There is, however, an increasingly extensive literature available in the global TJ debate that challenges some of the basic premises that underlie each of these processes and what they can be expected to deliver – including debate on the entire genre of TJ.

Arguments have been put forward that challenge the very premise of 'standard' TJ processes, seeing them as band-aid solutions that serve to particularise political violence into discreet instances affecting individual 'victims' and 'perpetrators' – in so doing, masking and maintaining the more profound, structural violence of these societies. Truth commissions can claim to 'heal' and/or 'reveal' historical truths via the accumulation of thousands of individual accounts of victimhood, while insidiously allowing underlying entrenched political, socio-economic and institutional inequalities and injustices to be carried forward into the new era, unhealed and only partially revealed.

It is not surprising that, in South Africa as elsewhere, victims who viewed testifying to a truth commission as one step towards a different, more just world, have been shown to be disillusioned years later when they are still poor, and one political and economic elite has simply been (partially) replaced with another.[30] Moreover, political violence can slide into criminal violence or new social protests when underlying economic injustices are not addressed, such as in South Africa and Peru.

> *New cycles of violence and repression in countries lauded for their transitional justice projects push us to ask whether these types of projects could do more to assure the goals of post-conflict recovery, such as reconciliation and sustainable peace.*[31]

This question needs to be borne seriously in mind and the issue of socio-economic rights – and wrongs – and how they are maintained by partisan state structures and historical realities, should be considered for inclusion in any TJ processes in Zimbabwe, along with the more usual inclusion of political and human rights. This is made more pressing taking into consideration that by far the worst and most widely felt impacts of the crisis of the last ten years, have been socio-economic.[32]

Colonialism entrenched the economic dominance of a white elite by dispossessing the black majority of their land and creating a poor underclass to provide cheap labour in the cities, via taxations. It was these injustices among others that drove Zimbabwe into a war of liberation, but after independence the structural injustices underlying poverty were only partially dealt with, even though strides were made in providing dramatically improved access to basic services via the state, and some access to land.[33] It was not only Zimbabwe's internal dynamic that worked to maintain structural injustices, but from 1990, also the international neo-liberal context.[34] In the 1990s, in Zimbabwe, there was once more a growing sense of economic inequality as a result of Economic Structural Adjustment Programme policies reluctantly negotiated with the World Bank, which led to job losses and growing economic hardship among Zimbabweans. This sense of economic disempowerment, together with a broader disillusionment about an increasingly powerful and unaccountable state, bolstered the rise of the Zimbabwean trade union movement, and its transformation in 1999 into a new political movement prepared to contest elections.

Along with political and human rights, economic rights have remained at the centre of what has driven the demand for democratic change since then, yet cataclysmic poverty has been the outcome of this struggle, as the government has systematically dismantled large parts of the economy, while simultaneously looting and plundering resources, including diamonds and gold, for the benefit of an increasingly small elite.

While Mugabe portrayed the land invasions post-2000 as a belated attempt to finally address the land inequalities left by colonialism, the outcome of the redistribution exercise remains highly contested. Over one hundred thousand previously landless Zimbabweans have indeed received land under this new system, but vast tracts of land remain idle, and the ZANU-PF elite have grabbed the best farms, allegedly including numerous farms each in violation of the 'one person, one farm' principle.³⁵ Clearly, while some corrections to the land injustices have been made, a new elite has become entrenched, leaving most Zimbabweans still impoverished, and the compulsory system of farm leases leaves farmers open to political abuse and sudden evictions. The land audit promised under the GPA remains an unaddressed issue, and could be helpful in guiding land policy into the future.³⁶

'Operation Murambatsvina', the government-orchestrated demolitions of 2005, displaced 500,000 people, while since 2002 between 2 and 3 million Zimbabweans have been forced to seek work abroad as Zimbabwean industry and commercial agriculture have collapsed. The hyperinflation of 2008 destroyed family survival mechanisms, and the introduction of new currencies with almost no warning – twice in succession – pushed Zimbabwe's poorest citizens into excruciating poverty, with sacks of useless bank notes under their beds. Health and education provision plummeted, and are now making a slow recovery although these services remain well below their 1990s heyday. The social fabric has been irrevocably changed, with families divided across borders and plunged into poverty not only at home but also often abroad.³⁷

There is increasing recognition in global TJ discussions of the need to transform the social conditions in a country in times of transition, and not simply to address the physical human rights violations of murder, assault and property loss.

> *Can transitional justice (TJ) today afford not to concern itself directly with social injustice and patterns of inequality, discrimination and marginalisation that were underlying causes of a conflict and that inflicted major suffering and victimization on vast swathes of a population? How can (or should) TJ have a more direct impact on reducing social and economic inequality?*³⁸

Mani goes on to recommend that TJ processes need to consider 'war economies and corruption, particularly the exploitation of natural and mineral resources, as these are often perpetrated by the same war criminals – and with the same abusive, violent and exploitative means and devastating effect on victims.' While Zimbabwe has not technically been through a war since 2000,³⁹ the ZANU-PF hierarchy has clearly used plundered mineral and other resources to maintain its grip on power.

Any analysis of structural violence that became incorporated into a truth commission process should:

> *... treat the root causes of political violence as more than just*

> 'historical context' for the study of civil and political violations, framing them in terms of state obligations that were not fulfilled and thus require redress. Second, this approach would increase attention to the oft-forgotten tasks of institutional reform and development in transitional justice processes.[40]
>
> The recognition at the centre of TJ discourse of economic, social and cultural rights, would allow demands for social change to be made 'through democratic mechanisms, not rejected as disruptive and subversive and thus made susceptible to repression.[41]
>
> Transitional justice thinking and practice needs to address privileged communities beyond the token criminal trials of select leaders. Already there are calls for forgiveness of ZANU-PF for the heinous crimes it has committed, but little has been said about correcting its contribution to existing economic inequalities. To fail to address these at this juncture, and with the current window of opportunity in Zimbabwe, would be just as erroneous as the original failures of transitional justice at the time of liberation.[42]

The preoccupation by victims of violence on the need for the socio-economic consequences of repression to be redressed, has been noted by previous research in South Africa, Sierra Leone, Uganda and elsewhere. Branch has noted that surveys undertaken in Uganda, which the researchers conducted intending to show that ordinary people wanted prosecutions, instead revealed that:

> ... only three percent of Acholi respondents named justice as being a priority for them, whereas peace, health, security, food, land, return, money and education were all named by between 32 and 45% of people surveyed.[43]

Similarly, in Sierra Leone, Shaw found that victims who testified to the TRC were preoccupied with getting financial reparations:

> Almost without exception, witnesses who spoke in the District Hearings I attended ended their testimony with pleas for material assistance, often expressing these pleas in a strongly felt manner more characteristic of [deep feelings] than their main testimony had been: 'I have nothing! What will be given to me?[44]

Many victims she spoke to told her that they had decided not to testify to the TRC because of the knowledge that there would be no recompense for doing so:

> If they want to heal the wounds, let them send jobs.[45]

In South Africa, too, victims have expressed disillusionment with their continued poverty and the lack of transformation in their lives more than a decade after the TRC. Reparations have remained among the contentious issues of the TRC, with Hamber noting that four years after the TRC, none of the recommendations regarding reparations had been acted upon. Eventually, seven years after the TRC began, a figure of about US$4,000 each was paid to those who testified, making a total payout of US$75 million – a fraction of the US$377 million recommended and set aside into a President's Fund by the TRC for this purpose.[46]

Khulumani Support Group, a nationwide grouping of over 55,000 South African victims, continues to seek redress from multinationals around the world that did not heed calls for a boycott of South Africa in the 1980s, and enriched themselves by trading and mining in the country. In November 2002, they lodged a case in the United States against 23 large corporations, demanding a retrospective Apartheid tax as a form of damages. After ten years of legal wrangling, in February 2012, the US courts finally ratified a settlement between General Motors and thirteen apartheid law-suit claimants, in which a symbolic amount of US$1,5 million is to be paid out in acknowledgement of the company's culpability of benefiting under apartheid.[47] Khulumani has said that the money will be put into a Trust fund to benefit victims and fund future actions.

Of course, one-time payouts are themselves only band-aids and can seldom be sufficient to transform the lives of even a handful of victims. The resurgence of social protests in South Africa in recent years, and the growing poverty gap, indicate that South Africa's transition has not delivered a better economic reality for most of those who suffered under Apartheid. Whether this is going to result in a threat to political stability in the decade ahead remains to be seen, but what is clear is that while the TRC may have enabled a smoothened political transition in the 1990s, it has not 'healed' the nation, although it is often popularly referred to as having done so. Archbishop Tutu has referred to the lack of general economic transformation as a 'powder keg' and has called on whites to voluntarily pay an Apartheid tax.[48]

> *In cases where economic exploitation has been systemic and institutionalised, individual reparations are inadequate. In fact, reparations, by individuating compensation, may impede systemic change by surrogating redistribution...*[49]

Victims of torture: the likelihood of reforms, reparations and justice

In Zimbabwe, the calls from political activists and civics, rather than referring to social justice issues, are currently focused on reparations for individual damage caused by political violence and repression. Calls for individuated compensation do not preclude recognising that what is fundamentally needed is the transformation of the militarised structures of the state to ensure that the state can never again violently repress its own citizens. Such transformation – and the separation of the state from the ruling party, no matter which party this is – has been acknowledged to be of paramount importance during any future transition: this failed to happen sufficiently in 1980, leaving the colonial apparatus of oppression conveniently intact ahead of Gukurahundi. [50]

In 1997, payouts under the War Victims Compensation Act acknowledged the suffering of individuals during the War of Liberation – but had nothing to do with the need to transform the structures of oppression: the army almost simultaneously went into action against citizens of the state yet again, killing and injuring civilians during the food riots of 1997. The payouts to war victims of Z$1.8 billion, after fierce lobbying by war veterans, also proved how problematic it can be to identify a 'true' victim and the level of compensatory damage owing, especially for 'invisible injuries', such as backache, stomach pain and Post Traumatic Stress Disorder (PTSD), years after the events.

> *The indiscriminate use of vague or false affidavits to confirm the place and nature of injury led to many abuses. The Commission is aware that it may not always be possible to find an eyewitness to an event that took place some eighteen or more years ago.*[51]

More recently, with incidents relating to post-2000 violations, civic organisations have had people claiming losses that later proved to be exaggerated or invented, simply because they believed that by so doing they would receive financial or other support from human rights NGOs.[52]

If individual reparations are agreed to in Zimbabwe as the way forward, there will be multiple complications: in many instances perpetrators are not known – this is the case with almost all Gukurahundi violations, where precise soldiers or commanders remained unknown to victims; furthermore, victimhood may now be difficult or impossible to prove. How does a villager in Matabeleland prove in 2013 that she lost her husband to the Fifth Brigade in 1983, and that as a result all the cattle disappeared? Or how does a family prove their homestead was burnt down in 1985 – or in 2002 – resulting in total loss of possessions? What medical record can irrefutably state that an unending backache is a consequence of being beaten by soldiers decades ago, and how does one measure the economic impact of failure to farm effectively for nearly three decades because of this? While international formulae exist for deriving amounts for injuries, the possibility remains of fraudulent claims, and of victims who are not informed being excluded, considering the large time scales involved here.

Gukurahundi impacted in complex ways on an entire generation, perhaps particularly on the children. The latest UNDP report (2012) indicates that children growing up in Matabeleland suffered permanent setbacks:

> *One study in Zimbabwe found that children who were exposed to shocks (civil war and the 1982–1984 drought) at ages 12–24 months completed 0.85 grades of schooling less and were on average 3.4 centimetres shorter than those who were not. This stunting was shown to reduce lifetime earnings by 14 percent.* [53]

Access to food was deliberately denied on a mass scale during 1984 – ZANU-PF's first foray into political abuse of food. Is it possible to financially compensate an entire generation of young adults for these losses, three decades later? Or, considering more recent events, what is to be done about assessing compensation for the 500,000 who lost dwellings and/or livelihoods, as a result of the government-orchestrated Murambatsvina?[54]

The legal precedent of victims successfully suing the state for damages has nonetheless been set over the years. Between 2003 and 2006, twelve victims of the Food Riots of 1997 were awarded damages by the Zimbabwean High Court for injuries caused by soldiers shooting or beating them.[55] However, only one victim was paid the damages, resulting in the Human Rights NGO Forum pursuing the cases through the SADC Tribunal. In December 2010, the Tribunal ruled that the Zimbabwe government was legally obliged to pay out the damages, totaling US$17 million – but to date, this ruling has been ignored. In November 2011, a 70-year-old man tortured by youth militia in June 2008 was awarded damages of over US$12,000, to be paid by the two aggressors.[56] To date, this money has not been paid and it seems unlikely that the perpetrators will ever raise or pay this money.

In May 2012, the South African courts ruled that South African police and prosecutors have a duty to investigate accusations of torture against senior Zimbabwean politicians, in a case brought by the Southern Africa Litigation Centre and the Zimbabwe Exiles Forum.[57] However, there is no political will in South Africa for this to happen at this time, and the ruling, while an important precedent, is unlikely to result in anything tangible, certainly during the existence of the GPA.

These cases highlight the gap between judicial rulings in human rights cases, and their implementation – as well as the time scales involved. The food riots were in 1997, and yet fifteen years later and despite various judgments in their favour, victims have not been paid out.

Furthermore, many cases of torture by the state or by various ZANU-PF-aligned groupings cannot now meet the criteria of proof needed by the courts. Notwithstanding excellent records held by some of the civic organisations for the more obvious physical injuries and losses caused by political violence since 1980, the burden of forensic proof may be hard to achieve at this point, perhaps in the majority of cases from all eras of violence. As illustrated above, legal processes are also costly and time-consuming and, in any era anywhere, only handfuls of victims seem to achieve court-based justice.[58]

Justice may well prove to be unachievable as a result of amnesties yet to be granted. Tsvangirai in 2001, ahead of the Presidential election, offered amnesties to Mugabe in exchange for being allowed to assume power in the event of winning.[59] Again, in early April 2008, amnesties were discussed during the brief window when it appeared that Mugabe might admit electoral defeat.[60] With the balance of power still remaining so strongly in the hands of the military in 2012, it is hard to imagine a transfer of power that does not guarantee their interests going forward, however repugnant this might seem.

A TRUTH COMMISSION

In other post-conflict contexts around the world, truth commissions have been instigated precisely to circumvent the need for victims to provide forensic truth and to face intimidating court processes, as well as to allow thousands of witnesses to be heard in a comparatively brief space of time: truth commissions allow for a version of history to be written that places victim experiences at centre stage. In Zimbabwe too, there have been calls for a truth commission internally, from both civics and the political opposition, as well as internationally. The parameters of such a commission remain to be agreed upon, although there has been robust discussion around the issue.[61] The united MDC devised a detailed Truth Commission policy ahead of the 2005 election,[62] and others have commented in detail on such a process, which seems likely to be part of any TJ package when the political space allows for this.[63] In May 2012, UN

Human Rights Commissioner, Navi Pillay, added her voice to those requesting a truth commission.[64] This, depending on its parameters and financial resources, could play a pivotal role in providing a public record of the atrocities of Zimbabwean governments over the last 40 years.

TRADITIONAL COURT SYSTEM

The possibilities of using the rural, traditional Zimbabwe court systems to hear cases and mete out local justice for political crimes along the lines of the Rwandan *Gacaca* courts have also been raised. While some version of devolved justice could be helpful, such a process needs to be carefully evaluated as many pitfalls have become apparent during the *Gacaca* process from which Zimbabwe could learn. While many scholars have lauded this community-based process, others have raised shortcomings. Problems of trials being conducted by people who are not sufficiently educated, lack of legal representation for the accused, reprisals against witnesses, and the ways in which the *Gacaca* courts have been used to settle non-political personal scores under the cover of a political alibi have been documented.[65]

> [G]acaca exposes – and perhaps deepens – conflict, resentment, and ethnic disunity. Lies, half-truths, and silence have limited Gacaca's contribution to truth, justice and reconciliation.[66]

Researchers have also documented that *Gacaca* processes, far from healing and improving mental health, have at times more than doubled the prevalence of depression and PTSD in communities where these courts are in weekly session.[67] This adverse mental health impact was found to be present for all involved – those sitting in judgment, those giving witness and those sitting in on sessions as community members. Justice at the community level may therefore make 'healing' among villagers more problematic, and while this should not preclude justice processes, it nonetheless needs to be borne in mind.

COMMUNITY REPARATIONS

Whether conventional justice, amnesties, a truth commission or some combination of these is arrived at as the way forward in the years ahead, the vexing question of who should fund payouts to what could be hundreds of thousands of victims is not an irrelevant one for a country in a state of economic hardship, in which it is not even possible to pay living wages to school teachers and nurses. If widespread individual compensation presents a difficult way forward, this leaves the option of community compensation. The precedent was set as far back as 1998, of recommending group compensation, for example in the form of improving regional access to development projects, education and social services, as compensation for the 1980s massacres. In 1998, *Breaking the Silence, Building True Peace: a report on the disturbances in Matabeleland and the Midlands, 1980-1988* was released. This was the first TJ document in Zimbabwe, and detailed the Gukurahundi massacres: the recommendations remain pertinent today. The report acknowledged the impossibility of verifying individual claims considering the time lapse involved – which at that stage was a decade from events – and instead recommended communal reparation in the form of a large, localised fund for development projects. The report recognised a generalised, ZANU-PF-driven neglect of the region, which failed to benefit during the first decade of independence when other parts of the nation were experiencing decentralisation of services, development and improved access to health and education. Instead, Matabeleland experienced state violence and death. Any future TJ process could consider this form of communal economic redress, for any period of violence.

In 1998, Amani Trust Matabeleland carried out a random survey in areas affected by Gukurahundi,[68] interviewing 740 people and asking what they wanted in the form of compensation for the massacres. *Fewer than a third of respondents were able to report on even one meaningful development project in their region, after almost twenty years of independence in Zimbabwe.* The overwhelming demand from this very marginalised and neglected part of Zimbabwe was for communal reparation in the form of water access – dams, irrigation schemes and boreholes – with grazing for cattle, better roads, new schools and electricity also high on people's lists. *Every person approved of some form of memorialising the dead, with most wanting exhumations and reburials, and others wanting ceremonies and shrines for the disappeared.* It is depressing to note that in 2012, fourteen years after the survey, and nearly thirty years after the massacres, all of these needs continue to be unmet in Matabeleland.

Where Matabeleland is concerned, the nettle of how state functioning may be maintaining ethnic divisions and inequalities needs to be grappled with, if this is not going to fester and resurface destructively in the future. Devolution of political power, and ensuring local control of local resources, could be part of changes to the currently very centralised state structure, and could be framed as redress. There is a perception very dominant in this region at the moment, that being Ndebele is to be part of a group that is deliberately disadvantaged and prejudiced against by the predominantly Shona state. Avoiding dealing with this burning issue is not a long-term solution, and those authors who have called for excluding the Gukurahundi massacres from future truth-telling processes on the grounds that this is too sensitive, are irresponsible to say the least.[69] In our own experience, which involves continuous interactions with Matabeleland rural communities since 1995, specifically around issues of political violence and mass graves, there is scarcely an individual in Matabeleland who does not want truth and accountability for these massacres.

Surveys on TJ

The ONHRI is clear that any TJ processes should encompass all eras of violence back to the colonial era.[70] Yet, as already alluded to, it is only in the Matabeleland provinces that strong calls are being made to include the Gukurahundi massacres of the 1980s, while most parts of the country believe that a truth commission and reparations should be limited to events since 2000 only.[71] Based on their survey, Du Plessis and Ford have strangely recommended that Gukurahundi is too potentially dangerous and inflammatory and should be left well alone![72]

Serious questions need to be raised about the likelihood of achieving 'truthful' findings on what people want in relation to the past, simply by conducting a random door-to-door survey as a stranger, or via a one-off workshop. Du Plessis and Ford's survey claims to have found that 30% of people in Matabeleland do not want the truth to be told,[73] and a ZHRNGO Forum survey puts the demand for truth in Matabeleland at only 16%.[74] Yet the level of fear of strangers is very high in Matabeleland, as a direct consequence of the massacres, and it is only by building trust over months and years, that people will speak from the heart about what they want. There is the need for detailed, ethnographic research to be done, as opposed to the quick administering of a questionnaire.

Between September and November 2011 Solidarity Peace Trust conducted lengthy, focused group discussions in a cross-section of rural districts in Matabeleland, where we have worked with partners for more than ten years. We asked around 200 participants in small groups over these months, what people thought should be done about the violence of the past. These groups always included one person already known to the interviewers, but most were new to us and, therefore, were not directly influenced by what they would have thought our expectations were in terms of replies. The groups included, variously, traditional leaders, members of ZANU-PF, both MDCs, ZAPU, various church groups. They included women, men and some were specifically for youth. *To a person*, including ZANU-PF supporters, people believed in the need for truth, an apology from the state and various forms of reparation. The vast majority of people wanted retributive justice. Villagers often commented on fear, remarking:

> *We are talking to you because you came with Mr M. If you had come on your own, we were not going to talk to you. We do not trust anyone...*
>
> *If I talk to a stranger freely then he will clandestinely organise people to come for me. Talking is the same as causing problems for myself...*

These heartfelt reservations should be borne in mind by researchers in this field! On the need to heal and move on, many expressed doubt that this could be done. The need for justice to include even the rich and privileged was stated clearly by many.

> *It is not possible for us to heal just like that because there is no one who is willing to apologise. In fact instead of apologizing they cause violence after violence. How can we heal? How can we forgive?*
>
> *The one who commits acts of violence must apologise and he must be arrested too, regardless of whether he is driving a car or is a pedestrian!*

Emotions around Gukurahundi still run deep, and the pain of victims has not perceptibly lessened in 25 years. What was startling was the reflection of ethnic suspicion and resentment, and the spontaneous way in which people would automatically and immediately respond to questions directly related to the consequences of political violence by commenting – 'the local headmaster is Shona and he beats our children', or – ' the local police are all Shona-speaking'. Being under the control of Shona-speaking civil servants is directly linked in people's minds to the fact that a Shona-speaking brigade came to Matabeleland to kill Ndebeles.[75] The implications of this for the future are sobering and cannot be dealt with by a determination to remain ignorant about it.

In addition to reservations expressed above, our recommendation is that surveys related to historical violence should be seen as the basis for debate, and not as a means of arriving at the apparently most popular position, which is then taken at face value. It could be that there will need to be different solutions for different provinces in Zimbabwe, for example, and for victims of different eras. As Branch observes about the situation in Uganda:

> There are political debates on justice and peace within every conflict-affected society – different concepts of justice between men and women, youth and the old, rebel and government sympathisers. It is this debate that researchers should pay attention to and, if invited, engage in, instead of seeking to determine a static set of preferences through surveys and basing their interventions on that.[76]

In general, surveys and discussions of TJ in Zimbabwe have not raised the issue of social injustices and how to repair them, including the issue of ethnic tensions rooted in our violent histories. Among ZANU-PF supporters, anti-white rhetoric, founded in the unaddressed grievances of colonialism has come to the fore in the last decade. If we want our TJ processes to lead to sustainable peace, then this ought to become a central part of the discussion in Zimbabwe as we head towards a more genuinely transitional space. More thorough, ethnographic research needs to take place as part of this process.

Whose memories count?

The experience of violence and its legacies, as already alluded to, has been and remains regionally different. In Matabeleland, for example, the multitude of mass graves in village settings cause deep emotional pain and fear, relating as they do mostly to post-independence massacres. These graves are threatening to the state, as they are evidence of its crimes. Their existence is routinely denied and hastily hidden when inescapable proof – literally – surfaces. In September 2011, the accidental uncovering of a mass grave in a football field in rural Matabeleland North resulted in an immediate clamp down of the entire area.[77] In January 2012, another mass grave dating from the 1980s became exposed, twenty kilometers north of Bulawayo.[78] In both these instances, the bones have remained where they are, and to date, it is impossible to access the areas.

However, in other parts of the country, mass graves are related largely to the War of Independence and are usually associated with a broader dialogue of national pride and sacrifice. In March 2011, the chaotic exhumation of a large mass grave in a mine-shaft in Mount Darwin, Mashonaland, became the catalyst for ZANU-PF propaganda about the war of liberation and occupied prime television news for weeks.⁷⁹ These dead were portrayed, almost certainly correctly, as the victims of the Rhodesian army, killed while fighting to free the nation from colonial rule.

Interestingly, the skeletons in ZANU-PF's own cupboard literally came tumbling out with this exhumation, as alternative dialogues sprang up as to who these dead might be: some of the remains were clearly still articulated, raising controversy as to the era of the remains. Activists in Harare claimed the bodies could include some MDC supporters killed by ZANU-PF during the intense violence of 2008.⁸⁰ ZAPU in Matabeleland brought an urgent court action to stop the dig, claiming that their cadres, including some of those killed during the 1980s, could be in the grave.⁸¹ Others wondered if the dead could include victims of the Chiadzwa diamond fields in the east of the country, where, since 2008, the Zimbabwean army is alleged to have shot in large numbers, villagers mining illicitly in the area. Unconfirmed rumours that some bodies were carrying Zimbabwe National Army ID cards, produced further speculation about how and when these dead might have come to be there.⁸²

The precise truth was not arrived at, as the bones were hurriedly reburied in mass graves – this time in coffins, and without forensic experts being allowed to solve the riddle. *However, what is noteworthy rather than any forensic certainty about the bones, is that they acted as a catalyst to so many conflicting historical claims and truths, bursting the lid off a noxious, boiling pot of stories of political murder that cut across forty years.* The history of violence in Zimbabwe is indeed a highly contested space, and ZANU-PF can clearly no longer control the dialogue around the nation's past. It is precisely for this reason that TJ remains fundamentally dangerous to ZANU-PF cadres, whose identity is based immutably on themselves as victims of the colonial era, who rose to become heroic, liberating forces – and whose leadership therefore cannot acknowledge their own massacres.

Zimbabwe's experience around the dead is archetypal: wherever in the world, certain dead are being denied, a certain version of history is also, inevitably, being denied. When the dead are given the opportunity to speak, they reveal the forensic truth in a way that can profoundly challenge the status quo and revise the national narratives.

Deciding whose memories count, and how truths should be labeled in official space in TJ exercises is one that has dogged previous TJ processes around the world. In South Africa, the marginalisation of women's voices, and the exclusion of rape and of forced displacement as political crimes that could be testified to during the TRC, has drawn negative commentary over the years.[83] The reluctance of the African National Congress, and refusal of the Inkatha Freedom Party to admit their crimes to official TRC processes created further controversy.[84] In Uganda, the Acholi citizens of the northern region continue to contest the government's official version of the Lord's Resistance Army (LRA) as the only perpetrators of atrocities: they have protested the indictment by the ICC of LRA leadership only, while the atrocities of the Ugandan army have been ignored.[85] In Northern Ireland, contesting positions on whether the Irish Republican Army on one side, and British troops on the other, are more perpetrators, or more victims, rage to this day.[86]

As Branch has pointed out, '... victimhood – like the identity of perpetrator – is a political designation, the result of political negotiation, contestation, and decisions.'[87] The discourse of 'human rights' (HR) that has prevailed in the world arena since the 1980s has serious limitations when confronted with the need to accurately portray a nuanced version of history, struggle and change. However, HR is the accepted dialogue among civics in Zimbabwe at this time, and bearing this in mind, it is worth considering, who are the 'victims' and who are the 'perpetrators'?

Members of the ZANU-PF leadership would argue that they were victims of colonialism, and that many of them spent years in jail during the 1970s and deserve reparation for this, while others suffered disabilities from the war. Yet, it is undeniable that since the 1980s the perpetrators of political violence in Zimbabwe have been overwhelmingly ZANU-PF, state agents and their supporters, with other political parties and their supporters being on the receiving end of this. The roles of being now victim, now perpetrator are more complicated in rural Matabeleland, where ZAPU were victims of the Rhodesians in the 1970s – and again of ZANU-PF during the 1980s repression – but some of their cadres became perpetrators of post-2000 violence in their new incarnation as ZANU-PF supporters. And some of these perpetrators have now rejoined the recently revived ZAPU, and are conceivably at risk of violence from their ZANU-PF ex-comrades in the run-up to any future elections. It is clear that the same individuals may have been now-victims, now-perpetrators over the years.

While the existence and extent of political violence by MDC in the last ten years remains an issue that civics in Zimbabwe is nervous to explore, at some stage in the future it will be necessary to confront this issue if we are to avoid another cycle of impunity under an MDC government. The MDCs have undoubtedly had the odds stacked massively against them, with the police, army and CIO all arresting, torturing and assaulting MDC supporters with impunity, as have war veteran groupings, youth militia, Chipangano, and other informal arms of ZANU-PF. But on the ground in some rural villages and urban suburbs, inter-party violence has become much more evenly matched in recent years,[88] and this is seldom admitted to by civics, on the argument that the ZANU-PF elements of the state have dishonestly blamed much of their own violence on the MDC, and to produce forensic proof of *some* MDC violence would be to add credence to the patently false ZANU-PF position that *most* of the violence is by MDC.[89]

Furthermore, there is an undercurrent of understandable sympathy for activists who have been repeatedly beaten and oppressed without justice or redress, who finally hit back physically at their perpetrators. However, this reciprocal violence can become provocation over time. The creation of MDC hit-and-run squads called DRCs – Democratic Resistance Committees – is generally acknowledged by civics, but there is scant, if any, acknowledgement of them in their HR documents. When such MDC violence has taken place, it has been seen as 'victims hitting back' and not as 'perpetrators' committing acts of violence – even though in our experience it can be innocent citizens who have at times been on the receiving end of MDC violence, simply because they support ZANU-PF. This has included old women and even children.[90] Clearly, there are some people in Zimbabwe who are justified in seeing MDC supporters as perpetrators. Furthermore, members of the MDC faction headed by Welshman Ncube would point to internal violence in the MDC as a major contributor to the split in the party: beatings and torture of MDC's own activists have taken place in their political headquarters and structures over the years, as several – largely uncirculated – MDC commissions of inquiry reveal.[91]

Our experience on the ground in rural Matabeleland shows that political violence is a complicated and messy business at the village level, with personal scores that have nothing to do with politics joining the mix. Indeed, over the decades 'in situations… in which violence may become the norm, perpetrator and victim identities may be ambiguous and shifting, and responsibility may be widespread.'[92] Arguably, we need to shift away from the simple HR approach that has predominated our accounts, with its categories and simple tables of 'victims' and 'perpetrators' and deal with our historical accounts in a more nuanced way.

Community-based healing: lessons learnt

Individual histories of violence are therefore best understood in relation to the histories of all others who have lived in the same space over the decades. Likewise, the consequences of political violence are multi-faceted and the process of 'healing' these consequences is a complex one, that can at times be best facilitated and promoted in the context of a community, rather than through individual interventions. One of the lessons that our organisation learnt during the 1990s, was that the emotional 'healing' of people affected by mass political violence was possibly not best done via hospital outpatient departments. In contrast, we began to have a dramatic impact, and to engage scores or hundreds of people in our processes simultaneously, once we were guided by the traditional leadership out of the clinic and under the trees, to talk to community members en masse.

From 1998 to 2000, we conducted an intensive programme of training and supervising rural nurses in clinic-based counselling of torture victims, but our own evaluation of this programme after three years, which included a random survey of clients counselled, found that few clients benefited from clinic-based counselling in any way that was meaningful to them.[93] It must be added that the immediate crisis of torture and organised violence was now years behind this client base, whose problems now were chronic. They had material and practical problems that needed resolving, such as needing death certificates for the disappeared, or material support for orphans, or the need to appease the spirits of the dead – and these problems were clearly beyond the capacity of a clinic-bound nurse to take forward.[94]

Once we dropped our western-centric approach in which we already 'knew' what the consequences of violence were – namely Post Traumatic Stress Disorder and mixed anxiety-depression disorder – and began to ask the community as a whole what their most pressing needs were in relation to past violence, we were told that the spirits of the angry dead in unmarked, unmourned mass and single graves was the worst social consequence of past massacres.

With this realisation, Amani Trust Matabeleland piloted a programme of exhumations and reburials of the murdered dead. In Zimbabwean culture, the spirits of the living and the dead are on a continuum, with the dead able to influence events in the lives of their descendants. To have thousands of murdered dead in unacknowledged and unmourned mass graves has reportedly caused a multitude of problems for the living. Failed marriages, infertility, illness, crop failure, droughts, failed development projects, are all blamed on the spirits of the angry dead.[95] In any culture, the right to mourn should be considered an essential human right, and many constitutions in Latin America now reflect this: in Argentina, it is a fundamental human rights violation for the state to disappear a person, to interfere with the right of citizens to mourn, or to withhold any information about the whereabouts of the dead.

This woman was murdered by 5 Brigade in Matabeleland South in 1984, and was exhumed in 2001 as part of a community healing process.

For four years, we conducted exhumations and tracked family and community functioning in response to these exhumations. This remains the most profoundly useful programme that we have undertaken. Each exhumation was in effect a small truth commission, in which all could bear witness as the bones were revealed and given their moment to 'speak' – to affirm and reclaim the version of history held by the villagers, which remains at odds with the official, national version of events during the Gukurahundi era. This vindication and reclaiming of historical memory at the local level was profound in its impact. It became politically impossible to pursue this programme beyond 2002, but we have continued to document graves against the moment when this exercise can resume.

Exhumations require experts, if the bones are not to be effectively silenced forever through commingling and destruction of evidence.[96] A mass grave is a crime scene and needs specifically trained individuals to analyse who, when, how, and what happened in all its forensic detail. The Argentinean Forensic Anthropology Team (EAAF) conducted the exhumations and began training us in these skills. Preceding and following on from any exhumation, there is a need for detailed, sensitive interviews and recording of data, so that all family members are involved in the process of reclaiming their dead loved ones. This process, which can continue for years, could, in western terminology, be seen as a form of grief counselling with a problem-solving, truth-telling purpose and a profound, tangible outcome, and we noted dramatic positive shifts in family functioning, as well as general community empowerment over the years.[97]

The burnt remains of five individuals were exhumed at Sitezi in Matabeleland South in 1999, and reinterred in the same site. This is the first formal memorial to victims of 5 Brigade."

While exhumations have not been possible in the last ten years,[98] we have taken our lessons learnt of engaging as many parties in the community as possible when dealing with political violence, and have continued with low-key processes of community conflict resolution and empowerment. In the space provided by the GPA, we have worked in several Matabeleland rural districts with an approach that has engaged the MDCs, ZANU-PF and ZAPU, as well as traditional leadership and the grassroots churches. We have created a mediated space in which grievances and conflicting versions of the 'truth' about the violence have been shared.[99] Through a lengthy process of working mostly in the context of visiting homesteads – even working alongside people in their fields if necessary – we have drawn rural villagers into meaningful discussions with their erstwhile enemies, and we have seen more positive relationships growing across party political lines in rural villages. We have seen this work culminating in joint meetings of ZANU-PF and the MDCs, at which their elected structures at ward level have taken turns admitting – without blaming the other – 'This is how **we** contributed to the violence in this area.' It can take months or years of discussions to reach this point. While replicating this work across all of Zimbabwe may not be politically appropriate at this time, we believe that the benefits of engaging directly and almost daily on the ground have been proven to have impact, resulting in behaviour change and reduced conflict at the local levels.

JOMIC and Peace Liaison Committees

In 2011, the GPA Joint Monitoring Committee (JOMIC), which has been mandated over the last three years to record and investigate all violations of the GPA, has extended its structures by opening offices at the provincial and district levels. JOMIC has, since 2009, built a reputation for itself as a credible structure capable of balanced interventions after political violence, and in many ways it has taken on some of the activities that might have been expected of the ONHRI. Since 2009, through JOMIC, all three of the major political parties have been investigating violent incidents together: after interviewing all those involved within the area where violence has occurred, all three parties have signed off on one agreed version of what actually happened. At the very least, these joint political reports on violence will form an invaluable archive in the future – and the exercise has served to highlight the need to probe below the surface to understand the multiple and often conflicting truths that precede and follow on from political violence.

The move to expand JOMIC to the district level is intended to be a proactive conflict prevention strategy and to build tolerance at the grassroots, a substantial shift from their previous, mainly documentary, role.[100] A pilot project in Harare and Chitungwiza has shown that where JOMIC-coordinated Peace Liaison Committees have been able to persuade local political actors to cooperate better, there have been drastic reductions in political violence.[101]

> ... members of the PLCs are always present on the ground, experiencing the points of tension and conflict in communities and living with both perpetrators and victims of violence in the communities. They are therefore in a vantage point to develop a proper perspective of the causes of tensions and conflicts in their local communities... At the same time, PLCs will also need to work closely with police and other security apparatus of the state as well as other institutions working for peace, such as the churches, civics, CBOs and the GPA's Organ on National Healing, for effective fostering of peace and security.[102]

Theories of change

The two above approaches of sustained and intense interventions, which are concerned with processes-over-time, stand in juxtaposition with the methodology of the one-to-three-day-workshop often preferred by many Zimbabwean NGOs in the burgeoning fields of peace building and TJ. There is a growing theoretical field examining complexity theory and conflict transformation, which aims to understand 'the nature of change processes in complex systems', such as in societies in conflict. Complexity theory has its roots in biology, physics, chemistry and computer simulation, and recognises the limitations of linear scientific approaches: the whole is more than the sum of its parts, and can behave differently – often unpredictably and surprisingly.[103] A society is a complex system, in which change and what will cause it, cannot always be reliably predicted.

> Lacking insight into the ongoing processes within a persona or social group, it is difficult to know what effect a given external influence is likely to have... Sometimes an external factor produces only resistance, with little or no change in the ongoing processes of the person or group... At yet other times, an external influence may initiate a process that unfolds according to its own pattern of changes, the effects of which may not be apparent for days,

minutes, or years, depending on the phenomenon in question.[104]

Social scientists have shown that 'it is simple social interactions over time [that] tend to promote the emergence' of group values and behavioural choices.[105] What will change social interactions cannot be definitively predicted, but it would be helpful for civics in the TJ and peace-building field in Zimbabwe to attempt to analyse more critically why it is that they are choosing one form of intervention (the training workshop, for example) over many other possible forms of intervention if they are to be realistic about causing durable changes in systems prone to violence, and if they are going to be able to reliably track that change over days and years.

If we, as practitioners, are genuinely interested in building new ways for people and political parties to relate to one another in a future Zimbabwe, we are talking of *behaviour change*. To remind ourselves of how hard behaviour change is to achieve, especially among adults with vested power interests developed over decades or generations, we can ask ourselves, *how would we persuade just one rural husband to stop beating his wife*? A workshop that teaches villagers about the Domestic Violence Act may well be part of working towards this change, but will certainly not achieve it. This will take long-term work with the wife, with the husband, with the children, with the neighbours, with the traditional leadership, with the police and with the magistrate, changing the way all of these parties react to violence. This is not a matter of simply giving information or a few hours or days of skills training, but of being there every week, so that when violence happens, you can intervene and mediate immediately. You need to have a *pre-existing* working relationship with all parties and *established neutrality* if you are to be taken seriously by everyone. You also need awareness of yourself as an actor in the events. Gender power relations at a national level and systems of poverty will also impact on localised violence.

Understanding more fully the systems in which we think we are trying to bring about change, and a more thoughtful theory of what causes change, are among the challenges that more NGOs in Zimbabwe need to take up, if we are to impact seriously on the patterns of political violence and impunity that exist in Zimbabwe. Changing established patterns of violence during periods of heightened political tensions, may take many years of weekly interventions at the local level. Moreover, the enduring consequences of political violence in the form of elevated levels of domestic violence and criminal violence in affected communities may pose a challenge long into the future. Peace building needs to be integrated into local functioning and is unlikely to gain traction if reliant on occasional visits and workshops from town-based NGOs.

Conclusion

A transitional space in which meaningful reconciliation among all parties can take place, does not currently exist in Zimbabwe, regardless of the GPA and its half-hearted commitment to 'healing'. The ONHRI, while it has well-intentioned Ministers, has had little official support, space or direction to implement any programme. Nonetheless, the ONHRI and the general impetus provided by the GPA have facilitated some useful discussions among Zimbabweans on what they believe TJ processes should include in the future. There is a broad agreement among civics and the churches that some version of the internationally established TJ 'package' is seen as desirable – involving a truth commission, institutional reform, some level of justice and reparations. Peacebuilding initiatives have become incorporated into this package.

However, civics in Zimbabwe could broaden their debate, and consider including social, economic and cultural/ethnic rights as centrally important to TJ, instead of the current narrow focus on documentation of individual violations. This is made more relevant considering the violation of social and economic rights, and the resulting destruction of social fabric and the cataclysmic deepening of poverty that are a direct product of the last decade of crisis – while acknowledging that poverty has its roots in longer-standing inequalities. There is a danger of masking deep-seated structural injustice by focusing on individual injustices and reparations. The cultural right to mourn the dead, among other cultural rights, needs to be part of policy debates. The issue of ethnic divisions should not be airbrushed out of this picture: there could be a need to restructure and devolve the state as one form of reparation for the massacres in Matabeleland.

If properly and openly consulted, rural communities who are those worst affected by political violence over the decades, have unusual and complex ideas as to what can help them move out of a state of oppression and fear and into a phase of positive development, where neighbours can once more trust each other. To reach these ideas requires prolonged engagements and detailed ethnographic research, rather than the implementation of prescriptive *yes-no* door-to-door surveys. Much challenging work remains to be done. In some parts of the country, the relative lack of violence in the wake of the GPA has allowed community TJ processes to take place that have facilitated resolution of old conflicts – while in other areas, tensions and sporadic violence have precluded this. Changing the way people understand the violence of the past and changing the way they will work together in the future is a profoundly difficult and complex task that requires modifying behaviour and transforming institutions: we should be prepared for decades of work to achieve this.

In all countries involved in TJ, the strength and determination of civics is recognised as a key factor in shaping the processes of TJ. Increasingly thoughtful, nuanced and encompassing debates and consultations need to continue, so that when a more genuinely transitional era arrives, we already have a clearer idea of our own lessons learnt, and best practices for the future. Finally, we need to acknowledge that world-wide, formal TJ processes tend to have more hopes pinned on them than can ever be realised: for citizens to feel better about their pasts and their futures, transformation is needed on a scale that involves reforming economic systems and rebuilding institutions at every level, which is beyond the scope of the usual TJ package. Economic opportunities and the delivering of basic services such as water and electricity, down to the level of rural villages, may do more to 'heal' people in Zimbabwe by removing the anxieties of every day, than a truth commission or other more conventional TJ deliverables can ever do: conversely, failure to deliver economic improvements may, over time, undermine any positive benefit from truth and justice processes, as has happened in South Africa. The years ahead will be challenging, but for the first time in over three decades of transitions, the opening to address and redress the violence and other injustices of the past in a broad and creative way, may be about to materialise.

Endnotes

1 Diplomats in Harare were able to visit hospitals full of victims with terrible injuries, as were a group of South African Generals who were in the country monitoring events. Civics produced scores of reports and gave video footage of events to international media. Around 9,000 people were ultimately treated for severe torture and other injuries, and around 200 people were killed.

2 Global Political Agreement, Article VII, 7.1 (c).

3 Interview with negotiator, August 2011.
4 Interview, April 2009. There was a scramble to include more people in government at the last minute, resulting in more ministers and deputy ministers than had been signed up to in the GPA. There is no particular reason why the mechanism of healing could not have been dealt with at the outset by setting up a National Peace and Reconciliation Council with appointed non-political commissioners, for example – a solution that was in fact suggested in 2011, in a policy document produced for the ONHRI by a UNDP consultant.
5 Jonathan Moyo is alleged by a WikiLeaks communiqué to have told the American Ambassador in 2007 that President Mugabe feared being hanged if he lost power. *The Zimbabwean*: 'Govt in dilemma over wikileaks', 9 Sept 2011.
6 In Sudan and Uganda, for example, premature indictments by the ICC have been perceived by some as not in the best interests of the civilian populations or of a lasting peace, but in a different historical context, prosecutions could become worth considering.
7 ZANU-PF clearly has a much longer and more violent history than MDC-T, including the massacres of the 1980s, violence around every election since 1980, and thousands of well-documented cases of torture since 2000. However, MDC has had five commissions of inquiry into its own violence and has not made these generally public, nor has it followed through on the bulk of the recommendations of these inquiries: *Report of the commission of inquiry into the disruption of the Harare Provincial Congress*, (MDC, Harare, 7 Nov 2001); *Commission of Inquiry into disturbances at Party Headquarters*, (MDC, Harare, 14 December 2004); *Report of the Management Committee of an Inquiry into the disturbances and beatings at Harvest House, Byo provincial office and in Gwanda at the late Maseru's funeral*, (MDC, Harare, July 2005); two further commissions of inquiry into violence against Trudy Stevenson in 2005, and violence around the country, running up to their 2011 national congress in Bulawayo.
8 '*Gukurahundi*' is a Shona word meaning 'the first rains of spring that wash away the chaff from the last season'. This is what Mugabe himself named the notorious Fifth Brigade at their pass-out parade in 1982. Those civilians who supported ZAPU were apparently the 'chaff' to be swept away.
9 CCJPZ and LRF, *Breaking the Silence, Building True Peace: A Report on the Disturbances in Matabeleland and the Midlands 1980-1988* (Harare, 1997) for a full history of this era.
10 Tichaona Sibanda, 'PM bemoans lack of rights and freedoms 32 years after independence': *SW Radio Africa*, 17 April 2012. In early November 2011 Tsvangirai submitted a dossier to the SADC mediation team and President Zuma detailing his sense that the GPA was failing and listing incidents of political violence that have

contributed to this.

11 Church and Civil Society Forum (CCSF), Report on CCSF Submissions, November 2009-April 2010, (CCSF, Harare, 2010) p. 41.

12 Ibid.

13 Ibid, p. 6.

14 Institute of Justice and Reconciliation, 'Report on Workshop for JOMIC District Peace Liaison Committees for Harare and Chitungwiza Provinces', (Harare, 7-8 April 2011)

15 The South African TRC had a slogan that 'revealing is healing'. While this was, and remains, a contentious claim (see ahead in this chapter), it is clear that truth-telling at some level is generally acknowledged as an essential part of transitional justice, and it is patently ridiculous that the Minister of Healing could be arrested simply for referring to the massacres in a church service.

16 Interview with Minister Ndlovu, May 2011; also observation. In May 2012, the case against Minister Ndlovu was finally dismissed for lack of evidence, after a year of him intermittently having to report to Hwange for hearings.

17 http://article.wn.com/view/2009/02/22/Zimbabwean_Minister_Sekai_Holland_speaks_from_Harare/, accessed 22 May 2012, has an audio clip in which Holland states that 'Mzilikazi's mobs' were professional at meting out violence and there have been no new torture methodologies in Zimbabwe since then.

18 Mark Schofield, 'Political rivals step up plans for peace rallies', Johannesburg, *The Sunday Times, Southern African Edition*, 4 March 2012.

19 Archbishop Tutu in South Africa famously introduced the notion of 'ubuntu' into what otherwise was a classic truth commission in terms of its enabling legislation.

20 Cited in Adam Branch, *Displacing Human Rights: War and Intervention in Northern Uganda* (Oxford University Press, 2011) p. 184.

21 From Robert Mugabe's speech to the 66th UN General Assembly, 23 September 2011.

22 There is general consistency among civic positions on what TJ should entail in Zimbabwe. See, for example, the CCSF summaries of provincial outreach meetings around the country (op. cit.).

23 The questionnaire focuses on enumerating HR abuses against the interviewee, asking about compensation, prosecution and using terms like 'perpetrator' and 'victim'. Only one response is allowed in the recording procedures relating to opinions on what needs to be done, severely limiting nuances of opinion.

24 UNDP, 'National Policy Framework for National Healing and Reconciliation', Harare, October 2011.

25 Personal information from a cabinet minister, 27 April.

26 Brandon Hamber, *Transforming Societies after Political Violence: Truth,*

Reconciliation, and Mental Health, (New York: Springer, 2009) for a critique of the TRC in South Africa.

27 Marie Trigona, 'Argentina Mothers of the Plaza de Mayo: Living legacy of hope and human rights', Women News Network, Oct 2010.

28 David Backer, 'Watching a Bargain Unravel? A Panel Study of Victims' Attitudes about Transitional Justice in Cape Town, South Africa', *International Journal of Transitional Justice (IJTJ)*, 2010 (4) 3 443-456.

29 CCSF, op. cit., with 19 civic and church members; 'Transitional Justice National Survey', (ZHRNGO Forum, Harare, 2011); 'Position on National Healing', (ZLHR, Harare, 2009); 'Pastoral letter on National healing and reconciliation', Zimbabwe Catholic Bishops' Conference, October 2009; Max Du Plessis and Jolyon Ford, 'Justice and Peace in a New Zimbabwe', *Institute for Security Studies*, Paper 164, June 2008; Max du Plessis and Jolyon Ford: 'Transitional Justice: A Future Truth Commission for Zimbabwe?', *International and Comparative Law Quarterly*, 2009 (58) 73-117 to list but a few.

30 David Backer, op. cit.

31 Lisa Laplante, 'Transitional Justice and Peace Building: Diagnosing and Addressing the Socio-economic Roots of Violence through a Human Rights Framework', *IJTJ*, 2008, 3 (2) 331-355.

32 Some civic groups in Zimbabwe have acknowledged the need to include economic trauma in the healing agenda: Institute of Justice and Reconciliation, 'Conference report: Towards a Shared Vision of National Healing in Zimbabwe' (Harare, 2010).

33 See Ismael Muvingi, 'Sitting on Powder Kegs: Socio-economic Rights in Transitional Societies', *IJTJ*, 2009, 3 (2), 163-182, for a detailed analysis of the link between social injustice and the role this has played in the current crisis. See also the *Journal of Peasant Studies*, 2011, 38 (5), special edition on land. There was some land redistribution immediately after independence, which transferred 23% of white-owned land to African use by 1996, for example, but land ownership nonetheless remained a pressing political issue – and one which ZANU-PF capitalised on – after 2000.

34 Lionel Cliffe, Jocelyn Alexander, Ben Cousins and Rudo Gaidzanwa, 'An overview of Fast Track Land Reform in Zimbabwe: editorial introduction', *Journal of Peasant Studies,* December 2011, 5 (38), 907–938

35 There are highly polarised descriptions of the outcome of the farm seizures: some see it as a welcome redistribution of land, others as a catastrophic destruction of agricultural production. See Cliffe et al. (ibid) for a collection of studies that provide what they refer to as a 'reality check', 11 years on. Clearly, some parts of the new system have proved productive, but political patronage and chaotic implementation

have undermined aspects of it. Only a land audit, and further time and research, will provide clearer answers to its successes and failures.

36 Three land audits already carried out in recent years have been suppressed by the ZANU-PF government, and the GPA-agreed audit has been prevented from taking place.

37 See Solidarity Peace Trust, *A Fractured Nation: Operation Murambatsvina -Five Years on* (Johannesburg, 2010); *Gone to Egoli* (Johannesburg 2009); *Desperate Lives, Twilight Worlds* (Johannesburg, 2010), for details of the impact of diasporisation on the social fabric.

38 Rama Mani, 'Dilemmas of Expanding Transitional Justice, or Forging the Nexus between Transitional Justice and Development', Editorial, *International Journal of Transitional Justice*, 2008 2 (3): 253-65.

39 ZANU-PF has persistently used the language of war in the last decade, referring to land invasions as a 'chimurenga', and labeling the MDCs as the 'enemy'.

40 Laplante, op. cit.

41 ibid.

42 Muvingi, op. cit.

43 Branch, op. cit., p. 208.

44 Rosalind Shaw, 'Memory Frictions: localizing the Truth and Reconciliation Commission in Sierra Leone', *IJTJ*, 2007, 2 (1) p. 201.

45 Ibid p. 199.

46 Brandon Hamber, op. cit.

47 David Smith, 'General Motors settles with victims of apartheid regime' (London, *The Guardian*, 2 March 2012).

48 BBC News: 'Powder keg in South Africa – Tutu', (London, 7 October 2006). Murray Williams, 'Tutu calls for wealth tax on whites' (IOL news, 12 August 2011).

49 Muvingi, op. cit.

50 *Breaking the Silence,* ibid, acknowledged this in 1997, as have many other commentators since then.

51 Government of Zimbabwe, *Report of the Commission of Inquiry into the Administration of the War Victims Compensation Act [Chapter 11.16]*, (Harare, May 1998) p. 47.

52 In our experience, the majority of victim testimonies appear to have been substantially true, from all eras, but there has nonetheless been a low level of false reporting over the years that needs to be acknowledged. Shari Eppel, 'A Tale of Three Dinner Plates: "Truth" and the Challenge of Human Rights Research in Zimbabwe', *Journal of Southern African Studies*, 2009: 35 (4) 967-76, relates the context and problems of accurately understanding what happens when political violence breaks out.

53 UNDP, *Human Development Report, 2011,* (USA, 2012) p. 60.
54 *The Standard,* 'Zimbabwe Obstacles for demolition lawsuits', Harare, August 2005. In this article, Zimbabwe Lawyers for Human Rights acknowledges the problems faced by potential litigants, even contemporaneously, or within a few months of the demolitions – never mind in 2012, seven years later.
55 ZimOnline, 'Landmark SADC torture ruling', 15 January 2011.
56 Radio VOP, 'Zanu-PF thugs to pay for torturing MDC activist', Harare, 29 November 2011.
57 BBC, 'South Africa court orders Zimbabwe torture investigation', London, 8 May 2012.
58 Comparatively few perpetrators have been charged with crimes in South Africa, for example; Dr. Wouter Basson – 'Dr Death' –was charged with 67 counts including using germ and chemical warfare for the apartheid regime, and was acquitted in 2002 after prosecutors failed to meet the burden of proof needed for convictions.
59 Personal information. WikiLeaks cable of 15 February 2001 from the US Embassy confirms that Mnangagwa approached Tsvangirai on behalf of Mugabe, looking for amnesties.
60 Personal information.
61 There is a 'Zimbabwe Truth and Reconciliation Commission' Facebook page, where Zimbabweans around the world can enter this debate.
62 Interview, David Coltart, who was Shadow Minister of Legal Affairs for the MDC in 2005.
63 Du Plessis et al., op. cit, 2009. The Institute of Justice and Reconciliation has stated that such a commission is essential to healing in Zimbabwe: Paidamoyo Muzulu, ' 'Truth commission essential for healing', in *Zimbabwe Independent*, 6 January 2011.
64 Gilbert Nyambabvu, 'UN chief urges truth commission', New Zimbabwe, 25 May 2012.
65 Max Rettig, 'Gacaca: Truth, Justice, and Reconciliation in Postconflict Rwanda?', *African Studies Review,* 2008: 51 (3) pp. 25-50.
66 Ibid., abstract.
67 Karen Brounéus, 'The Trauma of Truth Telling: Effects of Witnessing in the Rwandan Gacaca Courts on Psychological Health', *Journal of Conflict Resolution,* 2010: 54 (3) 408-437.
68 Amani Trust, Matabeleland: 'Preliminary Summary of Results of Survey', November 1998.
69 Max Du Plessis and Jolyon Ford (op. cit.) have written two papers expressing this view based on unconvincing argumentation. There would be such an outcry in Matabeleland if their history of oppression was left out of a truth commission – when

it has so clearly been the recipient of the worst abuses since 1980 – that this would create a threat to the state.

70 The relevant clause in the GPA itself specifies pre- and post-colonial violence must be considered, and this was also promoted at all public meetings of the ONHRI. See CCSF, op. cit.

71 ZHRNGO Forum, op. cit, found that 71% of respondents in their survey thought that TJ processes should be restricted to events since 2000, with predominantly people in Matabeleland wanting to include the 1980s.

72 Du Plessis and Ford, op. cit.

73 Ibid.

74 ZHRNGO Forum, op. cit.

75 The repression in Matabeleland was fundamentally about the destruction of ZAPU's support base and hierarchy, rather than being deliberately ethnic in conception – see *Breaking the Silence*, ibid., for a detailed discussion of the motivations for Gukurahundi. However, whatever was in the minds of those who orchestrated it, the common perception on the ground to date is that the motivation was ethnic.

76 Branch, op. cit., p. 210.

77 David Smith, 'Grave containing up to 60 people found at Zimbabwe school', London, *The Guardian*, 5 October 2011; see also Tichaona Sibanda, 'Police come under fire for blocking Tsvangirai rallies', SW Radio Africa, 31 October 2011. A rally scheduled to take place near this mass grave was tear gassed and dispersed, at St Pauls in Lupane.

78 Bulawayo24.com: 'Mass Grave at a Zimbabwe police post', 27 January 2012.

79 *Daily Mail Online*, 'Zimbabwe's killing fields: mass grave of over 600 bodies found in mine shaft', London, 31 March 2011.

80 *The Zimbabwe Mail*, 'Hundreds of exhumed bodies could be abducted MDC supporters', Harare, 3 April 2011.

81 *NewsDay*, 'Zapu plans parallel exhumations', 25 March 2011.

82 Interview with the ZIPRA Veterans Trust, March 2011.

83 Fiona Ross, *Bearing witness: Women and the Truth and Reconciliation Commission in South Africa*, (London, Pluto Press, 2003).

84 Antjie Krog, *Country of my Skull*, (London: Random House, 1998).

85 Branch, op. cit.

86 Interviews, Northern Ireland, Belfast and Derry, May 2011.

87 Branch, ibid., p. 208.

88 In our own experience in rural Matabeleland in particular, where most people do not support ZANU-PF, in 2008 violence was negligible but also rather even-handed when it did occur! More recently, in Nyanga for example, it is clear that MDC is

capable of 'giving' as good as they 'get'. Radio VOP, 'JOMIC investigates Nyanga violence', 27 February 2011, for example.

89 There has been some acknowledgement of MDC violence by civics: in various records of political violence, MDC are featured as perpetrators, but as ZANU-PF victims of MDC violence are very unlikely to approach civic organisations for help, these records are undoubtedly understated. The patently biased way that the state responds to any MDC violence also makes civics shy away from highlighting it themselves. For instance, the beating to death of a policeman in Harare ostensibly and very likely by MDC supporters in 2011 resulted in 58 arrests, most of whom were nowhere near at the time; many of these suspects were brutally tortured, and some were incarcerated for more than a year without access to a trial or medical treatment. Yet known perpetrators who have murdered MDC activists are seldom apprehended and even more seldom convicted.

90 see Shari Eppel, 'A Tale of Three Dinner Plates' op. cit., for a more detailed exploration of the relativity of truth and victimhood.

91 See note 7 for list of these inquiries.

92 Branch, op. cit., p. 210.

93 Amani Trust, Matabeleland, unpublished internal evaluation 2000.

94 The classic medical model of counselling has greater relevance if treating victims in the first few weeks, months or even years after exposure to TOV; our client base was more than ten years removed from this. However, while we had to remodel our psychological approach to care, we found that physically, people could still be suffering pain and disability caused by decades-old torture, needing treatment based in western physical therapies and interventions.

95 Shari Eppel, 'Reburial Ceremonies for Health and Healing after State Terror', *The Lancet*, 360 (9336), 14 September 2012.

96 See Shari Eppel, 'The silencing of the bones', at www.solidaritypeacetrust. org/author/shariep for a commentary on the disastrous consequences of amateur exhumations, such as that conducted at Mount Darwin during 2011.

97 Shari Eppel, 'Healing the dead: exhumation and reburial as a route to truth telling and reclaiming the past in rural Zimbabwe', in Tristan Ann Borer (ed.) *Telling the Truths: Truth Telling and Peace Building in Post-Conflict societies* (Notre Dame, Ind.: University of Notre Dame Press, 2006). Can be accessed via http://www.solidaritypeacetrust.org/488/healing-the-dead/

98 ZANU-PF's fear of being held legally accountable for these massacres in the future has grown over the last ten years as it contemplates the possibility of losing power; this has made exhuming and documentation of the massacres an extremely risky procedure, and one which would create security hazards for families that have already lost relatives to state violence. For this reason, the programme is on hold.

99 Shari Eppel, 'A Tale of Three Dinner Plates', op. cit..
100 Institute for Justice and Reconciliation, 'Workshop for JOMIC District Peace Liaison Committee for Harare and Chitungwiza Province', Harare, 7-8 April 2011.
101 Ibid.
102 Ibid, p. 2.
103 See Diane Hendrick, 'Complexity theory and Conflict Transformation: An exploration of Potential and Implications', Centre for Conflict Resolution, Working Paper 17, University of Bradford, 2009, for the summary given here of how this genre is developing and from where.
104 Robin R Vallacher, et al., 'The Dynamical Perspective in Personality and Social Psychology', *Personality and Social Psychology Review*, 4 (6), 2002, cited in Hendrick, ibid., p.12.
105 Hendrick, ibid., p. 12.

Select Bibliography

Abrahamsen, R., 'Blair's Africa: The Politics of Securitisation and Fear', *Alternatives*, 30, pp. 55-80, 2005.

Adelman, M., 'Quiet Diplomacy: The Reasons behind Mbeki's Zimbabwe policy', *Africa Spectrum*, 39(2), pp. 249-276, 2004.

Adolfo, E., 'The Collision of Liberation and Post-Liberation Politics within SADC: A Study on SADC and the Zimbabwean Crisis' (Stockholm: Swedish Defence Research Agency Research Paper, June 2009).

Alexander, J., *The Unsettled Land: State-making and the Politics of Land in Zimbabwe, 1893-2003,* (Oxford: James Currey; Harare: Weaver Press, 2006).

———, J. McGregor and T. Ranger, *Violence and Memory: One Hundred Years in the 'Dark Forests' of Matabeleland* (Oxford: James Currey, 2000).

Bourne, R., *Catastrophe: What went wrong in Zimbabwe?* (London and New York: Zed Books, 2011).

Bratton, M., and E.V. Masunugure, 'The Anatomy of Predation: Leaders, Elites and Coalitions in Zimbabwe, 1980-2010' (Development Leadership Programme, Research Paper, 9, 2011).

Chan, S., *Old Treacheries and New Deceipt: Insights into Southern African Politics* (Johannesburg and Cape Town: Jonathan Ball, 2011).

Cheeseman, N., 'The Internal Dynamics of power-sharing in Africa', *Democratisation*, 18(2), pp. 336-65, 2011.

———, and B-M. Tendi, 'Power Sharing in Comparative Perspective: The Dynamics of Unity Government in Kenya and Zimbabwe', *Journal of Modern African Studies*, 48(2), 2010.

Chikane, F., *Eight Days in September, The Removal of Thabo Mbeki* (Johannesburg: Picador Africa, 2012).

Chigora, P., 'On Crossroads: Reflections on Zimbabwe's Relations with Britain in the New Millenium', *Alternatives: Turkish Journal of International Relations,* 5(3), pp. 61-76, Fall 2006.

Chingono, H., 'Zimbabwe Sanctions: An analysis of the "Lingo" guiding the perceptions of sanctioners and the sanctions', *African Journal of Political Science and International Relations*, 24(2), 2010.

Chitando, E., 'Prayers, Politics and Peace: The church's role in Zimbabwe's crisis', *Open Space*, Issue 1, June 2011.

Cliffe, L., J. Alexander, B. Cousins, and R. Gaidzwana, 'An Overview of the Fast Track Land Reform in Zimbabwe: Editorial Introduction', *Journal of Peasant Studies*, 5(38), pp. 907-38, 2011.

Compagnon, D., *A Predictable Tragedy: Robert Mugabe and the Collapse of Zimbabwe* (Philadelphia: University of Pennsylvania Press, 2011).

Dansereau, S., 'Liberation and Opposition in Zimbabwe', in H. Melber (ed.), *Limits to Liberation in Southern Africa* (Cape Town: HSRC Press, 2003).

Dawson, M., and T. Kelsall, 'Anti-Development patrimonialism in Zimbabwe', *Journal of Contemporary African Studies*, 30(1), pp. 49-66, 2011.

Du Plessis, M., and Jolyon Ford, 'Justice and Peace in a new Zimbabwe', Institute for Security Studies, Paper 164, June 2008.

Eppel, S., 'Reburial Ceremonies for Health and Healing after State Terror', *The Lancet*, 360(9336), 14 September 2002.

———, 'Healing the dead: exhumation and reburial as a route to telling and reclaiming the past in rural Zimbabwe', in T.A. Borer (ed.), *Telling the Truths: Truth Telling and Peace Building in Post-Conflict Societies* (Notre Dame: University of Notre Dame Press, 2006).

———, 'A Tale of Three Dinner Plates: Truth and the Challenge of Human Rights Research in Zimbabwe', *Journal of Southern African Studies*, 35(4), pp. 967-76, 2009.

———, and B. Raftopoulos, 'Political Crisis, Mediation and the Prospects for Transitional Justice in Zimbabwe', in S. Eppel, D. Ndlela, B. Raftopoulos and M. Rupiya, *Developing a Transformation Agenda for Zimbabwe* (Pretoria: IDASA, 2009).

Evans, G., 'South Africa's Foreign Policy after Mandela: Mbeki and his concept of African Renaissance', *Round Table*, 35(2), pp. 621-38, 1999.

Freeman, L., 'South Africa's Zimbabwe Policy: Unraveling the Contradictions,' *Journal of Contemporary African Studies*, 23(2), pp. 147-72, 2005.

Gambahaya, Z., 'Tokenism and Deception: How women have been sidelined since the GPA', *Open Space*, Issue 1, June 2011.

Habib, A., 'South Africa's Foreign Policy: hegemonic aspirations, neoliberal orientations and global transformations', *South African Journal of International Affairs*, 16(2), pp. 143-59, 2009.

Hammer, A., B. Raftopoulos and S. Jensen (eds), *Zimbabwe's Unfinished Business: Rethinking Land, State and Nation in the Context of Crisis* (Harare: Weaver Press, 2003).

Kanyenze, G., T. Kondo, P. Chitambara, J. Martens, *Beyond the Enclave: towards a pro-poor and inclusive development strategy for Zimbabwe* (Harare: Weaver Press, 2011).

Kriger, N., 'Zanu- PF Politics under Zimbabwe's Power-Sharing Agreement', *Journal of Contemporary African Studies,* 30(1), pp. 11-26, 2012.

Laakso, L., 'Opposition Politics in Independent Zimbabwe', *African Studies Quarterly*, 7(2/3), 2003.

Landsberg, C., *The Quiet Diplomacy of Liberation: International Politics and South Africa's Transition* (Johannesburg: Jacana Media, 2004).

LeVan, C., 'Power Sharing and Inclusive Politics in Africa's Uncertain Democracies', *Governance,* 24(1), pp. 31-53, January 2011.

MacDermott, J., *Breaking the Mould in Zimbabwe – Pragmatic Engagement at a Critical Juncture* (Stockholm: Swedish Defence Research Agency, 2009).

Mandaza, I., (ed.), *Zimbabwe: The Political Economy of Transition 1980-1986* (Dakar: CODESRIA, 1986).

———, and L. Sachikonye (eds), *The One-Party State Debate and Democracy: The Zimbabwe Debate* (Harare: SAPES Books, 1991).

Masunugure, E.V. (ed.), *Defying the Winds of Change: Zimbabwe's 2008 Elections* (Harare: Weaver Press, 2009).

———, 'Zimbabwe at the Crossroads: Challenges for Civil Society', *Open Space*, Issue 1, June 2011.

———, and J.M. Shumba (eds), *Zimbabwe: Mired in Transition* (Harare: Weaver Press, 2012).

Matyzak, D., *Law, Politics and Zimbabwe's 'Unity' Government* (Harare: Konrad Adenauer Stiftung, 2010).

Mazarire, G.C., 'Discipline and Punishment in Zanla: 1964-1979', *Journal of Southern African Studies,* 37(3), 2011.

Mbeki, T., 'The Mbeki-Mugabe Papers: What Mbeki told Mugabe', *New Agenda*, 30, pp. 56-72, 2008.

McCandless, E., *Polarisation and Transformation in Zimbabwe: Social Movements, Strategy Dilemmas and Change* (New York: Lexington Books, 2011).

Moore, D., 'A Decade of Disquieting Diplomacy: South Africa, Zimbabwe and the Ideology of the National Democratic Revolution, 1999-2009', *History Compass,* 8(8), pp. 752-67, 2010.

———, and B. Raftopoulos, 'Zimbabwe's democracy of diminished expectations', in S. Chiumbu and M. Musemwa (eds), *Crisis! What Crisis? The Multiple Dimensions of the Zimbabwean Crisis* (Cape Town: HSRC Press, 2012).

Moyo, S., J. Makumbe and B. Raftopoulos, *NGOs, the State and Politics in Zimbabwe* (Harare: SAPES Books, 2000).

Moyo, S., K. Helliker and T. Murisa (eds), *Contested Terrain: Land Reform and Contemporary Civil Society in Zimbabwe* (Pietermaritzburg: S&S Publishers, 2008).

Moyo, S, and P.Yeros (eds), *Reclaiming the Nation: The Return of the National Question in Africa, Asia, and Latin America* (London: Pluto Press, 2011).

Moyo, J., 'Civil Society in Zimbabwe', *Zambezia*, 20(1), 1993.

\Mugabe, R.G., *Inside the Third Chimuranga: Our Land is our Prosperity* (Harare: Government of Zimbabwe, 2001).

Murithi, T., and A. Mawadza (eds), *Zimbabwe in Transition: A View from Within* (Johannesburg: Jacana Media, 2011).

Muvingi, I., 'Sitting on Powder Kegs: Socio-economic Rights in Transitional Societies', *International Journal for Transitional Justice*, 3(2), pp. 163-82, 2009.

Muzondidya, J., 'Zimbabwe's Failed Transition? An Analysis of the Challenges and Complexities in Zimbabwe's Transition to Democracy in the post-2000 Period', in Murithi and Mawadza, op cit.

Ncube, C., 'Contesting Hegemony: Civil Society and the Struggle for Social Change in Zimbabwe, 2000-2008', unpublished Ph.D. thesis, University of Birmingham, 2010.

Ndlovu-Gatsheni, S., 'Making sense of Mugabeism in Local and Glabal Politics: "So Blair, keep your England and let me keep my Zimbabwe"', *Third World Quarterly,* 30(6), pp. 1139-58, 2009.

Ndlovu-Gatsheni, S., *Do 'Zimbabweans' Exist: Trajectories of Nationalism, National Identity Formation and Crisis in a Postcolonial State* (Oxford: Peter Lang, 2009).

―――, 'Angola-Zimbabwe Relations: A Study in the Search for Regional Alliances', *The Round Table,* 99,(411), pp. 631-53, 2010.

―――, *The Zimbabwean Nation-State Project: A Historical Diagnosis of Identity and Power-Based Conflicts in a Post-Colonial State* (Uppsala: Nordiska Afrikainstitutet, 2011).

―――, 'Reconstructing the Implications of the Liberation Struggle History on SADC Mediation in Zimbabwe', South Africa Institute of International Affairs, Occasional Paper, No 94, 2011.

O'Donnell, G., and P. Schmitter, *Transitions from Authoritarian Rule: Tentative Conclusions about Uncertain Democracies* (Baltimore: Johns Hopkins University Press, 1986).

Phimister, I., and B. Raftopoulos, 'Mugabe, Mbeki and the Politics of Anti-imperialism', *Review of African Political Economy,* 101, pp. 385-400, 2004.

Raftopoulos, B., 'The GPA as a "Passive Revolution": Notes on Contemporary Politics in Zimbabwe', *The Round Table,* 99(411), pp. 705-18, 2010.

———, and L. Sachikonye (eds), *Striking Back: The Labour Movement and the Post-Colonial State in Zimbabwe, 1980-2000* (Harare: Weaver Press, 2001).

———, and T. Savage, *Zimbabwe: Injustice and Political Reconciliation* (Harare: Weaver Press, 2005).

———, and A. Mlambo (eds), *Becoming Zimbabwe: A History from the Pre-Colonial Period to 2008* (Harare: Weaver Press, 2009).

Ranger, T., 'Nationalist History, Patriotic History and the History of the Nation: The Struggle over the Past in Zimbabwe,' *Journal of Southern African Studies,* 30(2), pp. 215-34, 2004.

Sachikonye, L.M., (ed.), *Democracy, Civil Society and the State Social Movements in Southern Africa* (Harare: SAPES Books, 1995).

———, *Consolidating Democratic Governance in Southern Africa: The Case of Zimbabwe* (Johannesburg: EISA, 2007).

———, *When a State Turns on its Citizens: Institutionalized Violence and Political Culture* (Johannesburg: Jacana Media, 2011).

Saunders, R., 'Zimbabwe: Liberation Nationalism, Old and Born Again', *Review of African Political Economy,* 38(127), pp. 123-34, 2011.

Scarnecchia, T., 'Rationalising *Gukurahundi:* Cold War and South African Foreign Relations', *Kronos, Southern African Histories,* 37, pp. 87-103, November 2011.

Scoones, I., N. Marongwe, B. Mavedzenge, F. Murimbarimba, J. Mahenehene and C. Sukume, *Zimbabwe's Land Reform: Myths and Realities* (Woodbridge: James Currey; Harare: Weaver Press; Johannesburg: Jacana Media, 2009).

Solidarity Peace Trust, 'Walking a Thin Line – The Political and Humanitarian challenges facing Zimbabwe's GPA leadership and its ordinary citizens' (Johannesburg, 30 June 2009).

———, 'What Options for Zimbabwe?' (Johannesburg, 31 March 2010).

Spears, I.S., 'Understanding Inclusive Peace Agreements in Africa: The Problems of Sharing Power', *Third World Quarterly,* 21(1), pp. 105-18, 2000.

Tendi, M-B., *Making History in Mugabe's Zimbabwe* (Oxford: Peter Lang, 2010).

Tsvangirai, M., *Morgan Tsvangirai: At the Deep End* (Johannesburg: Penguin, 2011).

www.ingramcontent.com/pod-product-compliance
Lightning Source LLC
Chambersburg PA
CBHW051352290426
44108CB00015B/1985